W9-BAL-150

SMUGGLER'S BLUES

THE SAGA OF A MARIJUANA IMPORTER

JAY CARTER BROWN

ECW Press

Published by ECW PRESS
2120 Queen Street East, Suite 200, Toronto, Ontario, Canada M4E 1E2

LIBRARY AND ARCHIVES CANADA CATALOGUING IN PUBLICATION

Brown, Jay Carter
Smuggler's blues / Jay Carter Brown.

ISBN 978-1-55022-783-3

1. Brown, Jay Carter.   2. Drug traffic.   3. Drug couriers — Biography.   I. Title.

HV5805.B76A3 2007   364.1'77092   C2007-903491-8

Cover and text design: Tania Craan
Typesetting: Mary Bowness
Production: Rachel Brooks
Printed by Webcom

This book is set in Bembo and TradeGothic.

The publication of *Smuggler's Blues* has been generously supported by the Canada Council for the Arts, which last year invested $20.1 million in writing and publishing throughout Canada, by the Ontario Arts Council, by the Government of Ontario through Ontario Book Publishing Tax Credit, and the Government of Canada through the Book Publishing Industry Development Program (BPIDP).

DISTRIBUTION

CANADA: Jaguar Book Group, 100 Armstrong Avenue, Georgetown, ON, L7G 5S4
UNITED STATES: Independent Publishers Group, 814 North Franklin Street, Chicago, Illinois 60610

PRINTED AND BOUND IN CANADA

ECW PRESS
ecwpress.com

Table of Contents

He penned me a note and held it to the security window.
The note was simple.
"Buy life insurance."
But a few years earlier, I never would have thought about
    life insurance.
I was too busy living the high life and smuggling weed.

Chapter One

Feeding a Cop is like Feeding a Bear

I wrote a book once. Someone said that if you are going to write, then write about something you know. So I did. My novel, all twenty-seven double-spaced chapters, is about spies and drug smugglers operating between Jamaica and North America. Not that I was ever a spy. It has been suggested that with my background and connections I could have been an undercover operative or a spy. But I made my choice a long time before to operate on the other side of the law. Both my expertise and my background were to provide the drug smuggling aspects of my novel — cannabis smuggling to be exact. Cannabis has been my love and my business for most of my life. I may not have been a spy but I have rubbed shoulders with spies both down in Jamaica and over in Lebanon around the time when Uncle Sam began butting his so called isolationist nose into Third World politics. Or "poli-tricks" as the Jamaican Rastas like to say. The Rastas like to shorten and rearrange words to change and confuse their meaning. Like the expression "white white" or "white bread" that they use to describe a white person. Or "wha hap," which is short for "what's happening?" The most well known island saying is "soon come," which means that something is coming in Jamaican time, and that means very slowly. I spent a lot of time in Jamaica and I cannot remember ever having any fears or concerns about living and dealing there. There were times when I was the only white man in a sea of black bodies pressing around me. At rock concerts. In nightclubs. On the streets of Montego Bay and Kingston during rush hour. When I went into the hills where the marijuana is grown I was often the only white face to be seen for a dozen miles. I had no fear in Jamaica because I felt like I was kin to my black brethren who had joined with me to counter the downtrodding forces of Babylon.

Babylon is the name the Rastas give to the constabulary and soldiers whose duty it is to police the marijuana trade in Jamaica. During my smuggling years, Babylon seemed to be keeping a curious balance at play in its policing of drugs. The mountainous countryside around Saint Ann's and the area known as Cockpit country to the north of the island provided the cover necessary to grow the illicit marijuana crop. But there is no doubt the herb could easily have been eradicated with the use of helicopters and pesticides. In fact, the Jamaican government tried that once, just before the election of the great socialist prime minister Norman Manley. When the government that preceded Manley sent troops in by air to burn down the pot fields, the marijuana farmers quickly retaliated by lighting several mongooses on fire and setting them free to run through the sugar cane fields. The resulting fires quickly convinced the government of the day to end its marijuana eradication program before the entire island of Jamaica was ablaze.

It was this rebellious spirit mixed with a strong religious ethic that gave me a sense of security in dealing with the Jamaican people. I have always been aware of a spiritual calm when I am in Jamaica, as though the island is closer to God than is anywhere else on the planet. Even on my very first visit, I felt I belonged there somehow. While I was very comfortable amongst the Jamaican people, I was nevertheless careful to keep close to my Jamaican partner who showed me the ropes when traveling around the island and especially when going into the hills. My partner, "Righteous," was a tall and well-muscled man of lighter

SMUGGLER'S BLUES

complexion than most Jamaicans. In the pecking order of Jamaican society, a lighter complexion is often associated with higher intelligence and there was no doubt that this was true in the case of Randall "Righteous" Solomon.

I first met Righteous through another Jamaican who I had met during my early forays to the island. That man was a caretaker named Sunny. Sunny was a friend of Solomon's and he was also the gardener and houseman next door to a villa that I rented on the ocean near Hopewell. At that time, my friends and I were on a junket to bring some suitcases full of pressed weed back to Canada in an intricate scheme involving Canadian Immigration clearance cards. Passengers returning to Canada in those days were first interviewed by Canadian Immigration and then handed a three-by-five-inch card and told to proceed to customs for baggage inspection. The three-by-five cards had several boxes with numbers beside them, one of which was labeled E-24. It was discovered that if the E-24 was ticked off by the immigration officer, a passenger holding that card would be sent straight through customs without a baggage search. If enough people were in on the smuggling scam the odds were high that at least one in a group of seven or eight returning passengers would be handed an E-24 card. Brian Kholder and his cousin Alexandra were along to carry the bags of weed through Canada Customs once someone in our group had slipped them an E-24 card after clearing Immigration. There were about ten of us working the scam on this particular occasion, all friends from work and high school or college. There was my wife and me. Ryan McCaan and his wife Sally, and Phil Robson and his girlfriend Paula. My buddy Robert Bishop was along without a date, as was Ross Mitchell, who was dismayed to learn that "ross" was the slang word for shit in Jamaica. We had rented a seaside villa in the Jamaican parish of Hopewell that was ideally situated near a source of marijuana that was grown in the nearby parish of Orange Bay. We chose the Hopewell villa because we were close to the Montego Bay airport, yet free from the many prying eyes of the hotel staff in town. While we waited for Righteous to arrange for the marijuana to be pressed and packaged in Orange

Bay, the group of us lay about our rented villa in hedonistic splendor. As we lay lounging in ocean-side chairs, sipping brown cows by the pool and smoking copious amounts of weed, we discussed the possibilities of our impending wealth. We were smoking so much ganga that we found it expedient to pay Sunny to be our spliff roller.

Sunny was a solidly built man whose facial features looked carved out of dark stone. His demeanor was well suited for work as a caretaker and in the language of modern day psychology, he had more anima than animus in his character. Sunny was far from an ambitious soul. He had only one job to do for us, which was to roll joints, and whenever we asked him to do it, he would inevitably complain.

"You finish all dem spliff already, mon?"

Righteous was far more willing to work without complaining, and as time went on, I found myself relying more and more on Randall "Righteous" Solomon for many of my needs in Jamaica.

When I first met Righteous he was a "Moonie," which was a religious cult that was spreading throughout the western world at the time. His bright eyes, short-cropped hair, and a willing attitude gave me confidence in him and he soon became my right-hand man. I saw a lot of Righteous and Sunny that first year in Jamaica as our group strung the E-24 scam out as long as we could. We had several back-to-back successes before the smuggling scam finally blew apart in Toronto. That was when four suitcases full of weed slid down the baggage ramp to the circular pickup ring in the luggage collection area and one of the bags broke open, revealing sticks of weed poking out. We left the bags on the turnstile, pulled the luggage tags from the four suitcases, and went home broke. I was almost glad the trip folded just then because "Bish the Fish" Bishop and Marvin "Manny" Maniezzo had been playing poker with me on the way down to Jamaica, with the payouts due only after and if the E-24 scam paid off. I was so deep in debt after the two card sharks fleeced me, that just about all of my end would have gone to them anyway.

Other scams came and went, as fate sent one smuggling opportunity after another my way. Through Righteous and his connections, I met the people I needed to expedite marijuana out of Jamaica in larger and larger shipments. Righteous introduced me to customs agents, aircraft maintenance personnel, and shipping brokers. He had so many contacts that it seemed to me that the whole of Jamaica was like one large extended family tied together by blood relations, tribal ties and financial gain. Even the police were available for a price, although my bias against authority never allowed me to use any police help. Feeding a cop is like feeding a bear, everything is great until the food runs out.

The smuggling scams I was involved in grew to a level where I found myself flying in and out of the island on a regular basis. The smartly uniformed immigration and customs officers at Montego Bay airport had to know that I was into some kind of action. When asked the purpose of my trip, I always said pleasure. If I were a customs agent, I might wonder why someone would take several dozen pleasure trips to my country each year. But Jamaican Immigration and Customs never did. I remember flying into Jamaica on one occasion without my wallet and ID. Any other country would have turned me around and sent me right back home, but not Jamaica. The immigration officer simply waved me through to customs after I explained to him that I had lost my wallet. He recognized me, of course, which made his decision easier. But can you imagine trying to enter any other sovereign nation without ID when you are not even a citizen?

On that same trip the recently departed owner of Jamaica Car Rental rented me a car without a driver's licence or ID. Thank you kindly, Mrs. Chin, and rest in peace.

"Jamaica no problem" was the motto of the island and there was so much corruption that anything and anyone seemed available for a fee. Whenever I arrived on the island, my first order of business, after clearing Jamaican Customs and Immigration, was to pick up some ganga. Jamaicans call their weed ganga using the Indian word. They also call it herb, coli, lamb's bread, sensi and dagga. The stuff is everywhere. It's thrust into your face at the airport gas station. Don't ever buy weed at the airport. It's crap. Marijuana is also sold along the highways from thatched huts with fruit and sea shells hanging from their bamboo rafters. The huts are there due to squatter's rights alongside the road, and they operate without permits or licences. Marijuana can be bought in bars and restaurants. Taxi drivers sell it. Hotel owners and waiters sell it. Everyone sells it. But rather than buy the weed in town, I would drive up into the hills of Orange Bay just outside of Negril to get the good stuff. Not the lamb's bread sold for a small fortune in Montego Bay. Not the seeded coli from Saint Ann's that was being shipped north to Canada and the States by the ton. I'm talking about pure Jamaican sensimilla. Unseeded African ganga, lovingly nursed to perfection in a clearing behind some Rasta's hut. Watered by hand. Fed rat bat shit as fertilizer. Coaxed and pruned until the buds were thick with sticky crystals and smelled of cinnamon.

"You should leave your lungs to science," my buddy Bishop used to tease me, as I rolled joint after joint of the good stuff.

I was living the good life. Smoking the best herb. Eating in fine restaurants and hotels. Sleeping in king size beds in air-conditioned villas. Frolicking in swimming pools and being cared for by maids, butlers, and gardeners. Our wives and girlfriends would strut around the Jamaican beaches in their tiny bikinis looking like centrefolds, as so many Montreal girls do. My buddies and I mostly preferred to snorkel in the ocean rather than lie about in hammocks like the girls, who were trying to score a nice tan to wear home.

The first time we all sat down to dinner at our rented villa in Jamaica, the event was memorable for its excesses. There were two maids who came with the villa, one for cooking and one for serving. Our next door neighbour, Sunny, was dressed in his Sunday best and helping the two coffee-complexioned maids serve us that warm summer evening. It was a magical night, with the ocean ebbing and flowing to a rhythmic slap against the seawall outside the formal dining room. The pool lights were on, adding an eerie glow to a darkened horizon that sparkled with stars. Crickets and tree frogs serenaded us, and the warm Jamaican weather stood in sharp contrast to the bitter cold of the Montreal winter we had escaped. We were all in our early twenties and we snickered amongst ourselves about being served by a staff who were old enough to be our parents. I was confused at first when the maid brought a small silver bell to the table and placed it beside me. When I finally figured out its purpose, we all had great fun ringing the bell for water or tea or whatever we fancied. The table was laid out with white linen and china dishes, as course after course of Jamaican cuisine was ferried to us from the kitchen. The pace was slow and deliberate. Pepper pot soup with ackies and salt fish for a starter. The spicy starters were followed by a fresh tossed salad and then an entrée of grilled Caribbean lobster. The lobster was accompanied by several vegetable dishes of chocho, cauliflower, corn and fresh beans. All of the courses were spaced to allow joints to be smoked in between servings. The sumptuous meal was topped off by dessert, a homemade spice cake, and there were Tia Maria and Grande Marnier liquors to end the meal.

In the early days of my Jamaican experience, I was overwhelmed by this treatment, but I soon came to expect it as a way of life. I rented whatever car was available at the airport when I first flew into town, but as my trips to Jamaica became more frequent and lengthy, I took a long-term lease on an air conditioned Civic from Hertz Rent-a-Car. Then the first thing I did was to have the windows professionally tinted. The tint was so dark that you could not see inside the car even when it was parked and I got a kick out of watching people on the street peering in at me without knowing I was there.

One time I was driving the Civic to Negril when I hit a roadblock manned by machine-gun-toting cops and khaki-dressed soldiers who were stopping all drivers. The cops were looking for guns or ganga or whatever else they could find. Fridays were the worst for roadblocks because the cops would invariably be looking for entertainment money for the weekend. Any little thing they could find would lead to the inevitable bribe that left all parties happy and warranted few arrests. But it was annoying to have to throw away my spliff as I came across the roadblock.

I was asked by the first bribe-hungry cop how I could be

driving a rented car with such dark tinted windows.

"VIP," I remember answering with a grin, as I slipped him an American twenty to prevent a search of my car that could lead to my weed stash. It was not likely he would find my stash, which was hidden in the door panels, but I learned quickly that you always make your bribe to the first cop on the scene. Anytime you wait for the others to come over, it costs you a lot more. If you wait until the judge is involved, it is usually too late to work a deal.

Despite roadblocks and other small nuisances, life was grand in those days. I discovered Chateau Lafite-Rothschild wine, which even today is the standard to which I hold all other wines. I regularly ate curried lobster at the exclusive Richmond Hill Inn, which is perched on a mountain top with a view of the city of Montego Bay that is unparalleled. I remember driving home one night after an extravagant meal there, throwing Jamaican twenty dollar bills in a stream out the window of my rented car. It was my drunken tribute to the little man, the poor black Jamaican who saw little or none of the drug money that poured into the island. It was Jamaican money anyway, not real money. When my real money in Canadian and U.S. funds built up to an impossible level in my Jamaican safety deposit box, I would fly it to the Cayman Islands where I had a different safety box that held only thousand dollar bills.

Jamaica was like my home away from home, but let's face it, the island was a typically corrupt Third World country. That corruption is fine when you're trying to slip a load of contraband in or out of the country, but it can turn against you when you live there. Every time I went to my safety deposit box I had this sickening vision of finding it empty. It never happened, but the fantasy proved so powerful that I was always counting and recounting my money in the box.

On the other hand, Grand Cayman Island had a world-class reputation for legitimate banking. There are over 300 banks on an island the size of the city of Ottawa. On my first trip there I spotted the differences between Jamaica and the Caymans in a second. The Cayman customs officers reminded me of American customs officers: cold, alert, all seeing and all knowing. I took note of how they concentrated on those incoming passengers who fit a profile, like American hippies or Caribbean Rastafarians. Black passengers wearing jeans and gold chains received careful screening while white businessmen like me, dressed in slacks and a sports jacket, received only a cursory inspection. I was not really worried as I passed under the watchful eyes of these customs officers because apart from a personal stash of hash in my crotch, the only commodity I was bringing into the Caymans was money. And there is no law against bringing cash into the Caymans. The islands were built on foreign money. Drug profits money. Political payoff money. Embezzled money. Bribe money. Stolen money. Grand Cayman is an example of a Caribbean island living the American dream and it is all because of their banking rules, which allow the free flow of money in and out of the country. There is so much foreign capital flowing into the island that the smallest deposit required to open my first offshore bank account was fifty thousand dollars. It's probably higher than that today. The cleanliness of Grand Cayman's cobblestone streets and sidewalks were in sharp contrast to the goats and cows and dogs and pigs that wander freely along the litter-strewn streets of Jamaica.

Don't get me wrong. I loved Jamaica and I still do. I would never consider trading Jamaica's rural and hedonistic lifestyle for the sterile security of the Grand Caymans. Grand Cayman offers civilized efficiency, but Jamaica offers one of the last bastions of personal freedom in the world.

You can have it all in Jamaica. Pot. Hash. Coke. Mushrooms. Honey oil. Girls. Even young girls. Drinking. Drinking and driving. Swimming. Sun worship. Crack. Heroin, if you know where to look. About the only taboo on the island is homosexuality, which does not stop the practice but merely drives it back into the closet where, I must confess, I prefer it. Other than a Christian loathing of homosexuals, there is very little prejudice in Jamaica. Blacks can date whites. Asians can date South Americans. Old can date young. All without the critical stares that might follow elsewhere in the world. This liberal attitude towards interracial dating in Jamaica has led to the creation of some of the most beautiful and exotic women on this planet.

So how did I find myself in Jamaica working on some of the largest and most successful smuggling operations in Canada, you might ask. I can tell you that I did not become involved because of money. Barbara and I were in our early twenties when her aunt died and we came into a fifty thousand dollar inheritance. That was a substantial amount of money for two newlyweds. We had just returned to Canada from a year-long holiday touring North America and Mexico when the windfall hit. While Barbara and I were vacationing on our trip, my friend and ex co-worker Ryan McCann was busy scheming and scamming back in our home-town of Montreal.

I knew Ryan from a job where we worked together prior to Barbara and me leaving for Mexico. In fact it was Ryan who helped me get fired from my job and Ryan who helped me find the Volkswagen van we went touring in.

Once our trip was over and Barbara and I ended up back in Montreal, it was not long before I hooked up again with my old pal Ryan. The reunion was a festive one and we partied it up for a while on Barbara's inheritance money. Within a few weeks of our reunion, Ryan invited me to invest in a scam to run suitcases of weed from Jamaica to Montreal. Since I had no weed on hand and no immediate prospects for work, it seemed appropriate to jam down to Jamaica for a visit, especially since I could get money and smoke for doing so. There would be no risk to me, Ryan assured us. As the principal investor covering most of the expenses, I was not going to carry any bags through customs. Ryan had runners to do that.

The plan was simple and the first time we tried the E-24 scam, it worked like a charm. From that moment on, we were all hooked on fast times and easy money. Ryan and I were the best of friends; not only was it exciting to be making money hand over fist, it was pure pleasure to have a partner to share the good times with. I did not know at the time that I was on my way to new and unexpected heights that would eventually see me running one of the longest lasting and largest cannabis smuggling empires in Canada. And I had no idea that before the end of my lucrative career, Ryan would be a character in my fictional novel, receiving every imagined punishment I could possibly dream up for him.

When the E-24 scam came to an end I found myself out of a job, so to speak, as I was no longer needed by Ryan and his crew for investment purposes. The E-24 scam lasted long enough for all of us to make a little money, but money doesn't last long when it travels in one direction only. That's one of the problems with big scores that don't come every day. It is easy to burn through your earnings just on living expenses, especially if you like to travel first class. Add to this the inherent possibility of imminent arrest or death and the money is burned off even faster. With no jobs interfering with our social lives, there was no end to the parties and poker games that went on all night in Montreal. It was just prior to the Montreal Olympics, which esteemed Mayor Jean Drapeau had claimed, "could no more have a deficit than a man could have a baby." The Mayor must have been ahead of his time on the subject of men having babies because the roof of the Montreal Olympic Stadium is still not installed due to the debt that followed the games.

The E-24 scam left us with ample disposable income, so our crew sat in the best seats at stadium events and rock concerts and we were ushered through club lines by doormen who recognized us as free-spending high rollers. The Dark Side of the Moon concert that Pink Floyd put on at the Autostade in Montreal was typical of our evenings out, although it was without doubt the best concert I ever saw. Our crew was passing joints around with perfect strangers who were only too happy to share, as a full moon rose up over the open-air stadium in perfect timing with the music. I thought the moon was a prop, like the rocket that came crashing into the stage, but it was all real and larger than life. We partied like movie stars that warm summer evening in an atmosphere of peace, love and dope. We brought no booze to the concert because we were not into drinking yet. We did, however, begin experimenting with cocaine which was very new to the drug scene.

On our final trip down to Jamaica, our E-24 scam blew up and died. But Ryan was an enterprising and ambitious individual, and he had partnered with our pal Robby to finance a coke scam. We knew nothing of this at the time, until Robby showed up in Jamaica at the same time as the people in the E-24 crew arrived.

Phil "Robby" Robson was a unique and interesting character. He was twenty-two years old at the time and stood over six feet two inches tall. He reminded me of the character Ickabod Crane, in *The Legend of Sleepy Hollow*. Robby had curly black hair with bangs reaching to his eyes and a wide smile that softened his old man's face. He walked slowly and stood in a stooped posture, and in all the years I knew him, I never saw Robby run. Robby chain smoked weed or hash mixed with tobacco from cigarettes. He tooled around in a late model Corvette that he would leave unlocked and idling on the street for hours during winter because he did not want his car seat to get cold. For some mysterious reason, his car was never stolen.

His girlfriend, Paula, was a quiet girl with a pretty face and a body out of a magazine centrefold. Robby and his girlfriend used to get stoned on Quaaludes at our parties and would entertain us by acting as though they were going to have sex right there on the floor in front of us all. They never did complete the sex act with an audience watching, but they certainly came close enough to get our attention.

Ryan and Robby had arranged to have a kilo of pure coke stitched into the back panels of a suit jacket worn by a runner I had never met before. The runner had ferried the coke from Colombia to Jamaica and met up with Ryan and Robby in the hotel where the E-24 crew was staying. Their runner was in his early twenties, slim and clean-cut, with a cropped mustache and short hair. He came across as a businessman when I met him and he acted cool on the surface, but I could see by his mannerisms that he was nervous about his task.

Our E-24 crew was staying in Ocho Rios at the tip of the north coast of Jamaica. Our accommodation was at a small funky hotel on the water, with a billiard table in the main lobby and a swimming pool overlooking the ocean. The hotel was on two levels that were cut into a mountainside of lava rock deposited by past volcanoes. Our mixed group of young men and women occupied most of the rooms on the water side of the hotel, a setup that was reminiscent of a scene from Humphrey Bogart's *Key Largo*. The pool table took up most of the lobby. As visitors entered from the narrow, twisting road leading to the hotel, they could see right through the lobby to a swimming pool and bar that overlooked a turquoise ocean, pock-marked with pink coral reefs. The topography of Ocho Rios is very different from Montego Bay and Negril where the beaches are wide, shallow and easily accessible. In Ocho Rios, known as Ochi to the locals, the mountainous jungle rolls down to the sea where it slips beneath the deep and still water alongside a lava rock shoreline.

The first I realized that coke was going to be couriered to Montreal along with our weed was a few days after check-in, when Barbara and I were invited to a party that was underway across the street from the hotel. There were several of us at the house party including my wife, Ryan and his wife, and Robby and his girlfriend. My sidekick Bishop was there too, along with several of the others who were part of the E-24 scam. The party centred on the rear balcony of a rental villa that faced a yard with banana trees and palms. The glue that held the party together that night was a warm Jamaican evening, a vacation mentality and a medium-sized sugar bowl filled with Ryan and Robby's coke. I entered the house with my wife and we were introduced to Duane Allman, of the Allman Brothers Band. Duane was rapping with Ryan and Robby between lines of coke, which the three were snorting in the kitchen. I can't remember what my conversation with Duane was about, but he seemed very pleasant and we chatted and bumped lines until three in the morning. Unfortunately, Duane Allman returned to the States after this visit to Jamaica and was killed in a motorcycle accident within a few months of our meeting.

It was a relaxed atmosphere even as the coke took effect and the night became haunted with shadows and moonlight. Crickets were chirping and tree frogs were whistling as we snorted lines of coke on an Arborite kitchen table. The coke was much stronger than any drug I had tried to this point and the night sounds and moving shadows added to a disorienting high. The coke made me feel talkative. Friendly. Animated. Articulate. Insightful. Awake. Alive. It was absolutely nothing like the crap you get today that makes you want to hide in a corner and cover your head with a bag. We had ample opportunity to research the effects of Ryan's coke when we got back to Canada because, although his coke importing scam was successful, there turned out to be no market for the drug in Montreal. Cocaine was only just beginning to make the scene in the U.S. of A., and little sister Canada had not even started to wake up to it yet.

Even Ryan's well-connected loan shark buddy, Jean Paul LaPierre, was unable to find a buyer for the blow. Jean Paul was brought into our group after he met Ryan at a discount store that sold cut-rate stereos in Laval. Ryan had become kind of a salesman for the stereo store, and when he was not smuggling dope into Canada he was busy installing stereos for all of his friends in their houses and cars. The store's prices were great but there was no room for bad debt and that is where Jean Paul came in. Jean Paul was a collector for the store owner, as an aside to his own drug trafficking and loan shark business. Jean Paul drove a Cadillac which in some way compensated for his short stature of five foot eight or nine. If you are wondering how a little guy like Jean Paul could be a loan shark and debt collector, think of a pit bull terrier or think of Joe Pesci in the movie *Goodfellas*. Jean Paul was small, but he was dangerous. He didn't hang around much with our crowd, not until he began dating Manny Maniezzo's ex-girlfriend, which was an insane match if ever there was one. Go figure. Jean Paul, the sawed-off enforcer, and Susan Braun, a tall, attractive, intelligent college student majoring in psychology. I would usually run into Jean Paul when I visited Ryan at his home, where the loan shark dropped in to see him on business.

If it wasn't Jean Paul, there was always someone dropping in at Ryan and Sally's that summer. If the truth be told, we all came largely because of the coke buried in his back yard. The coke changed colour, turning from white to brown after being buried for a few days, but it lost none of its potency. It was so good I always wondered if it was cut with smack, especially after it turned brown. Like others in our group, Barbara and I would find ourselves calling Ryan and Sally even when we had seen them just the night before, as the urge to do coke overwhelmed our usual manners and discretion. We would party all night at Ryan's, doing coke and Quaaludes, and then drive home in the morning, cursing the birds for their singing. Our child-substitute Doberman would be waiting for us at home to be let out for a pee and a three minute crap in the yard. Then she was ushered back to bed where the three of us would sleep until late afternoon.

When I wasn't coking at Ryan's, I would meet my friends for daily get-togethers at Jeans Plus, a clothing store owned by David "Kaka" Klein and his partner Maury. Kaka always had a huge chunk of black hash as enticement to lure friends into his store because he was bored out of his mind staying there by himself all day. He generously shared his hash with visitors but he would never let anyone take a piece home with them, except as a consolation prize if he happened to win money from them at cards. I often left my money behind in games of poker or gin with Kaka and Maury, and I always suspected that they were partners at the card table as well as in business. "Two friends and a stranger" was the expression they used when they took my money and laughed about it. On the odd occasion that I won, they would pay the debt in stock, until I ended up with a closet full of cheap clothes. My buddies Bishop and Manny would drop by the store on a daily basis, along with a host of other players who came by to get high and play cards. There was always a lot of kibitzing going on at the card games, and I found the conversation interesting. Many of the people coming into the store seemed to know the details of major criminal events in town, from robberies to murder, and I soon came to the conclusion that criminals and cons are some of the biggest gossips in the world.

No wonder they always got busted.

Before he got into the coke biz, my friend Brad Wilder was

into some decent action pulling bags of weed from the bellies of Air Canada planes. It must have been a terrible blow to his father, who was a big shot with Air Canada, when his son got caught. While Brad was on bail for that bust, he hooked up with a school chum named Marty Ralston for a coke run to Colombia. A few months after his coke run, which judging by the coke in his sugar bowl was successful, the cops came looking for Brad with a warrant. He hid out at Derrick "the Doctor's" house for several months, before locating a safe house in the Laurentians.

Brad "the Wild Man" Wilder was a born showman, with endless stories about his travels and adventures. At six foot two, with blond hair and pale skin like an albino, he must have looked a sight walking around Bogotá, Colombia in a white suit and a Panama hat with his buddy Marty. According to the story mill, Marty also wore a white suit and Panama hat while in Colombia. At six four and fair-complexioned, he must have looked like Brad's twin. Talk about low profile. Brad had a habit of saying "hello" as a comment rather than a greeting. As in, "I answered a knock at my door and the cops were there. Hello!" His expressions were always animated and he spoke with much waving of arms and body movements. Brad was always a lot of fun to have around but unfortunately, a few weeks after he served his time in jail and was released on parole, he died of a brain aneurysm. He had turned himself in after several years on the run, in order to clear up his past and marry his new girl-friend and turn his life around. But when he was off hunting up north with Hoss and Derrick, he ran out of the house to watch some ducks fly overhead and dropped dead of an aneurysm. The last Derrick saw of the "Wild Man" was at his funeral, where Brad's girlfriend was tearfully telling everyone that the only memento she had from Brad was the ring he left her. Derrick was put in the uncomfortable position of asking for the ring back, after explaining that it was an heirloom from his grandfather that went missing during Brad's stay at his house. It was a bit of a shock to hear that the "Wild Man" would steal from Derrick after all the ear, nose and throat specialist had done for him, but it was par for the course with some of my friends and associates.

After the E-24 cash cow died, I was ready for some independence and came up with a scam of my own. There was no problem raising investment money. That's how it was done back then. Someone would come up with a scam and shop it around to all of their friends and associates for financing. With bank interest running at four per cent, there was no better action to be had on their money. The mooches were lined up three deep, hoping for a two-to-one return on their investment that I promised would follow within a matter of weeks. But it wasn't just about the money for me. It was about being into some kind of action. My buddies were scamming and scheming and gambling and I wanted to be dealt into the game.

A year prior to this time, Barbara and I were traveling throughout the U.S. and Mexico where we met lots of people, some of whom came to figure in my future ambitions.

We met one crew from the Ali Baba Head Shop in Phoenix, when we camped with them for a few weeks on a beach in Guayamus, Mexico. We were driving out of the campsite to continue on further south, when we came across their van coming in the opposite direction. A voice called out to us. "Turn around and go back to the beach," said one of them through the truck window. "We got hash." That was enough incentive to change our itinerary and we spent a few weeks hanging out with the Ali Baba group in a temporary commune on the beach. There were two guys and two girls in the van, all of whom shed their clothes as soon as they hit the beach.

After we returned from Mexico over Christmas, we went to visit our Ali Baba friends in Arizona. They welcomed us with open arms and invited us to stay for free at the living quarters above their head shop. The folks at Ali Baba were on the leading edge of the hippie movement, with employees and hangers-on wearing sandals and beads and long floral dresses or handmade clothing cut from leather. They were the kind of people who say "Have a wonderful day" and really mean it. The owners of Ali Baba were two Vietnam vets, Colin and Vince, who had returned from the war determined to live the rest of their lives enjoying the freedoms they had fought for in Vietnam. They told me during my visit to Phoenix that they had access to many tons of Mexican marijuana on the American side of the border. There was so much marijuana available that it was stored on pallets in an American warehouse and the dealers were on the honour system to just go and pick up what they needed.

It was Colin and Vince who I decided to visit with my friend Bishop from Montreal. Three of us were involved in the operation. Besides Bishop and me, our partner Ross Mitchell was waiting in Plattsburg to do his end. Bishop and I had money to invest but since Ross had none, we gave him the most dangerous part of the scam, which was running the weed across the Canadian border. The plan was simple. Buy the weed in Phoenix and have Bishop transport it to Plattsburg, a small resort town and beach just south of the Canadian border. I suggested that Bishop take the train, but he objected to the three-day trip and he complained that there were no direct rail connections from Phoenix to Plattsburg available. I took him at his word since he was taking the risk of carrying the contraband and after briefly researching train routes, I ended up agreeing with his decision to fly the weed back. It was way before the days of 9/11 and routine baggage scans, so I was not overly concerned about flying the weed back in suitcases. Besides, it was Bishop's ass that was going to be fried if he was wrong in his decision.

The boys at Ali Baba were happy to see me again and treated Bishop and me like family. They even took us sightseeing to Nogales, Mexico, where we spent a day soaking up the Mexican experience. When we were coming back through American customs, the Ali Baba crew were the epitome of professionalism, as they stopped short of the border and checked their vehicle over for any traces of drugs. The border guards seemed to see us coming and instantly shunted our truck to a checkout station, where we were interrogated by U.S. customs officers. There was no need to be concerned about the inspection because we had already cleaned out the truck, so it was quite funny when an alert customs officer singled out my buddy

Bishop for special attention. It could have been his disco clothes, which were so very different from our hippie hosts, or it might have been the nervous fluttering of his long feminine eyelashes. The customs officer checked our documents, and then directed his attention to Bishop, who was sitting by a window seat in the back of the truck.

"You're Canadian?"

"Yes."

"And you know these people?"

"No. I mean yes. I mean I just met them. I came down with my friend."

"What were you doing in Mexico?"

"Sightseeing."

"Anything else?"

"No."

"Step out of the vehicle, please."

"What for?"

"Step out of the vehicle."

Bishop complied with the order, while the officer frisked him and a second customs officer looked on.

"What's the matter, son? You look nervous."

"I'm not nervous," Bishop answered with a challenging stare.

Suddenly the Customs Officer slapped his hand over Bishop's heart and smiled over at his partner.

"Hey, Charlie. I think we're going to have a cardiac arrest here!"

The officer concluded that Bishop was clean and let us all pass back through the border into the U.S. Everyone in our van was laughing as we drove away from the customs wicket. I was laughing. The Ali Baba crew was laughing. Their girlfriends were laughing. Even the two Customs Officers were smiling. The only one with a scowl on his face as we re-entered the United States was Bishop.

Once we were back in Arizona, we purchased our first fifty bricks of Mexican weed and two hard-shelled Samsonite suitcases. We packed the suitcases with weed at the Ali Baba Head Shop and placed towels and limes over the red-wrapped bricks of marijuana. Then we bid farewell to the Ali Baba crew and drove our rented car to the airport. Bishop wheeled the bags into the terminal, where we both caught an uneventful flight back to New York. In New York we rented another car and ferried the suitcases full of pressed bud to Plattsburg just below Montreal on the Canadian border. There we met with Ross and we carefully stashed the bricks of weed under the springs in the back seat of his father's car that he had borrowed for the day. A few hours later, Ross drove the weed back into Canada, crossing the Canadian border on a busy weekend with the drive-in movie crowd. The plan worked flawlessly and the reunion in our hometown of Montreal was a happy one, as the parties continued and drug use escalated.

There was still plenty of coke and Quaaludes to go around at Ryan and Sally's house and we continued to gather there to party. When Ryan flew down to Jamaica for a scam, the parties continued without him. Ryan had no idea how close Ross and his wife Sally were becoming in his absence. I gave him a heads-up one time, but he was too busy with his scam to properly deal with the issue.

Meanwhile Barbara and I had rented a huge house in Beaconsfield where we had lots of room for guests and parties. I came home from a trip down to Arizona one time to find a mob of people at my house. I walked in with my suitcase and asked Barbara what was going on, what's with all the strange faces. There were Corvettes and Jaguars and a Mercedes-Benz in the driveway and I recognized none of them. My friends, Joe and Hymie, and a mooch named Izzy Solomon interceded to explain that the Rolling Stones concert was on that night and there was absolutely no weed or hash in town for the event. I was the only one in all of Montreal who had weed to sell. These people were all drug dealers working the show. I was angry that my friends had brought all of these strangers to my house but I made the best of an uncomfortable situation. I sold the ten pounds of weed that was in my freezer for full retail. Then I called Ross to run to our stash and bring over the rest of our supply, and we sold every brick of Mexican weed that night.

I went to the show with several of my friends, and I felt proud that everyone in the stadium was getting high because of us.

The house Barbara and I rented had three unused bedrooms besides ours, and as fate would have it, my friend and partner, Ross, needed a place to stay after his parents asked him to leave home. He had thrown a tequila party in their absence and his older brother had come by to find everyone drunk and half naked. Ross took offense to his older brother's objections and they had a punch-up that left Ross with his front tooth missing. Barbara and I agreed to let Ross stay in one of our many unused bedrooms. Since Ross was a bit of a flake and looked like a geek without his front tooth, I never considered him a threat to my relationship. Like Ryan, I should have paid more attention to the situation, but I was too busy working my scam.

Bishop and I returned several times to Phoenix for a refill of our illicit drug prescription. The last trip we took saw us take back one hundred and forty pounds of primo Mexican weed. We were so confident of our operation that we even made arrangements to have Colin and Vince come to Montreal for a visit on the next trip north. They were eager to come to Montreal and offered to ferry another two hundred pounds up to Plattsburg for us on a front. Up until this time, I had been accompanying my friend Bishop on the journey, but I never carried anything on my person. Bishop was the courier. My end was the "cap." I set up the purchase and I had the connections in Phoenix, as well as providing the bulk of the start-up financing. There was no need for me to stick my chin out, even a little. However, I am very quick to take on responsibility if needed, and when I discovered at the last minute that four suitcases of weed were too much for Bishop to handle with his bum leg, I did not hesitate. I didn't know about his leg, which had been injured in a motorcycle accident some years before but I suspect to this day that he was just nervous to do the run alone. I felt I had no choice but to help him carry the bags to the check-in counter. Flying with several suitcases was not unusual in those days. The airlines always accepted extra bags, sometimes without a surcharge if the plane was light on passengers. There were no raised eyebrows as we checked in Bishop's luggage. However our suitcases were so stuffed with bricks of weed that one of them was in danger of breaking open. Bishop and I taped it up at the airport counter to keep it closed. We could have gone back to the Ali Baba shop and left two of the bags of weed for a future run. It might have been embarrassing as well as costly, but it certainly could have been done.

Instead, I helped Bishop carry the bags to the check-in. I made certain the baggage stubs were on his person and in his name. We were the only people in first class when we boarded the plane and the stewardess sat down with us and began chatting freely. We were playing a game of heads up poker when she started asking questions.

"Where are you headed?" she asked. "What do you boys do for a living?"

"We're gamblers," Bishop answered, while trumping my pair of aces with three little sixes. We were gamblers all right. We were gambling on getting four suitcases of weed from Phoenix to New York without getting busted.

There were no customs checkpoints to worry about, but with several thousand miles to cover, it was still a dangerous mission. When we landed and deplaned in New York, we went looking for our bags. Much to our dismay, they were not with the other bags on the revolving turnstile. We waited until all the passengers from our flight had left the terminal and then waited around a little longer, thinking that our bags might still be coming. Just as we were about to give up hope, I spied our taped-up suitcase along with the three others sliding down onto a different baggage carousel about forty meters away. At first I figured that some member of the ground crew had placed our bags on the wrong incoming turnstile. I later discovered that it was no mistake and that some unknown but enterprising airport worker was intending to grab the bags himself.

Bishop and I quickly walked over to the adjacent carousel and scooped up the four suitcases, taking two apiece. We made a dash towards the escalators to make our way to the car rental agency. As I reached the escalators and I started to put my foot on the first step, I felt a hand on my shoulder pulling me back. I spun around, ready to take issue with this rather aggressive interruption of my journey and came face to face with several plain-clothes policemen. There were five or six of them standing by, as one of them flashed his airport police badge at Bishop and me. Our apprehension was a surprisingly civilized affair, involving no handcuffs. The other passengers in the terminal paid little if any attention as the detectives marched us back to a small room off a corridor in the terminal, where they opened our suitcases. The police officers seemed unsurprised as they discovered the weed. They removed it and carefully stacked the red-wrapped bricks on the desk. They interrogated us for a while, until they determined that the weed was destined for Canada rather than the U.S. At first they seemed certain that we had an inside contact working at JFK, who had put the bags on the wrong baggage turnstile. When satisfied that we had no inside contacts, the airport police consulted amongst themselves with resigned shrugs and came to the same conclusion that I did. An airport worker had spotted our bags and had tried to reroute them for a later pickup.

Bishop and I were charged with possession of narcotics with intent to traffic, trafficking, and interstate transportation of fruit, the latter charge relating to the limes we had placed in the suitcases to cover any smell. The cops found the remainder of a gram of coke in my wallet that the nice folks at Ali Baba had laid on us. The boys at Ali Baba did not deal in blow but had copped the coke for me as a favour. But the American cops wanted to know all about that coke. The cops played the usual head games to get Bishop and me to talk. They threatened us with five years in jail. They told us that our suppliers had set us up in order to take the heat off themselves, while they smuggled off another load. It did not take long to figure out that the cops were not at all interested in pursuing the marijuana trail. They were, however, keenly interested in the half gram of blow in my wallet that they later told me was one hundred percent pure cocaine. They offered Bishop and me a deal. Set up a coke buy for a kilo or two and they would spring us out of there. The thought was tempting and we told the cops we would think about their offer.

While they waited for our answer, Bishop and I were sent over to the Federal Detention Headquarters in New York City. We took the bus with no windows across town to a six story brick building that looked like it was built at the turn of the last century. There we were processed in and taught a little dance I called the Prison Polka. "Strip naked. Put your clothes on the counter. Step forward. Hands in the air. Spread your fingers. Open your mouth. Lift your tongue. Run your hands through your hair. Turn around. Lift your feet. Bend over. Spread your cheeks. Okay stand up and get back in line."

Once we were processed into the holding centre, the clock stopped until Bishop and I gave the cops our decision about helping them. It would have been totally unfair, of course, to set our Ali Baba crew up for a coke sting. They had been nothing but fair and honourable with us and they had made clear from the start that they did not deal in coke. But I came up with a plan to play along with the cops and then escape to Mexico when they brought us down to Phoenix for the sting. After some discussion with others in our cellblock, Bishop and I realized that we would not be staying in hotels and set free to run around loose in Arizona. They would watch us like hawks and we'd be housed in the local jail until we could be set like Judas goats upon our friends. After three days of agonizing arguments and rebuttals between the two of us, Bishop and I finally called the cops and told them no deal. We would bite the bullet and do our time. Bishop, who was single and who had attended boarding school in New York, accepted the decision more easily than I did. For me it meant living apart from my wife, family and friends in a strange state several hundred miles from home. I would be residing in a cellblock with a racial mix that consisted of twenty blacks and ten Puerto Ricans to every white person. As I looked around at my cell mates, I figured that I had to be some kind of fool to end up in this jail. Most of the other detainees were from some ethnic minority or other. There were very few other white boys in our holding cells besides Bishop and me.

Vinny, the jailhouse star, was one of them. Vinny, was a con-
sigiliere of a New York Mafia crime family. He was facing
twenty years in the slammer for the famous French Connection
heroin importing scheme and he took it like he was waiting for
a bus. You had to wonder why Vinny was in there because he
looked so out of place. He was tall, athletic, handsome and intelligent. He would exercise in a black belt routine every day
before leaving his cell, and when he could find a challenger, he
played chess like a master. I gave him a bit of a run at chess and
he seemed to enjoy the competition before finishing me off in
a few well-chosen moves. Besides Vinny, there were three other
Caucasian inmates. One was Robert Lieberman. Lieberman was
a white-collar millionaire who was awaiting sentencing and
incarceration for breaking antitrust rules and for tax evasion.
Lieberman had the dubious honour of a front page photo spread
in Time magazine to his credit, which made him a different kind
of jailhouse star from Vinny. Lieberman had been smuggling new
cars down to South America and bypassing customs on both
ends. He used to smuggle them in shrimp boats, he told us. He
took the decks off the shrimp boats in the U.S. and dropped two
cars per vessel inside. In South America he would remove the
decks again to recover the automobiles and sell them for several
times their value. He bragged to us that he was moving more cars
than the largest General Motors dealer in the U.S. and he heaped
scorn upon our drug business.

"Believe me, you can make way more money my way than
you can with drugs," he said, offering to take us under his wing.
He even offered us the use of his luxury apartment in
Manhattan, which was a necessary requirement for our bail
application. "Stay here in the U.S. and do your time," he said. "If
you stay, I will help you get transferred to Danamora Prison
which is where I'm going. It's the country club of federal jails.
It even has its own golf course. When you finish your time, I'll
show you how to make real money."

It was a generous offer, but not one Bishop and I were interested in under the circumstances. The remainder of the people
we met in the federal detention cells were all morons or worse,

except for Hans, a Dutch pilot who enthralled us with his tales of flying weed into the States from Jamaica. Besides Hans, the one other white guy in our eight-man cellblock was a twenty-five-year-old smack dealer and user from New York City. He was in for five years for trafficking and couldn't wait to get back out on the street for another run at the smack. He told us that his heroin supplier had given him a Cadillac to work with, but that the New York cops busted him, took the car and stole his money before letting him go without arrest. His heroin supplier gave him another Caddy following the shake-down but after a time on the street, the same thing happened. His heroin supplier bailed him out again and this time he gave the street pusher a Chevy 396 with a four speed and told him, "Next time, outrun the motherfuckers!"

"I couldn't buy the cops off the last time," the smack pusher told us. "They told me I had to go in." His attitude was so accepting and so matter-of-fact that I was somewhat taken aback. His stoic acceptance of his fate was something I had not seen before. It was an attitude that I could never imagine myself adopting.

Other than Vinny and Lieberman, most of the other detainees were black and Puerto Rican, several of whom were in for immigration violations. Like the commercial pilot from Panama who was in his third year of detention and walked around the cellblock as though the rest of us were all part of a great conspiracy against him. After three years of detention, the only English he could master was "I deed not know dere was coke on dee plane."

The detention facility we were in was the worst jail I have ever experienced. Even the condemned Bordeaux Jail and the inhuman Parthenais Detention Centre in Montreal looked good next to this hundred-year-old five-storey dungeon. Talk about a crowbar hotel. The entire building was made of iron bars and cages stacked top to bottom and side by side on five levels. There was an exercise yard on the roof but it was the equivalent of smoking two packs of cigarettes per visit. With the city traffic down below and the smokestacks from the adjacent buildings belching oil fumes on every side, there was no fresh air to be had. The roof was fenced off like a monkey cage, as if anyone was going to try to scale down five stories of rotting bricks in an attempt to escape. In addition to the monkey cage construction, armed guards were positioned in towers on each corner of the roof deck to prevent escapes and riots. There was nowhere to go and nothing to do. There were a couple of basketball hoops on the roof deck, but they were quickly taken over by the black population. As soon as the blacks were tired of playing, the Puerto Ricans took over the court. I think I threw the basketball once during my entire stay. One of the black inmates tried to intimidate me by suggesting that I had better watch my tight young ass at night, what with all the fags around.

"They better like fucking corpses," I said, "because that's what it will take before I let that ever happen!"

In spite of my bravado, I traded Bishop a pack of smokes for his top bunk and let him take mine on the bottom. From then on, I slept with one eye open to keep watch on the others in my cellblock. I was glad that Bishop was with me because I did not know another soul in the jail or in the entire state of New York. He used to piss me off by comparing the detention centre to his boarding school experience and saying that it was not so bad. Not so bad? It was fucking terrible! There was no privacy. The food was tasteless slop. The routine was totally boring, with nothing to do. The furnace fan dried out your nose all night until you could hardly breathe. There was constant noise and light, even at night. You were surrounded by illiterate idiots. The beds were like cots, with worn out springs. The floor was cold concrete. The walls were metal bars. Every smell was shared throughout the entire cellblock. On top of it all, I had no idea when it all might end.

My only salvation was in my dreams, which became more vivid and real than ever before. One dream in particular saw me diving from a sailboat into a turquoise Jamaican ocean. The experience was so real and refreshing that I was totally depressed when I awoke in the slammer. Nevertheless, I saw it as a certain sign of my future and I felt from then on that all was not lost.

One evening after supper, I opened my bunk drawer to get a bag of potato chips that I had been saving for a bedtime snack. The chips were gone and I was furious. I asked Bishop if he knew what had happened to them and he told me he had taken them to exchange for his cigarettes that he had lost in a game of gin. I was livid. I was ready to throttle him. That bag of chips was all I had to look forward to in that rotten cage and Bishop had taken them without even asking. I was working up to giving Bishop a well-deserved beating when his gin partner offered to give me my chips back in exchange for what was left of Bishop's smokes. It surprised me how far I was prepared to go over a bag of chips. That was the first and only time I can remember having an argument with my friend Bishop.

After several weeks of living hell, we made an application for a legal aid lawyer and applied for bail. After several delays, our bail was granted, but Bishop had no money so I called Barbara in Montreal and asked her to cover his bail too. She did as requested. But as soon as that happened, my legal aid was cancelled. The prosecutor insisted that if I could cover Bishop's bail, then I obviously had enough money for a lawyer. But in the end that didn't really matter much, because after one look at our fat slob of a legal aid lawyer in his oversized, rumpled suit, I knew I could never allow him to defend me. When we were ushered into his office I saw a half-eaten baloney sandwich on a metal desk that looked like it had been purchased for fifty dollars at a flea market. His office was a pigsty, with broken linoleum tiles on the floor and stains on pale green walls that had not seen a fresh coat of paint in decades. The lawyer's desk was covered with papers and books that lay disheveled and askew. He had thinning, greasy hair that looked like it had not been washed in weeks. To compliment an appearance that was less than fashionable, he had a slight lisp that caused him to spit when he spoke. And the only legal advice he offered was, "Plead guilty." When I made a derogatory remark about his office, he made some retort about having other clients outside of the legal aid system. I knew right away it was a lie. The guy was paid by the government to shunt people through the legal system. He did not even want to

 SMUGGLER'S BLUES

discuss the particulars of our case. He had no interest in checking into the legality of searching our bags without warrants. He had no concerns about probable cause for a search. He gave no consideration to the fact that Bishop possessed the baggage stubs and I didn't. He was like a bald, sweaty parrot that just kept repeating the same thing to both of us. "Plead guilty."

I left his office and made a call to my wife in Montreal. I asked her to check our situation out with a local criminal lawyer, and to her credit, she found one named Sidney Goldman. Sidney was a showboat and a legend in the underworld where he was considered an expert on drug cases. He had several very high profile clients and he seemed to revel in the attention from both the media and the ladies. Sidney was representing Ryan's loan shark buddy, Jean Paul LaPierre, and with Jean Paul's recommendation, Goldman gave Barbara some very sage and candid advice that he would not normally have given to a stranger.

"Tell your husband to get out of there," was the message. "Leave on the next bus. It takes telephone numbers to pay for a good lawyer in New York," and by that he meant lots and lots of cash. "Tell him to take his chances on extradition." He gave his advice without asking Barbara for payment or a retainer. "It takes lots of money and lots of time for the U.S. to extradite a Canadian citizen," he added. "With under two hundred pounds of grass, they might not even bother to pursue the case, and even if they did, you have a better chance to fight it from up here than you would in New York."

My wife flew down to meet me in New York with Sidney's message and we spent our first night together in weeks. We rented a deluxe hotel room, took a horse-drawn carriage ride through the city and then went to see the Broadway performance of *Jesus Christ Superstar*. In spite of the cost, the experience left me feeling empty. When it was time to retire, Barbara and I climbed into a king-size bed and after a long conversation, we went straight to sleep. I was so wound up over the whole experience of jail that I was not even interested in sex.

Before Barbara and I went out for the carriage ride, I discussed Sidney Goldman's advice with my friend Bishop. He sat in my hotel room and listened to my arguments but he was adamant that he was staying in New York to face the music. He had Robert Lieberman's apartment to live in, he told me, and added that he wanted to come back to Montreal, but only after he had cleaned his slate in the U.S.

"Remember when the federal prosecutor told us not to run home after we got our bail?" I responded. "Remember his sarcastic tone? Wasn't it you who said he was really telling us that he expected us to do just that? To run home to Canada. Wasn't it you who said he was actually telling us that that's what we should do?"

"Maybe so, but I've thought it over. I would rather do my time and have nothing hanging over me."

"Who cares what's hanging over you if you can slip the knot and go free?"

"I have my future to consider. Some day I might want to take a job in the States."

"Future as a jailbird," I replied. "Suit yourself, Bishop," I said with a resigned shake of my head. "But five years is a long fucking time."

In the end our Canadian lawyer had our case thrown out on a technicality relating to the improper search and we were deported back to Canada.

On Sidney Goldman's advice, Bishop and I both left Montreal pretty quickly after that to let the heat die down. Bishop went to Morocco for six months, and Barbara and I went first to England, and then to Bermuda and then to Jamaica where the high life and the action started all over again.

Chapter Two

When You Lose in the Smuggling Business . . .

My wife and I returned to Montreal where we cancelled the lease on our house in Beaconsfield and prepared to leave for Europe. That decision effectively put our houseguest, Ross, on the street. He was none too happy about it, but there was not much he could say under the circumstances. He ended up back home with his parents while Barbara and I discussed my legal situation and decided that it would be best to leave Montreal for a few months.

It was October, which is a good time to visit Europe because all of the summer tourists have gone home. The trip would allow us to recapture the same vacation that we'd had to cancel a few years before. Barbara's older sister, Margaret, was living in England and it would be a great opportunity to visit her. After starting off in England, we could decide later on which European countries we would visit next.

We landed in Scotland because the fog at Heathrow Airport was too thick to land there and we made our way by train to the north of England where Margaret lived with her banker husband. The two were very happy to see us and welcomed us into their home for the better part of a week. They took us sightseeing to visit a drafty old castle, with a torture chamber that was as cold as ice, and they treated us to our first taste of East Indian food, which left my stomach queasy and my asshole burning. After a pleasant stay with these in-laws in their small English cottage community, we made our way south to London where Barbara's younger sister, Brandi, had just arrived from Greece. Brandi was in the throes of a breakup with her Greek con artist boyfriend and was more than a little happy to see us. We stayed close to her fifth-floor walk-up bed-sitter flat in London, in a somewhat nicer but not much newer flat of our own. Both flats featured heaters that operated on meters activated by one shilling coins. Brandi's flat had a similar setup for her electricity and we howled with laughter every time the lights would blink off and we would have to search around for shillings in the dark.

I was very unimpressed with London which was crowded, expensive and cold. It was barely October and the chill and the damp cut through my sheepskin jacket like it was made of silk.

Our friend Bishop arrived at Heathrow airport a few weeks after we did and met us in London where we helped him find a cheap flat to rent. Bishop was on his way to Morocco to kill six months, and I was somewhat envious of his warm destination. When he noted my chunk of hash, which I had purchased from some Colombian exchange students who lived in Brandi's building, Bishop asked me to get him some. I kept my stash in a matchbox. Just to pull his leg, I told Bishop that I bought my hash from the store on the corner. "Just ask for a pack of matches and give the shopkeeper a ten pound note and tell her to keep the change. She'll hand you back a box of matches with hash inside, but don't open it until you're outside the store," I told him. My practical joke was interrupted by Brandi's arrival and the subject was dropped. But when I offered later in the evening to get Bishop some hash he answered, "Don't bother. I'll get some from the corner store on my way home."

If Bishop had possessed more money, I would have let him do it but under the circumstances, I didn't have the heart. Just as he was heading out to buy the hash I told him the truth and took fifty bucks from him to pass on to the Colombian exchange students.

I nearly got taken in myself, by those Spanish-speaking students

I was buying my hash from. In our hash-fueled ramblings, they told me of a scheme to import cocaine from Colombia to London, or Canada, in the linings of jackets made in some uncle's factory. I was not really interested in dealing coke, but the next time I phoned back to my buddies in Montreal, I passed the information on to Ryan. I hinted that I might be interested in setting up a deal if it looked good. Almost before I hung up the phone, Ryan's partner Robby hopped a plane to England to scope out the possibilities. When he arrived, I told Robby I had come to believe the deal was a scam by the South American students to rip me off, and I questioned why he had jumped on a plane so quickly. He told me Ryan had sent him and that he was going to be pissed off about the waste of an airfare.

After digesting this disappointment, Robby asked if we wanted to split the rent on a villa in Jamaica. He was planning on spending the winter there with his girlfriend, Paula, and asked if we would like to join them. Barbara and I had already discussed postponing the rest of our trip to Europe, because of the cold winter weather, and Robby's offer sounded tempting.

I also had five thousand other reasons besides the cold weather for going to Jamaica. While I was waiting for bail in New York with Bishop, Ryan had approached my wife in Montreal and talked her into investing five thousand dollars in a weed scam. While I was none too happy about Barbara proceeding without me on a business deal, the deed was done and I felt there was not much I could say about it. I consoled myself with the fact that at least we had something in the works to make back some of the scam money we lost in New York.

When you lose in the smuggling business, you lose big. You lose your investment money. You lose your product. You lose your savings, which your lawyer sucks up like a Hoover. You lose your livelihood, because you can no longer make an income. You lose your freedom, in some cases. You lose your girlfriends or wives when they get tired of waiting for you to get sprung from jail. Sometimes people even lose their lives.

In spite of all that, I decided to rearrange our vacation schedule and visit Jamaica to both enjoy the sun and to look in on our investment that was made with Ryan. It made more sense to be making money in Jamaica while sucking up a tan in a bathing suit than roaming around Europe in a sheepskin coat burning off money and killing time.

Before Robby left to return to Montreal, he passed on a request to me from Ryan for more money to cover shortfalls in the deal he was putting together with Barbara's money. I grudgingly gave Robby a couple of thousand more, which covered his London visit and I told him that was it. There was no more money to invest. I told Robby that if Ryan could not get his act together on the money we had already given him, then I would go to Jamaica and take care of business for him. The request for more money gave me a bad feeling, and I began to wonder what kind of a con we had gotten into.

My sidekick, Bishop, was getting ready to leave for Morocco and I could see that he was sad to part with us. Unlike Barbara and me, Bishop was on his own and had no one to run away with. We said he could stay with us in Jamaica, but he had no money to rewrite his airline ticket. His mother had given him a charter ticket to Morocco for a three-month tour and he had little choice but to see the tour through. After Bishop left, Brandi decided that she would like to spend some time in a warmer climate too, so she decided to come to Jamaica with us.

We phoned Robby in Montreal and found out that he and Paula were leaving for Jamaica the following week and that Ryan and Sally were coming down around Christmas time. Barbara and I were looking forward to sharing Christmas with our friends.

When we landed in Jamaica, after a three day stay in Bermuda, I could not have felt more alive. We stepped off the plane and smelled the fragrant tropical air. A warm breeze from the ocean blew across the tarmac as we made our way past the singing choir of welcoming hostesses. After an hour of milling around the terminal with several hundred incoming tourists, we finally exited Jamaican Customs and Immigration, rented a car and set about finding Robby's villa.

His directions took us to Hopewell, about fifteen miles from

Montego Bay. When we reached the villa, we saw that it was a two-storey white house situated right on the ocean. From the first moment I laid eyes on it, I knew we had made the right decision to come to Jamaica instead of staying in Europe. The ocean was an azure shade of blue and crystal clear. A fresh water swimming pool was situated right next to the salt water sea, with lounge chairs laid out around the perimeter of the pool apron. The sun was beating down, with temperatures of about ninety degrees that were offset by a refreshing ocean breeze.

It was great to see Robby and Paula again. Robby and I smoked a fat joint on the pool deck and discussed the contrast between London and Jamaica with congratulatory grins of satisfaction. Barbara and Paula made themselves each a Tia Maria and milk and started making up for lost time on all the gossip. My old friend Sunny from the days of the E-24 scam would come around to sell us weed. He had become a friend of sorts, as well as a guide to the customs and habits of his fellow Jamaicans. Ryan and Ross came down a few weeks after we arrived and they all stayed at the house with Robby, me and our wives. It was great to see Ryan again because he was always the life of the party. Ryan liked to do magic tricks and he was very good at the art of illusion. Unlike most magicians, Ryan would amaze you with his magic and then show you how the trick was done.

I spoke to Ryan about Barbara's five grand investment and he told me of a refrigerator compressor in Montego Bay that was ready to be shipped to Canada for repair after being filled with weed. The only thing holding him back was the cost of the weed. I found that a little disconcerting, since Barbara's money had been more than enough to cover twenty pounds of weed and a used compressor. From what I could see, Ryan was in Jamaica with Ross and Robby pulling off other scams. I couldn't help but think that he was using Barbara's money to pull off the other scams, without paying me any dividends. He told me not to worry, that he was coming back down to Jamaica with his wife Sally on a three-week cruise and that he would take care of business then. He said he was shipping his Thunderbird down to Jamaica, at the same time, to use around the island. That really set my warning bells buzzing. He was telling me that he was still seeking financing for the scam, but he had five grand to take a cruise with his wife and his car. I showed my displeasure but all I got was the cold shoulder. Finally I told Ryan that if something did not happen soon, I would take over the scam and ship the compressor myself.

A few days after he arrived, I had Ryan show me where the compressor was being stored. He led me to a house at the main intersection of the highway into Montego Bay. The house was on a hill where a lone Jamaican blacksmith, named Tyrel, looked suitably impressed as we pulled up in the T-Bird. He showed us a refrigerator compressor that was sawed into two halves and said that it was for sending weed to Canada. He said that he would fill the compressor with pressed weed and send it to any address that we gave him. It looked to me like an old piece of crap that wouldn't have been worth the money to send to Kingston for repair, never mind Montreal. But the Jamaican assured us that he had used this method to send weed to the States many times and he had never heard of a problem. He would weld the weed to the inside of the compressor where no one would think to look for it. He would press the weed really tight until fifteen or maybe twenty pounds would fit inside.

In hindsight, I realize why Tyrel had never heard of any problems. When a scam fails and someone goes down, the last thing anyone wants to do is go back to the scene of the crime and explain to everyone what happened. Most players write their bust off as a bad experience and never go back for more. But that was knowledge that came to me later in life, and while I had misgivings about their scam, Ryan and Tyrel almost convinced me that the idea was sound. But then Ryan asked for more money, saying that he had spent Barbara's earlier investment on the flight and cruise expenses. I was not very happy with Ryan's request for more money. This whole thing seemed like a throw-away scam, not one that required six months to set up. On top of that, he was staying with us and eating our food on the cuff, all the while asking for more investment money.

Eventually I put my foot down.

"No way. No fucking way."

I made it clear to Ryan that Barbara and I had no more money to give him and if he could not ship the load off with what he had, I would handle it myself. Ryan left Jamaica in a huff and I felt pleased to have told him how I felt, rather than keeping it bottled up. I had absolutely no worries about butting heads with him because he was a lightweight among the people we hung out with.

I contacted my friend, Jacques Laflame, back in Montreal, who had volunteered to store our furniture in his garage while Barbara and I left on our extended vacation. Jacques was a funny kind of guy. He was married to a cute little French girl and the two of them were into kinky games. They were always trying to get Barbara and me to take our clothes off and run around nude at their house. I suspect that had we done so, other moves would have followed. Jacques said he would be willing to receive the compressor from me. I told him not to attempt to open it under any circumstances. "I'll send it to your home," I told him. "It should arrive the day after I ship it. If there's a problem, there will probably be a two, or three, day delay while the cops examine the compressor before delivering it to you."

If such a delay happened, I told him to feign innocence at receiving the unsolicited compressor and if necessary, a smart lawyer would clear him of any charges. I offered to pay for a lawyer, at my expense, if there were any problems. If there was no heat on the compressor and it came through as planned, I told Jacques to leave it to cool off in his garage for a couple of weeks. Once the heat was off, I would contact our mutual friend, Ryan, to take the weed in the compressor off his hands. I told him I would pay him well for his trouble and not to worry as he had my furniture as collateral. I don't know if it was the money, the adventure or a chance to get into our pants that motivated Jacques to go along with the play. The guy was a straight arrow and the worst thing I ever saw him do was slip his wife some mescaline without her knowledge.

I shipped the load as we had discussed, and everything seemed fine. But then Jacques did something totally unexpected.

I was lounging on my pool deck in Jamaica and smoking a spliff when Ryan and Jean Paul walked unannounced onto my back patio. It was about a week or two after I had sent the compressor to Jacques and I was already on edge because I sensed something had gone wrong. Jean Paul had a serious look on his face and, without so much as a hello from either himself or Ryan, he urged me to come into an adjacent bedroom. As I followed behind Ryan, I was expecting to hear that Jacques had contacted Ryan about the compressor, but from the looks on their faces, I could see that something had gone terribly wrong. I asked what was going on and I was expecting to hear some bad news but Jean Paul's contorted face spoke more than his words.

"You want to know what happened? I'll tell you what happened. Your fucking friend got busted and he tried to take me down with him."

"Jacques got busted?"

"Yah, Jacques."

"I told him not to contact you or Ryan until the heat was off the load."

"He contacted us alright. And he had a fucking cop beside him when he called."

"How do you know that?"

"Because I know."

"What happened?

"You want to know what happened? I'll tell you what happened."

Jacques had called Ryan before he was supposed to and told him what was planned. Immediately following Jacques's phone call, Ryan called in his loan shark buddy, Jean Paul, to hijack the load. They coerced poor Jacques into going to the airport to pick up the compressor, even though it had been sitting in customs for days.

Poor, stupid Jacques. Poor, stupid, double-crossing Jacques. He was given the compressor by customs at the airport, after it had been emptied of most of its weed, and the cops allowed him to drive away with it. When he reached the Montreal Expressway, where it rises up to a right-of-way overpass that traverses

the city, Ryan, Jean Paul and another man closed off the highway behind Jacques. They accomplished this by stopping their
cars abreast in a line, thereby bringing the three lanes of expressway traffic to a halt, in order to give Jacques the time he needed
to escape any pursuers. It was a bold move, but the plan did not
work. Jacques was busted just outside Quebec City as he
checked into his motel room. He answered the phone when
Jean Paul called from a nearby phone booth and he invited the
loan shark to come and pick up the compressor.

One thing about Jean Paul: he may not have been the
smartest guy in the world, but he was cunning as a wolf.

"They're with you, aren't they?" Jean Paul growled into the
phone.

"What do you mean?"

"The cops. They're with you, aren't they?"

"No, no! That's not so," Jacques protested in French.

"They're standing right beside you, aren't they?"

"There's no one here."

"They're listening to every word."

"No, that's not true."

"Put them on the phone. I want to talk to them."

The phone suddenly went dead and Jean Paul knew it was a
trap.

Now I should explain a little about Jean Paul. This guy had a
sixth sense that warned him away from danger. It was not the
first time that his uncanny senses had saved him. There was
another time he had a premonition when he and Ryan were
about to pick up a load of weed that they had smuggled into
Canada. On that occasion, four hundred pounds of Jamaican coli
that Ryan had shipped north was waiting for pickup in a second
floor flat in the east end of Montreal. As far as they knew, the
load was secure, but at Jean Paul's insistence, Ryan and Jean Paul
both took a walk around the block before entering the apartment. It was cold that night and most people would have
forgone the walkabout and just gone inside to warm up, but Jean
Paul was adamant about the security check. About half a block
from the flat, Jean Paul walked past a car and saw two men in

suits lying sprawled across the seats. The story, as told later, was that the two men both had two-way radios in their hands. I don't know if he could have seen the radios on a dark and cold night, but Jean Paul kept walking straight to his car and he and Ryan drove away from the scene. They heard a news report about a four-hundred-pound weed bust at the same address the next day.

Not only that, but Jean Paul had a temper — a bad one. Jean Paul had a shootout one time with Charlie "the Weasel" Wilson over some weed that went missing in Jamaica. I suspect it was that same four hundred pounds of Jamaican coli. The shooting came after a meeting behind a restaurant that left Charlie's Porsche with three bullet holes in it. The way I heard it, Charlie pulled his gun and confronted Jean Paul, who pulled his own gun and started shooting. I suspect they were both surprised that the other guy had a gun and they can thank either good fortune or bad shooting that no one was killed.

So there I was standing face to face with Jean Paul and the little pit bull was working himself into a frenzy.

"The cops called your friend Jacques to come and pick up the compressor at the airport. They let him take it away and then they arrested him in Quebec City."

"What the hell was he doing in Quebec City?" I said.

"I sent him there to make sure there were no cops tailing him."

"I don't understand. He wasn't even supposed to call Ryan until the load was in his hands."

"Your rat friend called Ryan as soon as you hung up the phone. He told him that you were sending the compressor and he asked for our help."

"He wasn't supposed to do that."

"Yah, well he did, and then he ratted on us."

"I'm sorry to hear that."

"It's not as simple as that. You fucked up our scam and now you owe me."

"I owe you? Why would I owe you?"

"Because that was my scam you fucked up."

"I paid Ryan seven grand for that scam."

"That was my scam. I been paying two guys on the docks for weeks waiting for the right moment to send that compressor to them by sea. And you went and sent it by air. Now the scam is fucked up."

"I gave Ryan seven grand for that scam. He asked me for more money and I told him I was sending the compressor up on my own if he couldn't get it together. Tell him, Ryan."

I looked at Ryan. When he put his head down and turned away I was dumbstruck.

"I'm telling you, Ryan and I had a deal," I insisted.

That's when the sucker punch came. I was looking at Ryan when Jean Paul's fist came out of left field and caught me under the left eye. There was no pain, but I was in shock as the punch sent me reeling backwards. Before I could recover, Jean Paul grabbed a pair of scissors from our bedroom dresser and shoved me backwards onto the bed as he held the scissors in front of my eyes.

"You fucking owe me," he said.

I turned away and looked at Ryan for an answer to this mystery, but he just looked away again. I turned to Robby who was standing in the doorway. He, too, looked away with a shake of his curly locks. I felt alone. I felt deserted by my friends. Worse than deserted. They were in on the shakedown.

"You took our weed and you fucked up our deal," the little Frenchman raged on. "That weed was supposed to go north by sea freight, not air. No one sends a compressor north by air," he said.

It was a rip-off, pure and simple, and Ryan was using Jean Paul to pull it off. I could not bring myself to believe that Ryan was doing that. We were supposed to be friends. Best buddies.

When Jean Paul said he was paying two guys on the docks, I knew right away it was a lie. He talked on and on while I waited in subdued silence for the amount. I thought for a moment about fighting back. I figured I could take Jean Paul, even with the scissors in his hand. I figured I could take Ryan, too. But it wouldn't stop there. If I didn't kill the little Frenchman right then and there, he would come back and gun me down in

Jamaica or Montreal for sure. I waited to hear the amount, but first came the threats. He had two killers waiting in Montego Bay. I didn't believe him, but I let him think that I did. My allies and friends may have turned against me, but my loyal Jamaican gardener, Isaiah, heard the yelling and came rushing towards the commotion. He came bursting into the bedroom with his machete raised high and I saw Jean Paul looking concerned. Isaiah was a big man and with or without a machete, there was no doubt that he could have evicted Ryan and Jean Paul in a second. His appearance gave me a feeling of renewed confidence, but I would still have to face Jean Paul in Montreal later, as well as in Jamaica right now. I waved Isaiah away and told him it was just a small argument between friends and not to worry. He left reluctantly while I turned to Jean Paul and asked how much he wanted from me. The Frenchman was unable to conceal his pleasure, as the smallest trace of a smile washed over his face. He seemed to be musing over the amount he could gouge from me. He began with a bullshit story about paying his two guys on the docks five hundred a week for so many weeks and that, calculated along with the fee for my arrogance, would be six thousand dollars.

I thought about it. Six thousand dollars was possibly the maximum amount I would have gone along with under the circumstances, but it was affordable. I really had little choice but to pay the penalty if I wanted to avoid a war with Jean Paul. I pondered the amount for several moments before I agreed. I had actually held a lot of respect for Jean Paul up until this incident, and even though he professed to feel bad about it later, I never fully forgave him for what he did. I would also never forget that my good friend Ryan put him up to it and that Robby helped.

I felt like a dog that had been disciplined by the pack. The other dogs could smell that I was vulnerable, and they were taking advantage of it.

After the house was cleared of visitors, Barbara and I had a long-overdue talk about a lot of things, including our former friends and our future together. When you are an adolescent and still developing your character and personality, your friends will sometimes become closer to you than your family is. Friends will accept comments and behaviour that no one in your family would condone. Friends understand you. Friends accept you. But family will rarely turn on you the way friends can. At least not the way my friends did. I learned that friendship is often temporary. That friendship to some people is disposable. That there is a profound difference between friendship and companionship. That a real friend is worth their weight in diamonds. The people I had been hanging around with were not my friends. They were envious of me. They were spiteful towards me, all the while wearing a mask of friendship. After Barbara and I had finished discussing the issues, we decided to skip life in the fast lane and to quit smuggling drugs. We determined to get back to the basics that we had left behind, before we ever became involved with Ryan and his cohorts. We were going to return to Montreal and re-commit to our hippie attitudes that we had left behind after our trip to Mexico with our Volkswagen van. We didn't need money. We didn't need friends. We had our health and we had each other, and that was all that mattered.

Chapter Three

Hung for a Sheep, Hung for a Lamb

After several months in Jamaica, my wife and I returned to Montreal and found a townhouse in the West Island that we rented until we could find a house to buy. We had discussed the matter in Jamaica and we came to the opinion that we had wasted enough money on dope deals and partying. We decided that it would be wise to invest a part of Barbara's inheritance money in a home with some property. We began our house search in the west end of town where our friends lived.

I saw Ryan again. He was still living across the river in Laval, close to his psycho buddy, Jean Paul. I saw Robby again too. He was still living downtown with Paula in a two bedroom flat. When I saw them again, both Ryan and Robby acted as though what happened in Jamaica was no big deal. Ryan apologized for the shakedown, with the pitch that what had happened was all a misunderstanding. He even came over to my house with ten pounds of weed as partial repayment for the six grand he and Jean Paul had ripped off from me. I took the weed and accepted his apology, but inside I was still boiling about the incident.

For a while, I had daily fantasies about killing both Jean Paul and Ryan and I thought seriously about getting myself a clean piece for the job. Ryan's apology and the ten pounds of weed he laid on me made the entire incident even more confusing. One part of me wanted to continue on as friends with him, but another part of me wanted revenge. I figured that Ryan must have been successful in one of his importing scams and now that he was back in the chips, his conscience was bothering him. By dropping ten pounds of weed on me, he was trying to make up again. As time moved forward, I tried to forgive and forget, but the incident in Jamaica burned inside of me like a hot iron. Jean Paul's part in the shakedown was less upsetting than Ryan's betrayal because I saw that French little prick as a trained wolf rather than a person. I would have choked the life out of Ryan and Jean Paul in a second, if I thought I could get away with it. What Ryan pulled on me was an experience that left an indelible mark on my memory that no amount of time could wipe away. It wasn't about the money. It was about friendship and trust and loyalty. When Ryan called on me for backup at the printing supply firm where we both worked years before, I did not hesitate to help him, even though it cost me my job. When he was out of town scamming, I was available for anything he asked of me, including keeping an eye out for his wife. Ryan and his wife were like family to Barbara and me. We had spent countless hours together dropping mescaline and doing coke and laughing while we discussed our lives and expressed our innermost feelings to each other.

Before the Jamaica incident, Ryan and I once shared in the purchase of a board game called Swingers. After a little tequila and a lot of smoke, he and I ended up nude and making out with our wives on the carpet in the same room. Some people in our group actually thought we were swinging together, but that was never destined to be. After the shakedown visit from Jean Paul and Ryan in Jamaica, there were more poker games and there were more parties, but there was never again anything like that board game closeness Ryan and I once shared.

Shortly after Ryan's apology, I found myself invited to a birthday party at Jean Paul's house. The house was located on a cul-de-sac in Laval, and only the loan shark's closest friends were privileged to know its whereabouts. It was to be a surprise party, which was spoiled when Jean Paul and Ryan came across me and my wife as we drove into Jean Paul's subdivision. Ryan and Jean Paul were driving out for party supplies, when Jean Paul saw me and slammed on the brakes to ask me what I was doing there. I was secretly pleased to see what was, undoubtedly, a trace of fear and apprehension in Jean Paul's eyes. It lasted until Ryan explained to the loan shark that I was there for his surprise party. I could see that Jean Paul was angry about not being informed about the party and, particularly, about me coming. I thought the entire scene was as ridiculous as a Monty Python movie skit, and if I could have turned around and left right then, I would have. In my mind, throwing a birthday party for Jean Paul was like trying to domesticate a wild animal. I was only going to the party to break the ice, and I had gone there with mixed feelings.

I joined the party and spent most of my time in the kitchen with the guys while the girls sat in the living room doing their own thing. Ryan was there with his wife. Robby was there with Paula. Jean Paul's brother-in-law, Rene Lemieux was also there. At one point during his birthday celebration, Jean Paul separated the guys from the girls and sat us down in a little back den of his three-bedroom split level, where he treated the guys to some opium and jailhouse wisdom.

"Don't worry about going to jail," he said to the five of us with a wolfish grin. "Jail will be just like this. We'll sit around and play cards. We'll get high the same way we are now. And we'll shoot the shit the same way, too. It will be like hanging out in a men's club."

Jean Paul's comments reminded me of Bishop's comparison between the New York Detention Center and boarding school, but I curbed my impulse to make anything out of it. Jean Paul went on to say that he was going to jail soon. His lawyer had strung out his beef as long as he could and the end was in sight. Jean Paul was facing prison time for doing what he called a favour for some well-connected people. It was insinuated that the favour involved a murder but he was not going to jail for that. Jean Paul was taking the fall for a stock fraud conspiracy, and he treated his pending jail sentence as nothing more than payment for a cause, like going to college or apprenticing for a trade. He passed around a metal pipe filled with red opium to enhance the mood for some more of his jailhouse rhetoric. The only other insight into Jean Paul's character that I picked up that night was his penchant for fresh sheets and bedding every night, which Barbara thought excessive. I felt that Jean Paul was compensating for guilt, and no amount of fresh bedding would wipe his conscience clean.

Jean Paul told us the story of an undercover female agent who came onto him and became his girlfriend and what he did to her when he found out she was a cop. He told us that he beat her to a pulp, and when he was finished beating her, he washed her face with a damp cloth and then threw her from his car onto a street in front of the hospital. After Jean Paul's surprise party ended, I collected my wife and drove home wondering why I was associating with people that I so despised.

From time to time I played golf and poker with Ryan and Jean Paul, who both continued to be part of the mix of friends and associates I hung out with. You might wonder why someone would continue to hang out with the people who had screwed him. This type of Gemini behaviour is common in the underworld, where you can't just change jobs when you are pissed off with your associates or your working conditions. You either get out of the business completely or you put up with the working conditions and wait for an opportunity for payback. In the underworld, there are often undercurrents of unresolved conflict lurking just beneath the surface in many social interactions. Old animosities and unresolved insults die hard sometimes. Add to this an absence of legal recourse, and then factor in the usual petty human jealousies, and it's no surprise that double crosses and rip-offs occur all the time in the world of crime. Never mind honour among thieves, a thief's corrupted view of honour is like his corrupted view of respect. Respect equals fear in criminal circles and if you respect someone in the underworld, you must kill them if there is a disagreement. A murder like that is often called a settling of accounts by the local newspapers and broadcast media. The expression sanitizes and legitimizes the most heinous of crimes. In my opinion murder should be called what it is: murder.

When I first started in the smuggling business, there was no violence to speak of. It was just me and my buddies, a bunch of college dropouts and frustrated job seekers who became semi-organized in a joint endeavor to make money. When Jean Paul was brought into the scene, the game changed completely and became more serious. As the profits became larger and larger, there was a greater need for people like Jean Paul to keep some semblance of order in the drug dealing community. There were several criminal groups like ours working around Montreal who had heavies like him on the payroll. From time to time, these groups would divide and mutate into other cells or criminal groups which would often interact with each other on projects. For example, one criminal cell might be smuggling weed into the country while another cell would be selling it at street level to the local market. Or one cell might be printing fake documents which other criminal cells and groups would trade for drugs or unregistered guns.

Anytime two or more people were involved in a criminal enterprise, the local newspapers in Montreal lumped everyone together into a gang and then gave that gang a name. If you lived in the west end of Montreal you were part of the West End gang. If you lived in the east end, you were part of the East End gang. The Dupont brothers from Saint Henri had control of downtown Montreal and any trouble that occurred at the bars and night clubs was attributed to the Dupont gang. The Italians controlled Montreal North and criminal activity in that area was usually attributed to the Mafia. The South Shore and Laval both had their own local gangs. These groups would work together on occasion, but only when there was a mutual benefit. It's not as though you might offend someone in the West End gang and suddenly have a hundred guys after you. You would only have the hundred guys after you if the party you offended was willing to pay a fee or offer some other benefit as a reward for that service.

In an effort to make a quasi-honest living, I stopped smuggling cannabis for a while and started selling cars from my home.

The business is called "curbing" in the trade and the first few cars I purchased for curbing were from Charlie the Weasel's car lot on Decarie Boulevard. Charlie Wilson was a couple of years older than I was at the time and he was a hard-working man with simple tastes. He talked in the rough fashion of the east end, but he had a friendly face with slightly protruding front teeth that softened his features. He dressed in non-designer clothes and although they were not brand names, he always looked neat and I never saw him in jeans.

Charlie introduced me to his partner in the car lot, Irving Goldberg, who was fresh out of prison from a twelve-year bit for armed robbery. Irving was older than Charlie by ten years or so and Charlie often made reference to how dangerous Irving was. He did not look at all dangerous to me. I saw Irving as a clean-cut, slightly overweight man who looked like any other car salesman you might meet. He was of average height, with short curly hair and had a cherubic smile that projected a confident hospitality. I related well with Irving and with his partner Charlie, both of whom had criminal pasts that were more extensive than mine. My other friends from the West Island, who were mostly college and high school dropouts, were just playing at being gangsters and they were scared of Charlie. Charlie's pals were actually career criminals. I felt that Charlie understood the seriousness of the games we were playing, while my co-conspirators from the West Island did not.

The Weasel was given that name because he sought out money like a ferret searches out food. Charlie used to drive around to the places where my friends and I hung out and he would sniff around in the hope that he might profit by overhearing some scam or deal. Charlie Wilson had made his bones in the underworld as a young man. While working in a carnival, he was approached by some members of the notorious West End gang. They came to Charlie with a plan that was simple, and together they pulled off a score that went down without a hitch. Big Tommy Moore and Ryan Robertson put a guard's hat on Charlie's head and had him knock on the back door of a Brink's truck while the delivery courier was still collecting money bags in the store. Charlie was a short guy and all that could be seen by the Brink's driver was the top of his hat. When Charlie knocked on the bulletproof window, the driver saw the hat and opened the door. The rest is history. Charlie made over two hundred grand in less than a minute, and his reputation in the underworld became sealed and respected. The money Charlie made covered the inventory on his car lot and left a little extra cash for his other needs. As a result, Charlie Wilson, who quit school in grade ten, was well set up with a beautifully furnished apartment and a viable business, all before he reached the age of twenty-five. He drove a late model Porsche sports car, which made sense since he had no children. He was married to a lovely girl that he kept completely in the dark about his criminal activities. Unbeknownst to his criminal friends, who would have razzed him silly, Charlie had once been a teenage fashion model in the Eaton's department store annual home shopping catalogue that was sent to every home in Montreal.

I purchased several cars from Charlie and sold them privately from my home. I also bought cars privately through the newspapers and placed them on Charlie's lot to sell on consignment. I started hanging out at the car lot on a regular basis and when Charlie wasn't there, I would spend my time talking to his partner Irving. I came by daily to check on the needs of my consignment cars, grabbing a hose when necessary and giving them a quick wash or filling a deflated tire with air. I liked Irving and got along well with him. He was a straight-talking man who had a charming exterior that did not fit well with his reputation as a violent person. Irving had a large barrel chest with skinny arms and legs and eyes that were a bright sparkling blue. He had a mannerism that saw him turning his hands backwards like an ape when he walked that I suspect was developed to cement his image as a tough guy in the can. If he wanted to discuss something private, he would take me outside and walk me around the car lot, taking short, little steps that were a remnant of his prison experience. When faced with an uncomfortable situation, Irving would plant his legs firmly and stand his ground, while his face would flush a deep red showing his desire to leave. He was well mannered when he wanted to be, although that was often a ploy to get something he wanted.

Irv and Charlie were both a bit intrusive, in that they were inclined to walk into your house and help themselves to whatever was in your fridge without asking. One time Barbara and I unexpectedly met Charlie in Jamaica and he insisted on taking us on a sightseeing trip to Negril. He took it upon himself to act as our chauffeur and guide, even though he had never been to the west end of Jamaica before. Barbara and I were concerned about eating something before we left Montego Bay on our journey, but Charlie was adamant that we did not have to worry about lunch.

"They're all starving for company in Negril," he said in his most convincing voice. "Don't worry. Someone will feed us." The someone he was referring to were the white expatriates living in and around Negril. I thought at first he was joking, but when we arrived at our destination about twelve noon, the first thing Charlie did was hail down a white guy walking along the side of the road. The hippie-looking character greeted us with a cheery "Irie" and stopped to talk to Charlie through the car window. His appearance was a mixture of styles and cultures, with a dreadlock Rasta-type hairdo and Tilley brand designer clothing. He was a slim man, somewhat short in stature, who wore a braided beard that complimented his long, braided hair. His feet were shod with sandals made from Jamaican leather that were stitched to rubber soles made from a car tire. The hippie appeared to have plenty of time to chat on a pleasant day that saw shafts of sunlight spearing through the surrounding foliage. Charlie asked the long-haired man where we could find some food, and after a few minutes of conversation, we found ourselves sitting in the hippie's thatched home eating his food and smoking his homegrown weed. It was the first time I ever smoked a spliff wrapped in a pure, naturally grown tobacco leaf. The oversized joint was delicious and the tobacco leaf gave a much softer burn than regular rolling papers.

Negril is different from the rest of Jamaica both in topography and weather as well as in the attitudes of the people. Negril is considered country to the rest of Jamaica. There is none of the pushing and pestering that goes on in Montego Bay and the other tourist resorts on the north coast. Fruit grows larger and tastes sweeter in Negril. Weed tastes better too. In keeping with the laid-back attitude of the region, Ma Brown's famous mushroom tea shack carries on a prosperous business selling magic mushrooms. The shrooms are specially searched out in the surrounding jungle and pack a psilocybin wallop like nothing you have ever felt before.

The hippie's thatched house that we were in was completely made by hand, using the materials that grew on his property. He told us of his dreams to clear the surrounding jungle and make a resort consisting of thatched roof houses like his own. If you visit the hippie today, his property is on the cliffs and is one of Negril's most popular locations for the eco resort crowd. It is called Xtabi.

"How do you get along with the blacks?" Charlie asked the pleasantly stoned hippie.

"What do you mean?"

"You know. The niggers. How do you get along with the niggers down here?"

"Fine. I have a Jamaican houseboy and a maid."

"Don't they steal your food?"

"They don't have to. Most of my food is grown in the back yard. They can have whatever they want."

"What about stealing your money and your cigarettes?"

"I grow my own marijuana and tobacco on the property which the staff are welcome to partake in. There is little need for money here in Negril. Everything comes from the land."

"What about robberies?"

"It's no worse than anywhere else."

"As far as I am concerned, niggers are all thieves and they lie like a mattress."

"Why come to Jamaica if you don't like the people?"

"You know I have been asking myself that same question ever since I got here."

Charlie was candid in his dislike of blacks, unlike many of the tourists who refused to admit it, and his hippie host appeared to take no offense at that. Charlie hated blacks the way a junkyard dog dislikes trespassers. Sometime after our rendezvous in Jamaica, I saw him in a local supermarket in Montreal. "Tweet tweet," he said out of the blue.

"Tweet, tweet." He sounded just like the cartoon character stenciled on his briefcase. "Tweet, tweet! His canary sounds became angrier. "Tweet, tweet!" Suddenly Charlie began to rant about how he would like to kill all blacks, especially the ones from Jamaica. It was an uncomfortable situation for me as I had no ax to grind against black people and hoped that there weren't any in the store at the time.

It was a little after this incident that I was pulled aside by Charlie's partner Irving, for a walk around the car lot. He told me Charlie was out of town dealing with another Jamaican fuckup. Some video game machines that Charlie had smuggled into Jamaica were being ripped off by someone using a skeleton key to empty the coin boxes.

Irving was Jewish which meant he was a part of Quebec society that was often the victim of harassment and prejudice. I always thought that all Jews were meek and mild, but that was before I met Irving. Irv would have made a great soldier and commander. He was blessed with a charisma and charm that concealed his ruthless nature. Irv was a born psychopath and his stubborn refusal to comply with even the simplest of society's rules stood him at odds with all levels of authority. He once refused to pay rent and when the landlord threatened to sue him, he just laughed at him.

"I'm unseizable," he challenged. "I just got out of jail and I have no assets. I own nothing. You'll get nothing from me, and it will take months before you get me out of this house." He then made good on his threat by spending what remained of his rent money to hire a lawyer to stall his eviction.

In order to maintain unseizability, Irving used front men for everything. For the homes he owned. For the cars he drove. For the race horses he bought and gambled on. In order to protect his assets, he always had a "paper" drawn up by his civil lawyer which he would put away someplace safe until he needed it. Not too many people would challenge Irv over any of his possessions, regardless of whose name they were in, but the lawyer's paper seemed to give him peace of mind.

A true anarchist who lived by his own rules, Irv saved his greatest contempt for stoolies and rats. He was always talking about his disdain for this kind of person and made it clear that ratting was not something he would ever tolerate. His first bust for the armed robbery of a supermarket had come because his partner's younger brother had ratted them out. It had cost Irving twelve years of his life. He often expressed regret that he had let his partner talk him out of killing the younger brother and he swore that he would never make that mistake again.

Irving had learned the jewelry trade in jail, partly because his father was a successful jeweler and partly because it allowed him to have bartering power. Jewelers were the only convicts allowed to possess gold, which, like cigarettes, is another type of money in jail. Gold was even better than cigarettes, however, in that it could be used as a commodity on the inside as well as on the outside. What Irving did with his gold inside the pen was a mystery to me because he did not drink and he did not use drugs. He said he made jewelry with the gold to sell to the other inmates and I suspect that Irv came out of jail with a lot more money than he brought in.

Irving usually drank diet soft drinks except for the odd time when he chose to celebrate with one solitary glass of planter's punch. When I asked him why he did not loosen up more often he said he liked to keep his wits about him. I saw him stoned only once when he was taking some painkillers that I gave him for his bad back. He took his pill with a sip of rum and, under the influence of both codeine and alcohol, he was pleasant and charming. It was a side of him that Irv did not like other people to see.

Unlike most career criminals, Irving had a wealthy background with maids and butlers and he had lived in big homes in the nicest part of town. He had been given everything he wanted growing up, but along with his family's wealth came rules and authority. Parental authority. School authority. Legal authority. None of which Irving was going to stand for, with his disdain for following rules and his stubborn nature. He ran away from the family home at a young age and began living on the streets using his muscle and his wits. His addiction to crime followed an addiction to gambling, which Irving thought he had under control at the time that he met me. He used to own racehorses paid for with loot from his bank robberies and he gambled much of his stolen money away at the track. His racehorse was called Lucky which was a misnomer if ever there was one. Irving's racehorse never earned a dime in any of his races and the only person really betting on him was Irving.

When Irving and I first went into business together, he called me to a meeting at his apartment and sat me down with a solemn look. We were alone in his tidy unostentatious fifth-floor dwelling. There was a couch that looked nice but was uncomfortable and a teak dining table and chairs that looked like they were seldom used. The apartment came with wall-to-wall carpet and a small kitchenette that looked like it was not very well set up for cooking, with hardly any counter space. At that meeting Irv was wearing a terrycloth bathrobe which was complimented by a pair of comfortable leather slippers. Irving conducted much of his life in his bathrobe. He even came to poker games at my house wearing only slippers and a bathrobe. On this occasion, he was wearing his pale gold bathrobe and his brown slippers as he laid out the terms of our arrangement.

"Okay, here's how it is. We split the expenses fifty-fifty. We split the income fifty-fifty. Even-steven partners. Don't rat on me, and don't ever cross me. I've been crossed before and it never ends nice. They all cry and piss themselves in the end. But it's always too late."

As he spoke, he looked at me with a deadly expression in his eyes. It was a clear message and I knew that he meant what he said. But I was not worried. It was not my nature to rat, nor to be dishonest in my dealings, so I had nothing to fear from Irving. He told me he had already sent Charlie down to Jamaica to send up a four-hundred-pound load, but Charlie had run into major problems completing his task. It seems that Charlie had enlisted the help of Ryan McCann and his partner Robby to set up the purchase of the weed in Jamaica. The two men delivered the weed to Charlie, but when he went to pick up his weed at his rented Jamaican villa a few weeks later, someone had absconded with the stash. Charlie was told by Robby that a Jamaican must have swiped the load. But when Charlie questioned the Jamaican housekeeper at his villa, she described a white man with curly hair who had come by with a truck and taken the four suitcases full of weed from the garage. Robby had curly hair. And Ryan had a curly hair wig that he was showing off at parties. Four hundred pounds of cleaned and pressed marijuana was worth a sizable amount of money. Even in Jamaica, it was worth twenty thousand dollars or more. Irving must have been furious to have lost that kind of money, even if half of it belonged to his partner Charlie. He knew from Charlie that I had lived for a time in Jamaica and he had heard from Charlie about some of my smuggling successes.

I listened intently as Irving laid out the score. He had a door into Canada he told me. A couple of guys he knew from jail were working on the waterfront and were willing to boost a crate full of weed if someone would ship it to them. He asked me if I could put a load of weed together in Jamaica and ship it to his waterfront contacts in Montreal. He told me that he did not trust Ryan and Robby, who were just names he had heard from Charlie. Irv said he would choke Robby like a chicken if he ever came close enough. Irving had an interesting ability to crack his knuckles at will and he accompanied his threat with a pantomime of choking someone, complete with the finger-cracking sounds of breaking bones. Irving had arranged to have Charlie's Porsche repaired after Jean Paul LaPierre filled it full of bullet holes and he blamed the shootout on Ryan and Robby. Irving seemed to have little or no fear of Jean Paul, even while recognizing that the little Frenchman was capable of a showdown.

"If Jean Paul or anyone else ever bothers you," Irving told me, "just agree to whatever they want and then you leave them to me." The offer was music to my ears. Irving was just what I needed. Not only did he have a door into the country but he also had the wherewithal to deal with Jean Paul and his ilk.

"Just don't have anything to do with those two monkeys when you're down there in Jamaica," Irving instructed, referring to Ryan and Robby. "And don't be saying nothing about our conversation to your wife."

I assured Irv I would comply with his instructions and I shook his hand and left. But since Barbara and I are like two halves of the same clamshell, I went straight home and told my wife everything. I let Irv think that Barbara knew nothing until Irving came to know Barbara well enough to realize that his fears about her were unfounded. Before either one of them knew it, Barbara was treating Irving as she would a long-lost uncle, and Irving had given her stepdaughter status. Irving was very much like her recently departed father, who was gruff and sarcastic but straightforward with his thoughts and emotions. Both men had supreme confidence in their actions, and both had the same barrel-chested appearance. But there the comparisons stop, because Barbara's father was a hardworking family man whose conscience was regularly assuaged by prayers each evening.

Irving, on the other hand, was anything but pious. He had been divorced by his wife, after leaving her and his children on welfare when he went to prison. Irving had two children. A teenaged son named Aaron who was on anti-schizophrenia medication and who walked around in a lonely fog looking for a father substitute. And a daughter named Donna who was a remarkably well-adjusted young woman in her early twenties. Donna was a psychology major in university and I took her diagnosis of her father as a paranoid psychopath at face value, even before I looked up its meaning in a medical dictionary. Neither child played an active role in their father's life, although it was obvious they loved him in spite of his shortcomings. For his part, Irving treated his son about as well as he treated his dog, Nitro, and showed similar misgivings about the usefulness of either. Nitro had a habit of eating rocks until his teeth were worn down to stubs, which annoyed Irving to no end, while Aaron popped prescription pills in a fashion that led Irving to shake his head in disgust.

SMUGGLER'S BLUES

Irving had little to do with his daughter, who had reached a point in her life where she neither needed her father nor respected his way of life. Donna had educated herself into total independence and her only holdover trait from her father's influence showed up in her choice of men. I never knew whether she was being spiteful or if she was merely a victim of her own neurosis, but I found it curious that she dated men very much like her father. When I first met Donna, she was dating Irving's ex-con partner from his very first holdup who also was named Irving. Little Irving had turned his life around at that point and owned a moderately successful computer repair service. When Donna's father, Big Irving, tempted her boyfriend back into a life of crime, Little Irving was eventually sent back to jail. At which point, Donna started dating a career criminal named Ziggy Epstein, who was another member of our smuggling crew. Ziggy was a nice young man several years younger than Donna. He was kind and thoughtful, but I could never fathom why Irving's daughter chose men who were so far beneath her hard-earned station in life.

The first thing I did after getting tacit approval from Barbara to go ahead with Irving's proposal was to call Ryan. Even though I had lost faith in lyin' Ryan, he was the only person I knew capable of putting together a four-hundred-pound load of weed in Jamaica on short notice. I let him know from the outset that I was brokering a deal for some mob guys, and I gave him the same ominous warning Irving had given me. I told Ryan nothing of how the weed was being shipped. No timetables. No connections. I only told him what I wanted and when I wanted it and I promised payment upon delivery.

Ryan had our buddy Brian Kholder take care of our business. Brian had spent long hours in Jamaica overseeing the pressing of weed for some of Ryan's earlier scams.

Brian came from a good background, which does not refer to the lovely mother and hardworking father who brought him up. Brian's references came from his uncle Moe, a notorious gangster and pimp in the underworld and a wise guy for the Montreal Italian mob. Uncle Moe was dying of cancer when I first met Brian, but his uncle's reputation remained intact when, from his hospital bed, he sent shovels with red ribbons tied on, to those who still owed him money. Brian was not like his uncle Moe in the least respect. Brian was a philosopher by nature and the only one of my smuggler friends who actually had a university degree. He was soft-spoken and mellow, as was his wife Karen, who also had a degree. Brian and Karen had been the king and queen of their west-end high school before they moved on to Sir George Williams University. Neither of them ever held a real job that I was aware of, and I often wondered how they ended up in the smuggling business.

Brian and his wife were the first to wear Earth shoes, which were designed on a reverse incline with the toes up and the heels down. They were the first to buy a small Japanese car. They were the first of the university crowd to drop out of mainstream society and live in the underground society. Once in a while Brian would help his dad out on construction projects in Montreal, showing up on the job site wearing designer boots and a bomber jacket. His brothers, little Buddy and crazy Alex, would laugh at his disco dude appearance. But while they were toiling for peanuts for their father, Brian was raking in tons of cash dealing and smuggling marijuana.

Brian was a prolific reader with an interest in the philosophical side of life. He introduced me to books like *Autobiography of a Yogi* and Elizabeth Kubler-Ross's book, *On Death and Dying*. I did not like one of his favourites called *Seth Speaks*, by Jane Roberts, but I read it just so I could dispute and discuss the subject matter with him. I did not agree with all that Brian said or did, but I liked his character very much. He was a gentle person who retreated from life and its problems with downers like Valium, which he also took to avoid the comedown from cocaine.

I enjoyed discussing the deeper aspects of our existence with him, just as Barbara enjoyed the down-to-earth attitude of Brian's wife Karen. I had a lot of respect for Karen, who was an attractive fashion trend setter in our circle and the first person I knew who went out on the town wearing a silk scarf as a blouse. She tied the scarf around her neck and around her waist and let it hang loosely over her breasts. When she had finished knotting the scarf, she looked sexier than most other girls even though they were wearing designer blouses. When my buddies and I would drop by his downtown high-rise apartment to take Brian out for a drink, Karen would always encourage him to go with us. My own wife would often grumble and bitch when I announced that I was going out with the boys, but Karen was too cool for that approach. "Go," she told Brian. "Go and have fun with your friends." More often than not, Brian would choose to stay home with his wife instead of coming out with us, and I often thought that Karen's approach would work better on me than Barbara's did.

I had known Brian since the first E-24 scam. Brian was the one who grabbed the first two bags we shipped north and walked them through customs when his cousin Alexandra could not manage them because they were too heavy. I was right behind him on that trip and I was impressed with his stoic reliability when the chips came down. He looked like he was spacing out, as his eyes widened to the task and he carried the two suitcases straight up to the customs counter. His ice-blue eyes were tripping, but when he started talking to the custom's agent, his soft demeanor came through for him, along with the E-24 card, and he was waved through without a baggage check.

Brian Kholder's teeth were not in very good shape when I first met him, a trait that ran in his entire family, except for his sister Bonnie. One of the first things Brian did when he ran into money was to get all of his rotten teeth capped. When the dentist tried to tell him that choosing a shade of enamel that was too white would look unnatural, Brian ignored his advice and picked the whitest shade available. He ended up with the most beautiful smile I ever saw and I never once heard anyone comment that his teeth looked unnatural.

I came to rely on Brian for many of my needs in Jamaica when the scam that Irving pitched to me started to come together. After New York, I decided never to expose myself again in any future smuggling venture. I was a thinker not a mule. It was not a matter of fear, it was a matter of status. I was paying for the scam. I was running the scam. They were my contacts on both ends. I was not going to expose myself to arrest when there was no need. Not now, not ever.

Having arranged with Brian to have the four hundred pounds of weed cleaned and pressed, we went to check up on his progress in a small weed farming community north of Montego Bay. It was a pleasant drive in the cool morning sun and I put my little rented Civic through its paces. The roads of Jamaica lend themselves to spirited driving, with twists and turns and narrow switchbacks. It took about two hours to reach our destination, with the slowest part of the journey coming at Brownstown where the paved road turns to red dust. Brian guided me through the many towns and parishes along the way until we ended our journey high in the mountains of Cockpit Country. The Jamaican overseer in a mountainous parish outside of Browns-town was a young but very mature inhabitant of a small village that survived on growing marijuana. His name was Bossa and he pretty much ran the cultivation area like a general. He would give orders in the soft-spoken voice of a girl, and if they were not obeyed instantly, he would chastise the offender with a hard slap on the arm with the flat side of his machete blade.

The scene I came upon reminded me of movies I had seen about tribes in Africa who bowed to their chief. Everyone gave Bossa respect befitting a man of far older years. I could never put my finger on why he garnered so much respect from the other villagers until I came to realize the simple truth. Bossa was a born leader. He worked alongside his men, with twice the effort they put in. When they slowed down, he prodded them. When they asked questions, he knew the answers. Bossa was thick in the arms and chest and had a smile that came as easily to his face as did a scowl, if warranted. He was the same age as Brian, and I noticed he was captivated by the same interesting qualities in Brian that I saw. Bossa and Brian would talk about things as eclectic and diverse as God and the universe and death and rein-carnation and a thousand things that had nothing to do with smuggling weed. Brian returned to Jamaica one time without the hundred thousand dollars that he owed Bossa for a weed front and was forced to admit, "I'm sorry, man, your money went up my arm." Incredibly Bossa just smiled and said, " No problem man. We made lots of money together. And we will make money together again."

Brian had a helper in Brownstown, a quiet young man who hailed from Dollard des Ormeaux in Montreal. The young man's name was Bob McTavish and he was living with the villagers in one of the concrete block field huts that Bossa owned. Bob was busy building a latrine when I first met him. He told me that there was no running water and no electricity in the rural community, so he was helping them out. He also helped out with the pressing of the weed but his presence in the community had to be hidden from the local police. If the Jamaican police saw a white man in the area, they would assume that he was there on weed business. Once that became established, there would be no end to the bribes required from both the white man and Bossa himself.

When I met with Bossa and spoke to him for the first time, he told me that he wanted his money up front for the four hundred pounds of coli that Brian had commissioned him to deliver.

"No way," I told him. "You'll get your money when you deliver the weed to my stash house in Kingston." That put the responsibility of getting the weed safely to Kingston on Bossa's shoulders and off me. I told Bossa that I wanted the weed picked by hand, not chopped by machete, so as to get only the top most buds, without all the thick heavy branches and sticks at the bottom of the plants. "And don't press the weed when it's wet," I warned him. "It rots inside the bales when it's pressed wet."

I learned a lot about Brian on that trip to Jamaica. When we got off the plane, he had me stop at the first pharmacy he could find in Kingston. He loaded up on Valium, which was available without prescription in Jamaica, and he offered me some of the twenty milligram pills. I thanked him but declined the offer, being content to smoke a fat joint of weed. We were on the road to Brownstown, after Brian dropped several Valium and had settled into his seat to enjoy the ride. We took the main highway out of town that led into the mountains and I took pleasure in the winding, twisting road that felt like a race course with soft shoulders and deadly cliffs. A short distance into our trip, Brian spied two Jamaican girls walking by the side of the road. One was not bad looking, if you like the country girl type, but the other girl was not so pretty and she was clearly fat.

"Stop the car!" Brian said with such force that I thought it was an emergency.

"Pull over and stop beside that girl."

"You gotta be kidding me," I said, as I slowed the car down and pulled to the side of the road.

"Hey," Brian said, addressing the fat girl with his movie star smile. "Come over here for a minute."

The girl came closer with a shy grin, while her friend stood by, hoping for her own invitation to come over to the car. There was little traffic on the road and it was about twelve noon with the sun straight overhead when Brian asked the girl a question that needed no reply.

"How would you like to make some money?"

"Sure, why not?" the girl answered.

"I'll give you ten dollars if I can feel your tits."

"Sure," she answered with a big smile.

Brian reached out the window and took his time feeling up her big, heavy breasts before handing the girl her money.

"Okay, let's go," he said, as though he had just purchased a pack of cigarettes. Then he added. "Don't you just love Jamaica?"

After my visit to inspect the weed in Brownstown, I located a cabinetmaker in Kingston and consigned him to make me a large shipping crate. I told him that I was shipping home some personal effects and I gave him dimensions and my choice of wood. No knotholes, I instructed him, and the crate had to be solid with a lid that fit tight. Then I found a rental house in Kingston where the weed was to be stored until the next ship to Canada was ready to depart.

The house was on Old Hope Road, just a few miles from the Kingston waterfront and came with security grills and a yard that was fenced and gated, as were most houses in the all-white area. I told the rental agent that I had my own staff of maids and gardeners and declined her offer of some. I signed a one-year lease, with two months rent in advance. I did not quibble about the rental cost. I told the agent I was a writer and liked my privacy. She just handed me the house keys and went on her way to tally up her commissions. I located a shipping and customs broker on the Kingston waterfront and booked him to do the pickup and paperwork for the wooden crate which I labeled myself with stencils that I had preordered in Montreal. One stencil read Fragile and came with a wine glass symbol. The other one was the address of the recipient, a doctor whose name I had researched out of a Montreal telephone book.

Then I arranged with Brian to have Bossa deliver the four hundred pounds of pressed weed to the house I had rented. I paid for the weed only after it was delivered to the stash house. I put on gloves to cover my prints and helped pack the pressed and taped bundles into the waiting shipping crate. I threw in limes and mothballs for odor control, after which I ran a bead of wood glue over all of the wood joins and seams. Brian brought along his pal Bob McTavish to help out. I commissioned Bob to babysit the load and I came by to check on him every day. When the time finally came that the ship bound for Montreal arrived in port, I had my shipping broker send a truck to the house to pick up the sealed-up crate. Then I waited for the call from the broker to come down to his office and pay the shipping costs, once the crate had been weighed. This was the most dangerous part of the job because if there was a problem, it would probably show up after the crate was weighed.

The first shipment of weed was shipped off like clockwork and I flew home to Montreal to report my success to Irving. He was ecstatic at the news. The wait for the weed's arrival in Montreal was filled with jokes about our ship coming in. When the load finally arrived several weeks later, Irving was contacted by his dock connections. In order not to blow the scam, they needed us to send them a replacement crate with personal effects weighing what was reported on the shipping manifests for the crate of weed. The boys were going to grab the weed crate from Jamaica and replace it with a clean crate. I used my stereo and some small furniture items to comply with the request and had the replacement crate delivered to the boys downtown. We never referred to them by name. It was always "the boys downtown." Eventually the crate was delivered to us. I was informed by Irving at the last minute that we needed a stash house, and I quickly thought of a couple that Barbara and I used to get stoned with when we first started smoking hash. Alex Jones and his wife Suzette were people that we knew from my working days in the copier and printing machine business. Alex was a service technician who drove a Volvo and had about as much excitement in his life as a kindergarten teacher. He was a frugal Scotsman, and when I offered to pay him for looking after some weed, he asked how much money, not how much weed. He was tickled pink over the money he received, but he blanched pale when he first saw how much weed there was. The weed arrived in a panel van at Alex's house and we parked the panel truck in Alex's garage. Irving and I began unloading and as soon as Alex saw how much weed there was, he immediately protested. But his greed overcame his fear when Irving pacified him with an additional five hundred dollars.

"Hung for a sheep or hung for a lamb. What's the difference?" Irving told Alex while sweetening the pot with more money. Irving's ability to read people and cut right to the chase was spot on, because Alex pocketed the extra few hundred Irving gave him and never complained again. In fact, Alex was subsequently promoted to replacement shipping crate maker, as well as stash house provider, until the weed came in by container loads that were too large to fit in his attic.

After the weed was safely put away that first time, Irving asked me if I knew anyone who could sell it. I didn't want to handle any pot in Montreal while I was taking care of the expediting in Jamaica, so I told Irving about Brian Kholder and recommended him as our local distributor in Montreal. When it became obvious that Brian alone could not handle the volume of weed that was coming in, I subsequently arranged a meeting between Irving and Jean Paul LaPierre. I hated the thought of giving the little Frenchman an opportunity to make money off us, but he was, without a doubt, the most reliable weed wholesaler in town. Not only was he able to sell the weed in bulk, he also took care of any bad debtors.

Irv and J.P. met in a restaurant in downtown Montreal. The usually reclusive Jean Paul brightened immediately when Irving passed him a scrap of paper with three names on it as references. One of the names on the list was Jean Paul's friend and an ex-partner of his future brother-in-law named Roger Ouimet. Roger was a dangerous man who had done bank robberies with Irving and hits with the infamous Hells Angels' killer, Jacques "Apache" Francois. Roger Ouimet and Irving had also done scores together including debt collections, robberies and extortions. Irving never confided in me about any hits he might have done with Roger Ouimet, which I attributed to the fact that there is no statute of limitations on murder in Canada.

Small world, you might say of Irving's connections to Jean Paul, but like I said before, in the underworld, all roads seem to lead to the same places and the same people. My partner Irving and our new partner Jean Paul made a deal that day. Jean Paul would take all the weed Irving could give him and he would also take care of any collections and bad debts.

So there we were. We had the way in. We had the way out. We had the Jamaica end down. We had the Montreal end down.

Now all Irving and I had to do was collect up our rewards and spend our money.

Chapter Four

The Twilight Zone Incident

I suppose I have always had an affinity for roguish characters. I think that, to some extent, we all prefer the company of people who have a little of the Devil in them over the piously perfect and the politically correct. Rogues and Robin Hoods are far more interesting than their priestly counterparts and their errant behaviour is often forgiven by mainstream society, up to a certain point. Society displays a degree of tolerance for scofflaws who break unpopular laws, like the speeder who uses a radar detector to beat the radar trap or the businessman who cheats the taxman out of his fair share of taxes. These lawbreakers are not held up to the same contempt that we reserve for more serious criminals because the laws being broken are not necessarily popular laws. That is how I saw my situation. Like a modern day Robin Hood who was bucking the law prohibiting marijuana. Irving and I were supplying a product that people wanted and a service that the law arbitrarily decided should not be provided. Weed was a benign and harmless product, if we were to believe the report of the Quebec Ledain Commission into soft drugs. The Ledain Commission likened a toke or two of pot to a drink or two of wine and stated that marijuana and hashish were far less dangerous than tobacco. As far as I was concerned, the only one who was getting hurt by our activities was the taxman, and I went out of my way to give him his dues. I even invented a legitimate income so that I could pay taxes on at least a portion of my easily gotten gains, just to keep the taxman off my back.

After our first four hundred pound load of weed was taken from the waterfront by Irving's dock connections and handed over to us for distribution on the street, I hired my friends, Joe Dudley and Bob Bishop, to rent a truck to go down to the waterfront to pick up our replacement crate from Canada Customs. The boys downtown had already replaced the weed crate with a crate containing my stereo and some tables and chairs so that our importing scam would not get blown. But it still took some effort to convince my friends that the crate was clean. I finally gave Joe Dudley and Bishop the customs and excise documents needed to clear the cargo and told them that they could give me up to the Man if there was anything other than my personal effects inside the crate. In due course, Bishop and Joe returned with the switched crate. Joe laughed and said that while they were driving through the customs terminal, Bishop was vibrating so much it seemed like the truck was running even when it was turned off. Bishop sputtered his denials as they both argued playfully, looking happy and relieved to have completed their project without complications. I came to use my two friends many times to repeat the same exercise as subsequent shipments of weed arrived in Canada. My stereo and furniture were sent through customs so many times that the speakers ended up looking like Swiss cheese from all the test holes drilled into the wood cabinets by suspicious customs agents.

The crates we shipped became larger and larger, and then we started sending full containers of weed as our audacity and expertise improved. With each successful shipment of marijuana from Jamaica, the good life became even better, to the point where we became hedonistic. Irving and I had standing reservations at The Steak Place Restaurant in Pointe Claire. The owner of the restaurant, who was named Francois, had been involved in a scam some years earlier when Irving sold him a container load of stolen gin. That mistake landed Francois a heavy fine, after the

RCMP found a bottle of the stolen swag in his desk drawer at the restaurant office. The fine became even larger after the feds raided his home and hobby farm to find the rest of the shipment of stolen gin in his barn. In spite of, or perhaps because of his previous history with Irving, Francois treated us like royalty. His sumptuous service was rewarded with generous tips and we ate there at least three times a week. We went to The Steak Place so often that when I asked my wife if she would like to go there for dinner one night, she answered, "Not The Steak Place again!"

Can you believe it? You'd think I was inviting her to Burger King.

I bought Irving's eighteen carat gold pendent and chain from him. It was "legit," he told me, unlike much of what he owned in life. The medallion was comprised of two Austrian gold coins that were carried in a gold brace which was designed to hold the coins back to back. An eagle with spread wings decorated the faces of the coins which, at .999 fine, is the purest gold in the world. I also had an eighteen carat gold bracelet made for myself at a jeweler who was a friend of Irving's. The bracelet featured big chunky links of solid gold and an invisible clasp that made it look as though it was permanently affixed to my wrist. The bracelet weighed a total of five troy ounces and I often wondered if someone might contemplate sawing off my arm for the gold.

Irving exceeded my extravagance in jewelry by buying a new gold pendent for himself that was so excessively large that it looked like an Olympic medal hanging around his neck. The pendent was made with the horoscope sign of Libra stamped on it and came with an eighteen carat chain that weighed close to a pound. I used to laugh and kid Irv that the chain looked like a gold-plated dog leash.

In spite of Irving's warnings to me about showing off, when our moneymaking scam was underway, we both purchased late model Mercedes-Benz cars, completing the picture of our undeniable wealth. Irving figured that because we were in the car business, we could drive the cars without drawing too much heat but I didn't give a damn which police forces noticed me, as long as I had a nice ride. My Benz was a two-year-old 450 SL two seat convertible in metallic blue with tan upholstery. It was a beautiful automobile that commanded respect in a way that my Corvette never could. People actually stopped and waved me into traffic in the Benz. When I drove my Corvette it was like waving red flags at a bull. No one ever gave me a break in traffic unless I pushed my way through.

Irving's car was a brand new 450 SLC four seat coupe with silver exterior and black upholstery. The car was a dream to drive and afforded him the respect he had so long been denied. Cash money was coming in on a regular basis from the sale of our weed. At first I had so much money that I kept some hidden in my attic and some in my safety deposit box at the bank and I always had at least a few thousand dollars in my pocket.

As my trips to Jamaica increased in frequency, the size of our weed shipments increased as well. On my first trip to Jamaica, I shipped four hundred pounds north which I have already told you was brought into Canada successfully. Then I shipped seven hundred pounds. Then twelve hundred. Twenty-two hundred. Thirty-two hundred. Forty-four hundred. The last load I sent up totaled fifty-five hundred pounds of Jamaican coli. All told, Irving and I shipped eighteen metric tons of Jamaican marijuana to Canada over a five-year period and we never lost so much as an ounce. The boys on the dock took fifty percent after expenses and payouts, and in my opinion, they were worth every cent of their end. Irving and I split the other fifty percent after expenses and payouts.

My old pal Ryan McCann would have been enjoying at least a part of my good fortune had he not pulled his extortion tactics on me in Jamaica. I continued my charade of a friendship with him until Irving pulled me aside after one of our poker games. Irving told me that he could not understand why I was still associating with Ryan after what he had pulled on me. He made me feel like a fool and I had to agree with him. There was no need to entertain anyone I did not like any longer, and after Irving's words took effect, I called Ryan on the phone and told him not to come around anymore. I told him that I could forgive what he did to me in Jamaica, but I could not forget what he did. He tried to remind me that he had repaid my losses in weed, but I told him that that was not the issue. His breach of friendship and trust was eating at me to the point that I could not stand seeing him anymore. He was worried about my change of heart until I told him that I was not going to seek revenge on him. But I did not want him hanging around anymore, and I told him that Irving did not want him coming around, either.

I felt good telling Ryan off. It was long overdue, in my opinion. But banishment was only the beginning of Ryan's retribution for his sins. His real downfall came when he was found out to be a liar and a cheat by his partner, Jean Paul, and it happened in a most peculiar way. Charlie Wilson and Jean Paul were at war at the time, having both survived an earlier shootout over some four hundred pounds of weed. And then something almost miraculous happened. Even though he was close to losing his mind at the time and was running around saying, "Tweet, Tweet," Charlie came up with a real brainstorm. He called up Jean Paul and arranged a meeting. The last time the two had a meeting they ended up in a gunfight, so it is quite surprising that Charlie took this course of action. It was even more surprising that Jean Paul, who was a suspicious soul to begin with, agreed to meeting his enemy. I suspect that because Jean Paul was working with Irving and selling our weed, his allegiances had shifted away from Ryan and more towards our direction.

Whatever the reasoning behind their actions, Charlie went to Jean Paul's house and sat down for a coffee and some conversation. Charlie told Jean Paul about his four hundred pounds of weed that went missing in Jamaica. He accused Ryan and Robby of a double-cross that led to the shootout with Jean Paul and himself. Charlie came armed with some facts to back up his side of the story. He gave Jean Paul the phone number of the caretaker of his Jamaican villa and repeated the story that the caretaker told of a white man with curly hair taking Charlie's suitcases of weed. With the Jamaican maid's phone number in his hands, Jean Paul called Ryan over to his house on a pretext of business. When Ryan arrived, Jean Paul began to question him in the kitchen while Charlie hid in the hall closet to listen to Ryan's answers. Robby was called over to Jean Paul's as well, but fortunately for Robby, he was in Jamaica at the time. Jean Paul had his future brother-in-law, Rene Lemiuex, on hand as backup. Rene held a shortened baseball bat under the kitchen table while Jean Paul sat listening to Ryan explain how he had invested Jean Paul's money in buying their last load of weed. When asked by Jean Paul if that was the same four hundred pounds that belonged to Charlie, Ryan denied any knowledge of Charlie's missing weed and added that he was told by the maid at Charlie's villa that some black Jamaicans had stolen Charlie's weed. Ryan painted himself into a corner that day and Charlie stepped out of the closet to call him on his bullshit. A phone call to the maid in Jamaica confirmed that it was a white man who stole the weed. A white man with curly hair. Ryan's partner Robby had curly hair. And Ryan himself was known to possess a curly haired wig. It became clear to Jean Paul that Ryan had not spent the loan shark's money on weed. Ryan had spent Jean Paul's money elsewhere and then stolen Charlie's weed to ship north to Montreal.

It must have been a cold, sobering moment for Ryan when he realized he was caught in a fistful of lies and deception but there was little time for him to ponder his bad fortune. On a given signal from Jean Paul, Rene swung the baseball bat across the table catching Ryan across the temple and knocking him to the floor in one blow. Then Jean Paul carried Ryan's moaning body and dropped it over the railing to the lower floor of his split level home so as not to get blood on the living room's wall-to-wall carpets. Ryan's beating continued in the laundry room with blows from the baseball bat that were interspersed with questions. The vicious attack continued until Jean Paul was satisfied that he knew the complete truth. When he was finished his interrogation, the loan shark cleaned Ryan's face with a damp towel and dropped him at the Laval Hospital emergency ward with a warning about what would happen to him if he ratted. Ryan survived the beating, but just barely. The doctors at the hospital said one more blow to the head would have finished him. When he recovered enough to leave the hospital some weeks later, Ryan and his wife quietly vanished from the Montreal scene and moved to Toronto to start a new life.

If Jean Paul had had his way, Robby would have paid an even steeper price than Ryan. Jean Paul never did like Robby, who passed himself off as a bored and petulant college student and displayed a calculated arrogance in his every move. That Robby felt superior to Jean Paul was obvious but it was not personal: Robby felt superior to everyone. Robby was a college dropout who had been the former president of the Sir George Williams University's student union. He drove a Corvette that was fully paid for, and he came from a well off family in the west end. Robby had come down from a level of society that Jean Paul was still trying to reach up to. There was no doubt in Jean Paul's mind that Robby was responsible for the theft of Charlie's weed in Jamaica. This shifting of the majority of blame to Robby from Ryan was convenient for the psychopath who did not really want to kill his onetime friend. The blame shift was reinforced by Ryan during his baseball bat-inspired confession, but the truth was that Jean Paul hated Robby and was looking for any opportunity to hurt him.

Jean Paul was hanging around with a new friend at the time. The friend was an American visitor to Canada who was said to be a psychopathic killer who enjoyed torturing his victims. After dropping Ryan at the hospital, Jean Paul contacted the American hit man and gave him a contract to get Robby down in Jamaica. Jean Paul did not care about the expense, as the cost of the hit man was covered by the money that Jean Paul no longer had to pay his ex-partner Ryan for the last load of weed. A silenced .22 caliber pistol was smuggled down to Jamaica by Sammy Polanski to do the hit. Sammy was a small-time Montreal hoodlum with a penchant for publicity. When a newspaper crime reporter named Jean Pierre Charbonneau published a book called *The Canadian Connection* that had all of our names in it, most of us were choked about the exposure. Sammy on the other hand went around telling everyone which page he was on. Sammy was to set up Robby by offering him a free stay at a villa in Jamaica. Jean

Paul gave Sammy the money to rent the villa. Robby had taken him up on his offer and was staying at the villa with his girlfriend, Paula.

But before Jean Paul's American killer could arrive in Jamaica to meet Sammy and complete the hit, Robby received a warning telephone call at the villa. There was speculation that the call came from Ryan who had caught wind of Jean Paul's plot. Or that it came from my pal Manny, who was working at Jean Paul's furniture store and dealing Jean Paul's weed and hash on the side. However, I eventually heard that the tip came from a CIA agent named Sid. Sid was the guy who ran the other video and slot machines around Jamaica that were in competition with Charlie's. I once saw Sid riding a moped scooter through town, when he stopped to collect his winnings from the slot machine in Hopewell's general store and bar. Sid was a slim fellow. He was middle-aged and nondescript. He looked like a tourist. I never would have made him for a CIA agent if my Jamaican friends had not clued me in. After the call came from Sid, Robby wisely evacuated the villa that same day, escaping certain death just in time. The last I heard of Robby, he had moved to Vancouver Island to start a new life and, like Ryan, he was never seen again in the Montreal dope scene.

After missing Robby, Jean Paul's hit man left Jamaica and took on a contract for an Arizona judge who was feared for his harsh sentencing. He was hired by a Montreal drug smuggler and a Texas marijuana smuggler both awaiting trial. The hit man was caught after killing the judge and wounding the crown prosecutor, and I was surprised to learn that the guy was Charles Harrelson, actor Woody Harrelson's father. Harrelson senior got several life prison terms for the killings in Arizona. His son bankrolled an appeal, which failed, and Charles died in prison in 2007 of a heart attack. I saw a television interview with the American hit man, some years after he was jailed, and I was chilled by his calm demeanor and his intelligence. He seemed too damn smart to be doing what he was jailed for and I figured he was typical of many of the criminals and social deviates I have come to know. They are all in it for the rush more than the money.

SMUGGLER'S BLUES

With revenge being a dish best served cold, I should have been happy that my enemies were vanquished. Robby and Ryan were out of the game and Jean Paul had done my dirty work for me, while my conscience remained clean as a whistle. You would think I would be forgiving of Jean Paul who had done the right thing in many people's minds. But I was still uncomfortable around him and I let Irving deal with Jean Paul exclusively.

A strange though unrelated occurrence that same summer saw me looking through the want ads for a gun. It was late in the summer and the fields around my dead-end street house were motionless in the still night air. I had been out playing poker that night when I made my way home at around 1:00 a.m. I parked my Mercedes in the driveway and started walking to my front door. The entrance was only a few steps away, on the side of the house, facing the surrounding fields. Suddenly I heard the sound of a gunshot go off that seemed to be right beside my ear. I know gunshots when I hear them and I instantly dropped to the ground with my heart racing. I scurried around my car on hands and knees and then ran into my house. Once inside, I realized that I had nothing for protection other than a machete and a spear gun. I waited for hours inside the house, unable to go to sleep while I wondered if the shooting was random or if it was a murder attempt that had failed. I did not call the police, who would have asked too many embarrassing questions and I was walking on eggshells for a week until I read in our local papers that some kid had been apprehended for running around our neighbourhood firing gunshots. But by then I had already found and purchased a gun of my own. It was a .30 caliber deer hunting carbine like my father used to own. As there were no children around my house, I felt it was safe to keep the rifle loaded in the hall closet. The purchase of the rifle was timely, because although I did not know it at the time, I had good reason to have one. I was successful at dodging the cops and Canada Customs but what I did not know was that someone else was stalking me. A crew of young American guys who were hanging out in Montego Bay and Kingston had successfully strong-armed some of the west end wannabees who were trying to run their own dope scams out of Jamaica. The Americans had already put the west end kids on the arm in Jamaica and had even followed them to Montreal to coerce more money out of them. The Americans must have thought that all Montreal men were meek and mild, because they actually had the nerve to approach Big John Miller and me when we were sitting at a fashion show in the Pegasus Hotel in Jamaica. One of these clowns recognized Bob McTavish, who was sitting at our table, and came over uninvited to talk to him. I could not believe my ears when Bob leaned over to me to announce that the American wanted a piece of our action. It was not a request. The little goof was trying to put us on the arm. I was disappointed by Big John's response when I whispered Bob's message to him. He just laughed like I had told a joke and went on watching the fashion show. I looked at Bob McTavish and said in a voice loud enough for his American visitor to hear.

"Tell your friend to fuck off, unless he wants to get hurt." I felt confident with Big John at my side and a sharp buck knife in my pocket. I expected a problem in the parking lot later, but the American must have thought better of his idea because he left with his buddies. I found out a few weeks later that the Americans were preparing to kidnap me and hold me for a ransom in Montreal. Not only that, but they were going to use my friend and ex-partner Ross to set me up. Ross, if you remember, was the driver who ferried the Ali Baba weed from New York to Montreal in the back seat of his father's car. Ross was still my friend . . . or so I thought, until Bob McTavish clued me in. Bob was supposed to be in on Ross's scheme but then he told me that he had changed his mind. Bob was a strange guy like that. I found out once that he was hanging out with the federal Crown prosecutor in the west end and was going to parties with him. I was invited to these parties by Bob on several occasions and in a more than casual way. "Come on to the party," he urged me one time. "It's a celebration for this guy who just got out of jail. Everyone is going to be there."

Yeah right, Bob. Just what I wanted. A party with a Crown prosecutor, a bunch of lowlifes I did not know and some heat score who just got out of prison. Many years later, I read a tell-all book that described how a stoolie came out of jail and started working for the Montreal RCMP. He wrote about a coming-out-of-jail party that he threw on behalf of his RCMP handlers and how he snagged a Montreal Mafioso and put him away for a long time. It was the same party that Bob had invited me to in the west end and I thank my stars that I hadn't gone. I heard from Bob after that party that the Crown prosecutor would be attending another party and that he was very interested in meeting me. I can only speculate as to why. Maybe he was expecting to hear some unwise bragging or a confession perhaps. Since I didn't go, I will never know. After Bob told me about the kidnap scheme, I called Ross over to my house for a little talk. He brought his girlfriend along and a bag of acid which the two were popping like vitamins. I suspect he wanted the security of the girlfriend in case I had something nasty planned for him. He denied his part in the whole kidnap story, of course, while admitting that the Americans were in fact planning to do just that. He had no answer as to why it was Bob who came to me with the warning and not Ross himself. I warned him that if anything happened to me, my partner Irving and his gang would kill him and his American flakes and not to forget it. Then I told him to fuck off and never come back into my life. He and I were both very fortunate that I didn't know about him making moves on my wife when I was in the U.S. federal detention centre. If I had known that, Ross would possibly be dead and I would be damned to hell for doing it.

In spite of this small hiccup, my life was going as well as I could ever have expected. I had an endless supply of money and all of the backup I could want with my growing list of acquaintances in the underworld. There was just one little problem that remained to be dealt with. You might remember that when Irving and I started our business arrangement, he sent me down to Jamaica behind Charlie Wilson's back. Irving never actually told Charlie that he was dissolving their partnership and starting a new one with me. I felt like a two-timing whore between my loyalty to my new partner Irving and my friendship with his business partner Charlie.

However, I did not allow my discomfort to interfere with my responsibilities. Some time after our second or third successful load of weed was smuggled into Canada Charlie came by my house with a friend. His visit came a few weeks after a *Twilight Zone* type of meeting between us on an Air Canada flight. I was flying down to Jamaica to ship off another load of weed for Irving's contacts to grab, only this time I had my father along as a front for the shipping arrangements. It would not make sense for the broker to see me shipping another load of personal effects so soon after the first load without arousing his suspicions so my father was going to be my front for the broker. You might wonder how my father came to be helping me out on an importing scam. I can't really answer that question except to say that later in life I became closer to both of my parents, who seemed very supportive of my chosen career. To my parents it was all about a harmless drug called marijuana and after all, didn't the Seagrams and the Bronfmans make their fortune by smuggling liquor into the U.S.? The only negative comment I can remember my mother making was, "Whatever you do, son, don't get caught." I suspect she was more concerned about what the neighbours thought, than about the right or wrong of the situation.

Anyways to get back to my story about the Twilight Zone incident, my dad and I were sitting in the middle of Air Canada's economy class, or the cattle car as I call it, when the strange coincidence with Charlie Wilson began. I could see that the plane was completely full as we boarded in Montreal. My dad and I were practically the last ones on the plane. It was not hard to find our seats as there were three empty seats by a window and all of the rest of the seats in the aircraft were full. For a moment I thought that I had lucked out, with an empty seat between my dad and me, but then I saw a briefcase lying on the window seat. It was a black Samsonite briefcase, like the one that Charlie the Weasel carried with him wherever he went. It was identical, right down to the distinctive decal of a Tweety Bird from the Tweety and Sylvester the Cat cartoon. What are the odds that someone else had a briefcase exactly like that, I was wondering, when Charlie came back from the washroom and slid past my dad and me. He excused himself as he sat down beside the window and did not even recognize me at first. Charlie was as amazed as I was about the coincidence of our sitting together on the same plane, side by side. After introducing the two I told him my dad was coming down to buy some land in Jamaica. Charlie accepted that without argument and after that it was an interesting ride. I heard all about Charlie's problems with his gaming machines that he had set up in Jamaica and the problems with his attempted dope deals. "No more dope deals," he said. The Jamaicans were too corrupt and the dope dealers in Montreal were too dishonest and unreliable. The car business was no good, either. And his partner Irving was no good. It was an interesting ride, but I was only too happy to see the last of Charlie when I left him in the terminal at the Montego Bay airport, while I headed on to Kingston with my father.

Three weeks after that plane ride, Charlie was at my door telling me that he had a friend in the car who he wanted me to talk to. Talk is often a euphemism for much more than just words in the underworld, so there was no way I was agreeing to that. I could see that Charlie was agitated. He told me the guy in the car with him was Robert Lavigne. I did not know the name at the time but I heard later from Robert's own partners that Lavigne was a very dangerous man. I was firm in telling Charlie that I would talk to him but I would not let his friend into my house, and I took comfort in knowing I had the loaded rifle in my hall closet. It took thirty minutes to convince Charlie that I was not his enemy, while Robert Lavigne waited outside in the car.

"Yes, I am working with Irving," I told Charlie, "but I was instructed by Irving not to tell you or anyone else what we were doing. It's just business. It's nothing personal. You would have done the same thing in my shoes," I told him. "If you have a problem with Irving because he dropped you from your scam, work it out with him. I'm not the one you should be mad at."

I reminded Charlie that he had already stated his intentions to quit the drug business and I suspected then as I suspect now that he was angrier about being left out of the loop than anything else. He must have heard that Irving had a load of weed in town. Everyone in Montreal was selling the Jamaican weed and everyone was talking about it. Now that he realized that Irving had pulled off their scam without him, Charlie was understandably angry about it. But if he had any idea how much weed Irving and I had actually brought into Montreal, I have no doubt he would have been much angrier than he was. When he started with Irving they were trying to ship off four hundred pounds of weed and Charlie could not get the job done. Now Irving and I were shipping entire containers full of weed to Canada on back-to-back runs. Charlie told me he was pissed off at Irving for going behind his back and that he was pissed off about Jean Paul ending up with his four hundred pounds of weed that Ryan and Robby stole from him in Jamaica. Before he left my house, he said he was going to get his pal Robert Lavigne to take care of both Irving and Jean Paul.

"You don't know this guy," he said pointing to Robert who was waiting in the Porsche outside. "You think Jean Paul's tough? This guy will eat Jean Paul for breakfast."

When they left I immediately phoned Irving from a cool phone. He seemed unfazed by the news of Charlie's visit and his threats. Irving acted like Charlie was a pussycat and told me not to worry. He said that he was going out of town to Ottawa for a few days to take care of the house of a friend who had recently gone to jail. He gave me the phone number there and told me not to call him unless it was an emergency.

"I'll deal with Charlie when I return," he told me. I thought he took the incident rather frivolously, until two days later when I got a phone call from Irving in Ottawa.

"Did you hear the news?" he said in a voice that was heavy on drama and light on surprise. "Little Charlie is dead. Someone shot him and his pal Robert Lavigne last night at a bar north of Montreal. I heard it this afternoon on the one o'clock news on the radio."

Irving gave me a few more details, but as soon as he hung up I switched on the radio to hear the news reports myself. My mind blurred with the news that Charlie, "the Weasel" was dead. The thought that I had spoken to him just the day before overwhelmed me with wonder and surprise.

I was getting the vibe that Irving was involved with the Weasel's demise because he was giving me his report as though he had personally solved our problem with Charlie and Robert Lavigne. But how could that be when Irving was in Ottawa, which was several hours drive from the crime scene? It seemed highly unlikely that he would have done the deed himself and then driven back to Ottawa on icy roads for several hours. And then to brag to me about it on the phone. Irving was smarter than that. But he could have made a phone call to some of his underworld buddies in Montreal. I was hoping to hear some answers before I was picked up for questioning by the police, who I expected on a daily basis after Charlie's murder. I knew they were coming. I was one of the last people to see Charlie alive.

But before the arrangements for Charlie's funeral were even complete, I heard news of two more murders on the radio. This time the reports stated that Jean Paul LaPierre and his girlfriend Susan Braun were found shot to death in her Habitat apartment complex, which was built as part of Expo 67. The news reports said their bodies had lain undisturbed for days. I did not know what was going on at this point. It seemed like people all around me were dying and I had no idea about possible motives or who was behind the killings or who was next. I called Irving in Ottawa again to tell him about Jean Paul and Susan and he seemed genuinely surprised to hear of their deaths. I was not sure if I believed him in his denials about Charlie's murder, because in that case, Irving had motive. However when it came to the deaths of Jean Paul and Susan, he had no motive I could think of. But Irving was the only connecting thread between all four victims.

Except for myself.

"Don't call me from your house anymore," Irving said, after I contacted him about the second set of murders. "In fact don't call me at all unless it's absolutely necessary."

A few days later I was picked up by the Montreal Homicide Squad at my home in the west end of Montreal. I had cleaned house already while waiting for the cops to show over Charlie's murder, but they took so long to come for me that I had moved my weed stash back into my bedroom. I saw the police edition Ford with the dish-plate hubcaps through the front window at the same time as I saw two strangers marching towards my door. They were wearing cheap sports jackets and I knew they were not coming to sell insurance. I went to the bedroom and dumped a half a pound of primo weed down the toilet, most of which floated to the top of the bowl after the flush. When I answered the door, the two homicide detectives were agitated.

"You saw us coming and made a call. Who did you call?"

"I didn't call anyone."

"Yes you did.

"No I didn't."

"You are under arrest for the murder of Charlie Wilson and Robert Lavigne."

"You gotta be joking."

"This is no joke."

After giving me the routine about a lawyer being provided if I needed one, the cops handcuffed me. I knew I had nothing to fear since I was not involved in any way with Charlie's killing. I had been at home with my wife and my friend Bishop when the dirty deed was done. But I did have secrets to protect, not least the purpose of Charlie's last visit to my house with Robert Lavigne. The cops started out by asking me why I had not attended Charlie's funeral, to which I answered that I did not like funerals. The cops were angry at my reluctance to cooperate and so they took me in for questioning. Inside the police station I maintained my silence, but it was only a matter of time before I needed a bathroom break. I was taken to the washroom by the police officer who had been interrogating me. He was a big bruiser of a detective who looked to be a surly pessimist with a stoic resolve to do his job. I was washing my hands when he came over to stand beside me.

"So, you don't want to talk, eh?"

I looked at him with suspicion. "It's none of my business," I said. "I don't want to get involved."

He swung his open hand as hard as he could and hit me on

the side of my head. I have been punched, but I had never been slapped that hard before. I saw stars. Dazed, I staggered a couple of feet away from the big cop and stared back at him in shock.

"This is murder," he said, looking squarely into my eyes. "We don't care about your other little games. This is the homicide squad. We are the cream of the crop. An innocent young girl and several other people are dead," he said. "We want answers."

I could see he was working up to another swing.

"All right, I'll tell you what I know," I replied, sparing myself another blow to the head. "But not in here. Take me back out there and I'll talk."

I pointed to the outer office where the other detectives were seated. I dried my hands and half expected another shot to the head, but instead I was escorted by the bull back to the interrogation room. I was asked why Charlie had come to visit me the day he died and what we talked about. I told the investigating officer that Charlie and I were friends. That we talked about his car lot and the cars that I bought and sold through him. They asked who I thought had killed Charlie and I told them about the shootout between Charlie and Jean Paul. It was common knowledge amongst Charlie's friends that the gunfight had occurred. With both Charlie and Jean Paul dead, it gave the cops something to work on that led nowhere. Realizing that I was offering nothing further, the interrogation was halted with one last question.

"Where is Irving Goldberg?" The burly cop hissed Irving's name as though he was talking about something lower than a snake. I told the cop that I could provide an alibi for Irving because I had phoned him in Ottawa at the time of the murders. I regretted giving any information about Irving's whereabouts, but I suspect that they already knew that information after three weeks of phone taps. They asked me for Irving's address which I would not have given even if I knew it. They asked for his phone number but I told them I did not remember it. After several hours of interrogation, the homicide squad eventually released me, right after plucking a hair from my head. When they led me to another room for the hair sample to be taken, I was surprised to see a man in a white lab coat removing a hair from my buddy Bishop's head. I found out later that they had brought Bishop in for questioning, too, after I gave him as my alibi on the night in question. The homicide squad released Bishop and me at the same time, with a warning not to phone Irving. On the way home I made sure we were not followed, and as soon as I could, I stopped at a pay phone to call Irving in Ottawa. It occurred to me that if they had wanted to, the cops could have put out an alert for any phone calls from Montreal to Ottawa, and at two in the morning mine would likely have been the only call. Under the circumstances, it was a chance I felt was necessary to take. I found a hotel that was open and I went inside to use the lobby phone.

He answered my phone call in a sleepy voice "Go to a pay phone," I told him. He was reluctant to drag his warm ass into the ten-below-zero weather outside his Ottawa bedroom but my persistence got his attention. "Go to a pay phone," I said, "and call me back at this number."

It took about ten minutes for his call to come through. Irving was impatient. It was 2:30 a.m. and I knew by his nature he went to bed around ten. He had been fast asleep when I called him, and he was in no mood for twenty questions.

"What's up?" he demanded.

I told him the cops were looking for him. I told him that they probably knew he was in Ottawa. "Hide the book," I cautioned him. "They want to know about Charlie, but they don't know anything about our scam unless they find the book." The book I was referring to was a small notebook that Irving kept on his person at all times. The book contained all the records of our weed transactions, including collections and payouts that were too numerous to trust to memory. Irving snorted at my concerns about the cops and acted like I was overreacting. But he hid the black book before he went back to his friend's home to climb back into the king size bed. The next morning at six o'clock while he was fast asleep, the Ottawa Provincial Police came for Irving. He answered the door in his robe and let them in before they broke the door down. Irving made only one statement.

SMUGGLER'S BLUES

"Do you know what an ironclad alibi is?" he said to the cops. "Well that's what I got" he responded, answering his own question. "So save your questions cause I ain't answering them." Having nothing on him, they took Irving in for a few hours before letting him go without charges.

I will never know for sure if Irving was behind the hit on Charlie, but I was told later that he was. I eventually learned that Jean Paul killed Charlie along with an accomplice who was an ex-partner of Irving's from his bank robbing days. Jean Paul's accomplice was never caught, but it was probably his brother-in-law Rene's friend, Roger Ouimet, or Rene's older brother, Joseph. It no longer matters. Both men are dead today. Roger died in a shootout with the cops during a bank-hold up and Joseph died in a jailbreak attempt.

I know that at least two men drove to the club the night of Charlie's murder. Jean Paul and someone else. It was 3 a.m. and the club was still open, being in a Laurentian town where the closing hours were relaxed. The informal establishment was only a half hour's drive from Montreal and enjoyed a reputation as a fun place to dance and rock the night away. Charlie was seated at the bar with his back to the door when two men wearing hoods and carrying machine guns entered the bar. Before anyone in the club knew what was happening, Jean Paul, wearing a hood, ran up behind Charlie at the bar and smashed the back of his head in with the butt of a modified M-1 carbine. Jean Paul had showed me that weapon at his birthday party. The M-1 was unlike any I had seen before and had been modified to fire on full automatic and used a belt of bullets rather than a clip. It was the same M-1 that Jean Paul had used previously to drill multiple rounds into a cop car that was chasing him after a bank job in the Laurentians. Jean Paul stepped back after clubbing Charlie and then blasted him with several rounds of .30 caliber ammunition. Poor Charlie died before he hit the ground, mortally wounded by the blow to the head even before the automatic fire finished him off. Jean Paul's partner gunned down Robert Lavigne, who was running to Charlie's defence, or running from the dance floor where he had been dancing with an unidentified woman, depending on whose story you believed. Either way, he was hit in the back. Some say Robert was beating on Jean Paul and pulling him off Charlie when he was shot by Jean Paul's partner. Some say Robert was bolting away across the dance floor towards the exit when he was hit.

After Charlie and Robert were felled by a volley of gunshots, the two gunmen left the bar. In typical fashion, the bar patrons cleared out as soon as the killers fled in a waiting car. Only the waiters and bar staff remained by the time the cops showed up to take a report. On their escape out of town, Jean Paul's getaway car slid off the road into a ditch and his accomplice's gun discharged, sending a bullet through Jean Paul's leg and into his balls, which eventually swelled up like grapefruits. A mortally wounded Jean Paul and his partner made their way past the Operation Intercept roadblocks that were supposed to prevent exactly these kinds of escapes after crimes in the Laurentian villages north of Montreal. I imagine Jean Paul's partner was apologizing all the way back as they drove to Jean Paul's girlfriend's apartment in Montreal. When they reached Susan Braun's apartment, Jean Paul was put into bed and his false teeth removed to help with his breathing. A telephone call was made to a third accomplice and a doctor was summoned to the apartment at gunpoint. When the doctor pronounced Jean Paul to be dead of shock and blood loss, the accomplice promised to take the doc home and took him instead to a garbage dump and shot him dead. Jean Paul's partner was intending to take Susan to her parent's home, but when it was time to leave Jean Paul's stone cold body, she started screaming hysterically. The accomplice put a silenced twenty-two to her head and pulled the trigger half a dozen times to silence her cries. According to the cops, Susan Braun died in a most cruel way, with defence wounds through her hands.

Any unfulfilled aggression I had towards Jean Paul died with him that day as I heard the circumstances of his suffering departure. After their deaths, I doubted that Jean Paul and Susan would meet in an afterlife because, by my interpretation of karma, they were going to different places. I am certain that it

SMUGGLER'S BLUES

came as no comfort to the parents of Susan Braun that the police had come to warn them about the danger their daughter was in only a week before her murder. They told the parents all about Jean Paul and his violent criminal past and urged them to warn their daughter. I, myself, could never understand how an intelligent, college-educated, pretty girl like Susan could ever hook up with a menace like Jean Paul. It bothered me that her fourteen-year-old brother refused to even talk to me at her funeral, as though I was somehow involved in her death.

There was a period of quiet for sometime after the murders, until everyone's fear subsided and business started back as usual. But the murders had changed those of us who remained in the game. There was no room for amateurs in the smuggling trade, now that violence ruled the roost. Irving was my insulation from violence. He had no fear of anything or anyone. At best, he showed a measured respect for someone else's abilities but never any fear. He warned me about the Mafia in very serious tones.

"If the wops ever get wind of our scam, they will try to take it over, sure as shooting. And I ain't gonna let that happen without a fight. We'll all end up dead if that happens. So don't ever talk to anyone about what we got going. Especially the wops."

Irving was a leg shaker. I have met a lot of leg shakers and foot tappers and they usually have something on their conscience. Irving used to sit opening and closing his legs like a schoolboy. Even when he was playing cards and supposedly relaxed, Irving would be moving his legs constantly. I met lots of leg shakers in the underworld. It's as if they can control every aspect of their lives right up to murder and then the leg shaking starts.

I also met dozens of interesting characters who were not leg shakers. I met them as they came out of prison and came by our car lot to visit Irving. There was Freddie Peters and his brother Gary who had both done time and gone on scores with Irving. Gary was a career convict, with a recidivism rate that required a revolving door on the prisons. Gary had done B and E's, holdups and robberies. He did some with Irving. He did some with others. And he did some on his own. One time Irving sent his jailhouse crony on a warehouse score. The warehouse was in

Laval, which was some distance from where Irving lived and since Irving was on parole with a 9 p.m. curfew at the time, he decided to hand the score off to Gary. While Gary went to work late one night, Irving waited at home to hear about the successful break-in. In due course, he received a phone call from a panicked Gary.

"Where are you?" asked Irving.

"I'm in the warehouse."

"Why the fuck are you calling me from the warehouse?"

"Something's wrong. A red light came on."

"What do you mean a red light came on?"

"It's the alarm system. I think it's activated."

"Get out of there," shouted Irving. "You tripped a silent alarm."

"I can't leave. I think the cops are outside."

"Hang up the phone! Hang up the fucking phone!"

And that's how it is in the underworld. A shortage of brains and an overabundance of daring.

Speaking of brains, I met Ziggy Epstein and his sister Ruby through Irving. Their older brother Simon was said to be a genius with safes and alarm systems. Simon died soon after his release from prison. The sister's story was that her brother Simon tried to pull off another vault job and blew the money up with the safe. Then he became depressed and committed suicide. But the word on the street was that his buddies had spent his end of his last score while he was in jail taking the fall for the job. They killed him with cyanide when he came out looking for his end.

Simon's younger brother, Ziggy, was a quiet young man with a dry sense of humor. He became our jack-of-all-trades, installing my electrical lights along the driveway and tending to odd jobs at our homes and at our business. He drove cars to wherever we needed them ferried. He walked our dogs for us and washed our cars. Ziggy's loyalty was his strong point, and he also knew his way around the streets.

Ziggy's sister was going out with a scam artist nearly twice her age named Julius. He was always coming by with hot merchandise to sell, from leather jackets to diamonds and jewelry.

Julius looked too old to pull scores, with his gray hair and his bifocal glasses. I always wondered if Julius didn't buy those coats wholesale and just pretended they were hot.

Irving was a drawing card for colorful characters and miscreants of all shapes and sizes. Like Sonny the Booster, who was legally blind but drove getaway cars for Julius. The two boosters used to come to our car lot and laugh about the scores that had put them in prison. There was one story where Julius was throwing stolen booty from the car, while blind Sonny was trying to lose the cops and hitting every other car on the road.

Irving was like a father figure and mentor to all of these strange lost souls, as well as to me, to some degree. My own father and I were not as close as we might have been at the time, and when Irving came along, he filled a gap in my life. Seeking direction, as most young men do at certain times in their lives, I latched onto a mentor who showed no doubt as to his own direction in life. With Irving it was full speed ahead at any cost. The man showed no fear. He had belonged to the infamous Stopwatch Gang, whose members were famous for remaining in a bank for less than one-hundred-and-twenty seconds. He survived the dismantling of that gang when their last job saw them getting caught in the act. Irving was with the other members of the gang, waiting for an opportunity to enter a bank that was located in a small shopping centre in Montreal. He noticed something was amiss. It was winter and there was a crew of workman doing some work on the hydro lines. Irving noticed that they all sported bright new yellow work gloves. He told the other gang members about the new gloves but they said that he was just being paranoid. Irving backed out of the score, while the others questioned his manhood and entered the bank with guns drawn. They all ended up in jail. The hydro workmen were all cops. The gang had been staked out. They all went to jail, except Irving.

I met Myron Wiseman through Irving. Myron was another con out of prison who had been Irving's cell mate. It was Myron who wrote Irving's parole release application after reading Irving's own attempt, which pretty much said, "Give me parole or go fuck yourself." Myron was a paper hanger and counterfeiter and he was handy for obtaining phony licences and documents. He was always chuckling about being "rehabilitated" as if the word were an oxymoron. Myron was an incorrigible criminal in the purest sense of the word. To Myron, it was a courageous act of defiance to break the law. Any law that was broken was another blow struck for anarchy. Myron was a revolutionary spirit who was totally against the accepted corruptions and class distinctions that exist in Western society. If he had owned a bike it would have been a Harley, just for the sheer spite of it, but he was more likely to sit down at a grand piano than ride a motorcycle. Myron was cultured and refined. He was a quiet man who always dressed in a suit. He even wore a suit to work cleaning and detailing our cars on the car lot that Irving and I opened together.

The car lot was incorporated in my name as Modern Motors and dealt in high-end used cars. Our premises were rented on the second and third floors of an old car wash location on Decarie Boulevard. Unlike most car lots in town, our showroom was indoors and the cars were parked on the second and third floors. It was an ideal location for selling cars in a hostile winter climate. It was also perfect for visitors, who came and went without being seen clearly as they drove in and out of our garage.

One such unusual visitor to our garage was Randy Segouin. I was going to set Randy up on a date with Barbara's girlfriend, Heather, the stewardess, until I found out he was a stone-cold killer.

"Don't fuck around with him," Irving said one day. I had made a smart-ass remark to Randy, and he had turned his cold eyes on me. Randy's eyes had a way of glazing over when he was in a foul mood, and many people who had seen that look were no longer around to talk about it. I heard from one of his partners that Randy used to stand in front of a mirror with his gun in his hand saying, "Are you looking at me? Are you looking at me?" Then he would pull his gun out and make like he was drawing down on and shooting his imaginary adversary. Randy was bad. Randy was so bad that even the Hells Angels threw him out of their club. Randy's previous partners in crime had been only too happy to see him go over to the biker gang when he got the itch to ride a Harley. Within weeks, the Angels were calling his partners up and begging them to take Randy back. They would have killed him if his partners weren't supplying them with bargain basement prices on weed and hash.

"We got only two fucking rules," they said. "No ripping off other club members and no fucking around with another club member's girl."

In two weeks Randy had broken both of those rules. Randy and his partner, whose name I do not remember, eventually killed so many people that paranoia was ever-present. Around then his partner ended up killing Randy in self-defence. They had been drinking for days in a New Brunswick cottage. Randy and his partner had already killed the landlord and his son a few days earlier in a drunken fight and then cut them up and buried them somewhere on the farm. When Randy gave that look of his to his partner, it was the end of the line for Randy. His partner killed him with a couple of rounds from his .45 automatic. Eventually Randy's other pals from Montreal came looking for him and the partner confessed his crime to them. They had no choice but to forgive him, as Randy's pals knew only too well that the partner was telling the truth. If Randy gave you that look, it meant the end if you didn't move fast. Randy's partner ended up in jail for killing his landlord and confessed everything to the New Brunswick police before killing himself in prison.

Another of Irving's jail friends who came by after his release from prison was Richard "Chico" Perry who smoked tobacco and weed mixed in a pipe and walked around all day stoned and smiling. I didn't see Richard around for very long. Shortly after being sprung from prison, Richard told his local banker that he wanted to open a line of credit. Being a career criminal, he did not stand a chance of collecting any money from the bank manager but Richard would not be warned off from his delusions, even by Irving. Chico threatened the bank manger and when he went to pick up his line of credit funds, the cops came to arrest him. When he turned around with a gun in his hand, they shot him twice in the stomach. Richard fell through the swinging gate in front of the manager's office, shooting the cop who shot him, as he twisted and went down behind a counter. He ended up being shot nine more times through the body, as he hid beneath a secretary's desk all the while continuing to shoot it out with the police. When he ran out of bullets, they arrested Richard with an empty .45 in his hand and a pipe full of tobacco mixed with weed in his mouth. Richard lived through the shootout and the cops put him in hospital with his legs and his arms in casts and then handcuffed him to the bed. Somehow Richard got loose, however, tied his bed sheets together and scaled down the four-storey hospital building to a second-storey rooftop in the dead of winter. He dropped from the roof to the ground and made it four blocks before the cops caught him again and brought him back . . . to jail instead of the hospital.

As the money began to roll in for Irving and me, some of the friends who came around visiting were given a place in our organization. We had need of more personnel to handle pickups and deliveries and collections, as well as others to look after the needs of our car lot. The lot was an impressive front for our weed business, with thirty to fifty high-end cars in stock at any one time. We had a Mercedes-Benz and a Dino Ferrari on the lot as well as high-end domestic cars. I drove a Rolls-Royce for a while just to see how it handled. I was surprised to see that it could peel the tires, but I found it too large and ponderous for my liking. The nicest car I ever drove in terms of performance was a Dino Ferrari, and the closest I can come to describing its handling is to compare it to a bumblebee. It stopped, turned, braked, and cornered like nothing I had ever driven before and made a Porsche 911 feel like a truck by comparison. Big John Miller laughed at me when I took an interest in the car business and stayed around at night selling cars. I took the five-to-nine shift, until I couldn't stand it anymore.

"What are you doing?" John asked when he saw me staying behind in the office one evening.

"I want to learn the car business."

"You got a business already. You don't need to be doing this shit."

It took almost a month before I agreed with him and quit the five-to-nine sales shifts. I couldn't stand hanging around that stinky garage all night, and I hated haggling with customers who were getting a good deal and acting like I was screwing them. Irving used to handle those jerks much better than I did by using reverse psychology. When customers tried to bargain on a car with Irving, they would invariably come up with a story about a comparable car they had seen at a lower price.

"Oh yeah?" Irving would say, without missing a beat. "Then go buy it."

Our cars were in superb condition when we sold them. After all the money we put into them, after buying them wholesale and selling them retail, there was hardly any profit. When our accountant, Abe, who was Irving's cousin, did the books for us in our first year, we made $331,000 in income and spent $332,000 in expenses. And that wasn't even counting the off-the-book expenses for Myron and Ziggy's salaries.

For several years I had Abe the accountant invent an income for me so that I could pay my fair share of taxes. How can you drive a Mercedes and live in a beautiful home without paying taxes? Irving taught me many other wisdoms as well, such as never showing off my money when I was into a good scam.

"Wait until the scam is over before you flash your cash," he advised. Meanwhile, at the height of our operation, we bought ourselves new homes, new Mercedes cars, new furniture and we both sported enough 18 Karat gold jewelry to sink a small boat. Irving had an affinity for the glitter, and John Miller and I followed his lead with dutiful respect, in that our gold chains were always less flashy than Irving's were.

John Miller became part of our operation halfway through our scam with the boys on the dock. It was me and Irving equal partners all the way at first. But then a situation arose where someone had to be killed and I didn't want any part of it. The boys downtown who lifted our containers from the waterfront were in a bind. A new supervisor was placing them at different positions on the waterfront and they could no longer function as needed to pull our loads off.

"No problem," said Irving. "I'll take care of it."

"What are you going to do?" the boys asked.

"I am going to kill him," said Irving. "I'll walk right up to his door, ring his bell, and when he opens the door, I'll drill him."

He was serious. No fucking around with Irving when it came to money. That was one Jewish stereotype he followed religiously. To coin one of Irving's favourite expressions, he'd kill his own mother if the price was right. But I could not go along with Irving on this one. I wanted money, but not enough to kill an innocent man who was just doing his job. I argued against Irving's plan and I stoutly refused to drive his getaway car.

"It's not right, Irving" I said, as I asked myself why the fuck he couldn't drive his own getaway car. I offered to give up the scam if that's what it took in order to stop Irving from killing an innocent man, but there was no convincing him. He was gonna do what he was gonna do, no matter what I said, and the Devil be damned if he didn't like it. When Irving realized that I was not budging on the issue, he contacted Miller and asked him to be his getaway driver. Miller's compensation for the job was to be made a full partner in our scam. John Miller agreed to take the job, but in the end, the dock supervisor was transferred to another location on the waterfront and the problem was solved on its own.

John became a thirty percent partner in our scam, all for doing nothing. And boy did he love the change in lifestyle. John was driving an old shitbox Oldsmobile when I first met him. A few months later, he was driving a new convertible Cadillac Eldorado, and he was decked out in gold jewelry and puffing fatties. I didn't mind sharing my booty with John. There was more than enough money to go around and John Miller changed my somewhat tedious job with an edgy partner into a job that was fun. Irving had the door. Irving sold the weed and collected the money. Irving had control. John and I were like his assistants, for all intents and purposes.

Irving kept records in his little black book, but there was never much cash given out because we were always investing the bulk of our profits back into the scam, paying for subsequent shipments that grew larger and larger every time. We drew enough money out to support our lifestyles, and every now and then we would pull a chunk of money out of the kitty for a larger house or a better car.

For me it was not about money so much as it was about the game. My future was riding on a life-sized magic carpet, with heavenly rewards and deadly consequences. The protagonists kept changing as I evolved through different sets of friends and business acquaintances. From Ryan and Robby I moved on to Bishop and Ross. From Bishop and Ross, I moved on to Irving and John Miller. Our antagonists were the police, Canada Customs, Immigration, the Mafia and all of the other lowlifes and criminal groups who wanted what we had.

"Don't let the Mafia get wind of our scam," Irving always preached to me. "I ain't giving up nothing to those wop bastards," he promised. "There will be blood everywhere if it starts up with them."

Irving knew what he was talking about. The mafia had cost him several of his friends. One of Irving's friends, Adam Schidlenski, survived a beating and stabbing that saw him left for dead in a car trunk at Dorval Airport. When the Mafia tried to extort money from Adam a few years later at his bar in Saint Jovite, he threw the Mafia enforcers out of his bar at gunpoint and told them to check with "the old man" and see who the fuck they were dealing with. Old man Vincent, the reputed head of the Montreal mafia, told his boys to leave Adam Schidlenski alone. "That guy is too crazy," he said at the time. The Mafia eventually blew Adam up on the Decarie Expressway using a remote-controlled bomb to do the job. The hit was ordered when Adam would not pay tribute to the mob for a scam he was involved in where he melted down Canadian quarters for their silver content and then shipped it to the U.S. My friend, Big John Miller, used to chuckle at how Adam had offered him the job of driver, which was a euphemism for bodyguard or enforcer.

"No fucking way was I taking that job!" laughed Miller, finishing with a loud snort. "I knew what was happenin'. Two fucking weeks later, the guy was dead."

John Miller was a nice guy who had the misfortune to be born with a pug's build. Powerfully strong, with massive arms and shoulders, he had a striking appearance, even though he stood no more than five foot ten. Miller was a good-looking man for his size. He had prematurely white hair and a quick, easy smile with nice white teeth. He was a learned man, with a sardonic wit and a sarcastic view of life. With his menacing looks and jailhouse demeanor, John Miller didn't stand a chance in the straight world. I always believed that he was doomed from birth to lead a life of crime. On the outside, Miller had the looks of an enforcer. On the inside, he was a hippie. He loved to burn weed and hash. He liked snorting a line of blow from time to time, but weed was his thing. Proud as a peacock, he liked wearing flashy gold jewelry and driving his purple Cadillac Eldorado convertible.

"A pimp's car," he used to laugh. "I have to drive it like an old whore," he would snort, as he spread his legs wide to clear the low steering wheel.

John was down with the blacks and spent a good deal of his time at Rockhead's Paradise Bar, near the rough quarter of Montreal known as Saint Henry. Rockhead's was a club that catered to a mainly black audience, and many a time, when I went looking for Miller, I found him there. He was comfortable in that black environment that had the whores and the patrons swapping outrageous lies and generally laughing it up.

I started bringing John down to Jamaica with me to break the monotony. He was a little older than I was and I used him to dispatch a couple of the container loads of weed we sent from Kingston to Montreal. We were supposed to keep a low profile in Jamaica, but that was difficult with Miller around. His personable nature and his enjoyment of a good time led him into the centre of most gatherings.

One time we were at the Pegasus Hotel in Kingston, with Miller at the pool bar and me in my room smoking a joint. I was listening to the police band that was playing by the pool. Suddenly they stopped and I heard a commotion going on down below. I looked over my balcony and saw the police band running in scattered directions and, a short distance away, I saw John Miller watching them from behind a palm tree. I found out later that John was having a friendly conversation with an Australian gentleman at the bar. Somehow the conversation became heated, and when the Australian said that all Canadians were shits, John decked him into the pool. As soon as that happened, the police band scattered and the show was over, pending the arrival of real policemen.

I had many good times with John Miller. He was a good friend and he was as solid as a rock when the chips were down. John was one of the few business friends I kept all my life and I am only sorry that he is not around today to continue the good times.

Chapter Five

Holiday in Beirut

We had to do something. We had weed coming out of the wazoo and more was on the way. There was too much to fit into Alex Jones' attic so we rented a house and we had Bishop babysitting the stash, or "sitting on the bomb," as John Miller and I used to laugh. The house was a modest two-storey Tudor, with an attic that held several hundred pounds of our pressed marijuana at any given time. But Bishop needed to go out on occasion, and the thought of leaving all that weed untended was a little disconcerting to all of us. At first we had Bishop call Irving or me when he needed relief, but that soon became unworkable. The poor guy could not even go to the store for a pack of smokes without planning it and he soon began to complain that he felt like he was sitting in prison. Before he became crazy with boredom and quit, Irving and I found a solution.

"Let's get him a dog."

Irving and I were both dog owners and we saw this as the best answer to Bishop's problem. Irving had a German shepherd called Nitro and I had a Doberman called Max which was short for Maxine. They were both spoiled house pets, but they both had been trained to bark and growl at strangers. Max came with Barbara and me when we went on our sabbatical to Mexico. We used to leave the dog in our camper in Mexico with the side doors wide open and we never got robbed. The Mexican children loved to tease Max to get her to start barking and frothing at the mouth and then they would laugh and exclaim "El Lobo" which means wolf.

Irving's shepherd, Nitro, was also trained to guard the house and car. Once, when Big John Miller and Irving were out for a drive, they stopped at an intersection near a bus stop. Some poor guy was waiting for the bus when Nitro suddenly jumped out of the car window and with no provocation at all, ran over and bit the man on the back of his leg. Irving called Nitro back to the car and John Miller opened the passenger door to let him in. Before they drove off, Irving leaned across John Miller and addressed the bus rider in a concerned voice. "Gee, that looks pretty bad," he said. "You should have that looked at." Then without even offering the man so much as a ride to the nearest hospital, Irving stepped on the gas and drove away.

After much searching, I located an ad in a local newspaper for trained guard dogs. The dog breeder lived in Rosemere, a picturesque little village in the Laurentian Mountains north of Montreal. On a bright winter afternoon, Irving and I drove out to see the dog trainer who met us with an affable smile. He greeted us in English, laced with a strong Quebecois accent. "What kind of dog do you want?" he asked. It didn't really matter, we found out later. He had only one dog available. When we first laid eyes on Marquis, he was locked in a cage in the kennel quarters, where there were no other dogs at the time. Marquis was a black-and-tan Doberman that weighed in at about one-hundred-and-fifty pounds, which is large for that breed of dog. He had a cropped tail that was longer than normal and a left ear that flopped over his eye while the other ear stood straight up to a point. His stance was solid, with feet that were like bear paws. His legs were like gnarled tree trunks, covered with black bumps and warts. His black-and-tan coat was coarse and thick and oily and he smelled of unwashed dog. His head was massive and when he snarled his fangs hung below his lips in a menacing manner. He immediately went for us as we

SMUGGLER'S BLUES

approached his cage. As we came closer, the Doberman began barking and snarling and frothing at the mouth.

"Marquis down!" the dog trainer said, as he bent to open the cage.

The trainer slipped a choke chain around the dog's neck, to which was attached a sturdy leather leash about ten feet in length. When he brought the animal out of its cage on the leash, Marquis became docile and friendly, like a big clumsy kid that kept stepping on everyone's toes.

"Why is he for sale?" I asked

"This dog is not for everyone," he said. "He needs a strong owner. As long as you hold him by his leash you are safe. But don't drop the leash. The first guy I sold him to was too old. The dog was too strong for him. The second guy was a bread delivery man. He bought the dog to prevent people from stealing from his truck when he made house-to-house deliveries. One day he calls me up and tells me, 'Come pick up your dog. He won't let me back into my truck!' I had to take him away," the trainer continued. "He's a good guard dog, though. He just needs a strong owner."

Irving and I studied the animal some more, but we did not take the dog right away. After I looked in the papers for another week or two and found nothing, Fast Freddie Peters and I went back at a later date to pick up the dog. We brought along fifteen hundred dollars cash to pay the trainer. I am not afraid of dogs. I have always had dogs in my life. But Freddie had never owned a dog and this one was terrifying to him. I sat in the front passenger seat, with Freddie driving the big Mercury sedan that was used as our lot car, and I put the Doberman in the back seat. I held on tightly to the leash, but I did not feel especially safe with the Doberman standing at face level on the back seat of the car. To placate the black-and-tan beast, I had purchased a box of dog biscuits. I fed him along the route to our destination, which was Bishop's house. As I fed Marquis, I noticed he was wagging his tail throughout the journey. He was docile, for the most part, except for attacking the car window every time he saw another human on the side of the road. However, he went absolutely wild when we were stopped by a road work crew and were forced to wait beside a mechanical man, with a robot arm that raised and lowered a red metal flag. I thought the dog was going to go through the window to get at the mechanical contraption. Freddie was ducking forward in the driver's seat yelling,

"Hold onto the leash, hold onto the leash!" The ride was uneventful, for the most part, until just before we arrived at the stash house and we ran out of dog biscuits. Freddie was more than a little concerned about the dog biscuits running out, so when Marquis suddenly leaned over the back seat and planted a long wet lick on his ear, poor Freddie nearly drove off the road.

When we got to the West Island house where the weed was stashed, we gave Marquis to Bishop, who was thrilled to have his own dog. Now he could leave the premises whenever he wanted, without having to worry about security. One look at Marquis and we knew that no one was going to come around the house while this dog was inside. After Marquis became adjusted to the house, he would come barreling up to the front door, barking and snarling and jumping against the door, whenever the door chimes rang. He hit so hard and high that he damaged the door jam above the top sill of the door. When Bishop took the dog for a walk around his residential neighbourhood, the brute would pull against his choke collar the entire way, growling and straining towards everything that moved and even some things that didn't. The dog would try to attack mailboxes, cats and other dogs, men, women, cars and children.

One evening, Bishop tried to domesticate his workmate by having him sit down before his meal, in the same way that I had trained my Doberman to sit and wait politely for her signal to eat. Marquis became impatient with the idea and jumped up and bit Bishop on the arm, causing him to drop the plate of food he was offering. As soon as the plate hit the floor, the dog let go of Bishop's arm and immediately began to wolf down the food. The attack left two puncture wounds in Bishop's forearm that looked exactly like .38 caliber bullet wounds. To Bishop's credit, he did not give in to fear of the beast. After the dog bit him, he threw some more dog food down the basement stairs and when the brute ran down after the food scraps, Bishop slammed the basement door closed on him. From that time forward, the basement became the dog's quarters when Bishop was home. When Bishop was out of the house, the dog roamed freely throughout the living quarters, with access to all the rooms and all of the doors and windows.

For one brief period, the dog was kept at Irving's house when the stash house was empty and Bishop was out of town. Irving had some guests over for a barbeque and let Marquis run around on the lawn with his dog Nitro and my dog Max. Before long, Marquis tired of doggy play and began to run over to Irving's guests, jumping up on them and humping their legs. If my dog or Irving's dog had jumped on me like that, I would have kneed the animal in the chest, but I was not ready to try that with Marquis and neither was anyone else. I kind of felt like a rape victim after Marquis was through humping my leg and I could finally get him off me.

One time, I received a call about the dog from Irving, and I could tell by his tone that he had a serious problem.

"Come over here right now and take care of this dog or I'm gonna take my shotgun and shoot him!" I rushed over to Irving's house, which was only a block away from mine. When I arrived, the dog was in the lot car which was parked in Irving's two-car garage. Our lot boy, Ziggy Epstein, had taken the dog for a walk and he was returning with the dog in the back seat of the car when he stopped at a shopping mall to have a coffee with a friend. When Ziggy tried to get back in the car, the dog would not let him in. Ziggy might have shown some small amount of hesitation and fear when he approached his car or perhaps the people walking by the car in the shopping mall had triggered a reaction from the Doberman. But when Ziggy tried to open the car door, Marquis began snarling and frothing at the mouth and acting insane. Ziggy tried to calm the dog, but Marquis just tore both of the shoulder belts from their attachment harnesses with one bite each. With help from his friend at the coffee shop, Ziggy managed to wedge a piece of plywood between the front and back seats of the big four-door Mercury. Ziggy and his friend then drove the car back to Irving's house, with the dog snarling behind the wood barrier the entire way.

When I arrived at Irving's, a small crowd was standing around the car. There was Ziggy and his friend David, Irving and his girlfriend Jane, Freddie the Booster, Barbara and me. The back door of the car was open and the dog was standing on the back seat with a bloody knucklebone from the butcher lying between his legs. Irving had thrown the bone into the car to placate the beast, but the bone became an item to guard. Now the Doberman was snarling even more aggressively at anyone who came close.

"Jane, get me my shotgun. I'm going to kill him!" said Irving as I entered the alcove that led to the garage.

"Hold on," I told Jane before she went for the shotgun. "Let's see what's going on here."

"The fucking dog's gone crazy. That's what's going on," growled Irving. "Look."

He threw the dog a piece of cheese, which Marquis wolfed down in an instant and then returned to snarling at everyone again.

The women were standing behind the men who were watching from the garage alcove leading into the house and no one dared get too close to the dog. I studied the situation for a time until I noticed that even though the dog was snarling and frothing at the mouth, his little stump of a tail was wagging. That told me that Marquis thought this entire charade was a game and as far as he was concerned, he was just doing his job. The cheese and dog bones were his reward for guarding the car, therefore feeding him only caused more aggression. Using a little dog psychology, I took a piece of cheese from Irving and threw it to the dog, who inhaled it in one bite. The dog was drooling and frothing in between bites as he growled and snarled all the while wagging his tail. I threw the next piece of cheese on the ground beside the car and Marquis ran out of the car to get his reward. He gobbled up the cheese and then hopped back into the back seat of the car to recommence his guard duty. The Doberman stood splay-legged over the knucklebone and began snarling again as I approached closer. I stood a moment and watched and observed his behaviour, until I finally devised a plan that required a certain amount of risk. I threw another piece of cheese on the garage floor. This time when the dog ran out to get it, I quickly slammed the car door closed behind him. The trick worked and the dog immediately became docile again and ran around the car looking for more treats, while slobbering licks and kisses on anyone he passed. I gave the Doberman a final piece of cheese and patted his head. The crisis was over.

After Irving and I successfully imported our shipments of weed into Canada, we fronted it to two high-level street dealers. One of them was Brian Kholder, who I liked very much. Barbara and I hung around with Brian and his attractive wife Karen for quite some time until they got into smack and lost interest in us. I can honestly say that I have never had any desire to profit from something like heroin, which causes such devastation in people's lives. That being said, I had no idea just how addicting the stuff really was until I saw the changes it effected in my friend Brian. The drug made him surly and stubborn and took away his ability to function, and it reduced his energy levels to near zero. Irving was somewhat responsible for Brian and Karen's addiction. He had Chip "the Limey" Jenkins, who was a friend of Simon Steinberg's, bring an ounce of pure heroin from London to see if there was a market for it in Montreal. Irving gave Brian the ounce of smack to move and I heard from Brian later that he never sold a gram of it. He used the whole ounce himself and by the end of that ounce, he and Karen were hooked for life.

Simon Steinberg was a gentleman who purchased and traded in several cars from our car lot. Simon began to hang around our office, playing cards and listening to the war stories being traded around by the boys. He was a well-dressed and well-groomed young man with a nice smile and the unfortunate distinction of having the worst breath I ever smelled on a human being. As pleasant as Simon Steinberg was, how he endeared himself to Irving was a mystery to me.

As I mentioned earlier, when I first met Irving he had overcome a gambling problem. At first Irving stayed out of the gin and poker games that went on between the boys who came around our place of business to play cards. For a while, Irv was content to observe. But the whooping and the laughing and the friendly banter of the card games drew him in, and before long, he began to join us at play. When it came to cards, Irving played conservatively and he played well. He was extremely disciplined and never bluffed that I could see. In fact, he did not play like a gambling addict at all. But I soon became aware that Irving was still very much addicted to gambling. Only he was not gambling at the card table. He was gambling with our scam.

Irving was never satisfied with what we were making and kept upping the size of the loads I was sending to Montreal. We went from shipping crates full of weed to shipping containers filled with weed, and still he was looking for more. Each time the size of our shipments increased to a new level, it tested the boundaries of chance. It is only because the boys on the docks were so good at what they did that the container scam never blew up in our faces. When the RCMP wanted to look at a container, they would have to ask our dock worker contacts to go and fetch it for them. If the container was one of ours, the boys would tell the cops that they could not find it or they would stack it in such a way that another container had to be moved before either of the container doors could be opened. Then they would stall the cops until the container was emptied or hidden again somewhere else in the yard. The boys downtown were good at their job. So good that we eventually had so much weed on hand that it began backing up on us. Our last load of nearly six thousand pounds left us with so much weed that several hundred pounds spoiled and went rotten before it could be sold.

At the same time as the weed bales began stacking up, Irving began bitching about having to pay out fifty percent of our earnings to the boys on the docks. Brian Kholder's younger brother, Buddy, was making a name for himself by smuggling large loads of hash through Russia and the Netherlands into Montreal. Buddy was knocking off back-to-back container loads of hash without a miss and he was getting rich. Buddy was once asked the secret of his success by Bob Bishop and his answer was typical of his attitude.

"I just watched what you guys did and didn't make the same mistakes," Buddy laughed.

When Irving wanted to start dealing in hash, I had no problem with it on a moral level. Grass and hash are both the same, only one is cannabis sativa and the other is cannabis indica. Besides, hash does not spoil like weed does and hash is worth a lot more per pound. So when Simon Steinberg offered us a way to bring some hash into Canada by air, Irving was all ears. I could see nothing wrong with trying something new, but I did not want anything new to mess up the good thing Irving and I already had going. Simon told us he had a jet rated pilot's licence and access to a DC-8 in London. His parents were the owners of a chain of gas stations across Canada. Like Irving, Simon had been brought up rich. He was receiving an allowance of thirty-eight hundred dollars a month when we met him, which is no small change even today. He drove a late model Mercedes-Benz and he had no need of money. But boys will be boys, I guess. Simon had a zest for adventure and he wanted to join us in our little games outside of the card room. He traded in his Benz on a pretty little BMW CSI we had for sale and paid us cash for the difference.

It just so happened that Shaun Palmer was around at the time of the purchase and the two started talking about drug deals. Shaun was an Irishman, with the gift of the gab and a thousand one-liners in his joke repertoire. He inherited a senior position in our organization when Jean Paul died. Shaun had been working with Jean Paul for only a short while when his opportunity for advancement came. Shaun knew little about moving weed, he confessed later, but jumped at the opportunity to make some real money. The Irishman was tall and well built with a cheerful grin and a boxer's face. He looked like he belonged in the underworld, but in truth, he came from a very different background. Shaun was a drafting equipment salesman before he started working for Jean Paul as a furniture salesman in Jean Paul's store. He had helped Jean Paul with some weed deliveries in the past and since he knew some of Jean Paul's customers, he was able to take over when his boss dropped permanently out of the scene.

Within a few months of taking over as our main wholesaler, Shaun lost six hundred pounds of our weed all in the same week. Two hundred pounds went down in the trunk of a car belonging to one of his deliverymen, and four hundred pounds went down in a motel when a maid found the marijuana in the room and called the cops. When Shaun came to meet with Irving to discuss the losses I waited as cover, with a loaded shotgun in a car on the second floor of the garage where our office was located. We had no way of knowing who Shaun really was, or if he was going to settle the debt or try to erase it at gunpoint. Irving was furious and ready to kill Shaun, but the Irishman soothed him into submission with his gift of the gab. When Irving started ragging on him about the losses, Shaun retaliated in kind.

"What are you complaining about?" he said in a voice equally as loud as Irving's. "It's my responsibility that the weed was lost. I'm the one who has to pay back the debt."

When Shaun didn't try to weasel out of the debt, it caught Irving off guard. Even though Shaun did not have the money to cover it, he came to an arrangement with Irving about how to pay us back. Shaun agreed to pay an extra twenty dollars a pound for all future weed fronts, until the loss of the six hundred pounds was made up. This still left a hefty profit margin for Shaun to make some decent money, as the weed he was selling at street level went from two fifty to three hundred a pound and he was paying only two hundred to two ten to us.

Shaun was back in good stead with Irving once he paid back most of his debt and he came to Irving with an offer of a hash supplier in the Middle East. Shaun's offer was timely and he was instantly taken in as a partner on Irving's new hash scam with me, John Miller and Simon Steinberg. After consulting with Simon and Shaun, Irving came up with a plan. Simon would fly by commercial airliner to England, where he would use his pilot's licence to charter a commercial DC-8 jet and fly it to Lebanon. According to Simon, there were tons of places where we could stash the hash in the wings and fuselage of a big DC-8. Shaun's friends in Beirut included a captain in the military who would help us expedite the hash from the city to the airport and onto the plane.

The scam sounded pretty good on the surface but with a little digging I saw flaws. For one thing, Irving and I and Big John Miller already had a good scam going, so why fuck it up? For another thing, there was a serious war going on between the Israelis and the Lebanese so it was not the best time to try something sneaky over there. I had no confidence in Simon Steinberg and I told Irving so. But Irving was my friend and mentor and he was adamant that we should try to import some hash. Irving could not go to Lebanon himself as he was on parole and unable to leave Montreal. Big John Miller was in the same position, although he was free to travel with me to Jamaica.

"Go and oversee the project," Irving practically begged of me. "If it doesn't look good you can scrub the mission, but I know I can trust you to make it happen."

Irving had made me a lot of money up to this point and if he was right about the hash scam, I stood to make even more. So I updated my passport and booked a flight to London, where I had arranged to meet with Simon Steinberg in a hotel restaurant.

As I look back on my past, I find it hard to understand all the risks I have taken. Many could have landed me in prison for a long time. They were calculated chances, I liked to think, and I felt I was smart enough to pull off my scams without getting caught or resorting to violence. But I knew, even then, that my reasoning was flawed, just like everyone else who ends up in prison. I know now that it was not so much the money that I craved as it was the action. The money was a reward that came along with bragging rights for having won at a game, but the game itself was more the draw than the monetary reward.

Hurting people was not my thing, and yet I have to admit that I had been prepared to stand by while Irving and John Miller killed an innocent man who just happened to be in the wrong place at the wrong time. Not that Irving would have stopped his plans because of anything I said. When he was convinced of something, there was no changing his mind. Nevertheless, I do not feel I have the right to stand in judgment of Irving or John Miller, who risked their everlasting souls by offering to ride along on a hit together. We all shared in the shame of that decision but mine was a convenient position, where I stood to benefit from Irving's crime without wearing the guilt.

It was all business with Simon Steinberg when I met him in England, even though we were meeting over a sumptuous dinner at a five-star hotel.

"Where's the plane?" I asked.

"Don't worry. It's all taken care of. I will be flying it into Lebanon."

Simon's promise was given to me with a reassuring grin as we dined on rack of lamb. While we talked, Simon showed off his experience in fine dining by recommending our meal and ordering it. Then he began instructing me on some of the finer points of English social graces, including an explanation about all the cutlery. It pissed me off that even though I was paying for all this fine dining, Simon was talking down to me like I was some poor slave and he was the rich white master. I found myself resenting the little prick more and more for butting his rich white ass into my arena. I could only speculate on why Irving had ignored my warnings and gone into business with him. Was it because Irving and Simon came from such similar backgrounds, both having been raised with maids and servants and both being Jewish? Why was Irving being taken in by this little con man, I wondered, as my own sense of greed and duty kept me from abandoning the hash project in spite of my misgivings. After our meal was over, I booked my ticket to Lebanon and left Simon with his promise to fly the DC-8 to Beirut ringing in my ears.

It was a long flight to Lebanon and I slept through most of it. When the plane touched down at the Beirut airport, I was concerned that customs might find and seize the hundred grand or more that I had on me. But I was treated with courtesy and respect as I was whisked through the Lebanese Customs and Immigration stations in an expedient fashion.

Being in Lebanon back then was probably one of the few times in my life where I felt in real peril. I was entering war-torn

Beirut during the war with Israel, with over one hundred grand cash in my pocket and not so much as a stick to defend myself with. I was booked in at the Intercontinental Hotel, where my associate from Montreal, Shaun Palmer, had flown in a few days earlier to connect with his Lebanese contacts who were supplying the hash. I took a taxi from the airport and checked into my room before meeting Shaun in the hotel bar. When I found him, I had to tear the Irishman away from a few gentlemen in suits who were laughing at his jokes. The hotel bar was filled to capacity with men in suits and I wondered out loud to Shaun what they were doing here during a war.

"They're spies mostly," said Shaun with his usual cherubic smile.

"What did you tell them you were in Beirut for?" I asked him, fearing the worst.

"I told them I'm selling fire trucks," he said with a grin. "No one knows anything about fire trucks and I'm sure they need them around here with the war going on."

I liked his answer and my confidence level edged a little higher.

"How is your military friend who's going to deliver the hash to the plane?" I asked.

"Not too good," said Shaun without blinking. "He was killed in the war. We'll have to make do without him."

"Jesus Christ, Shaun! That's a major change in plans! What about the fifty grand we paid for the hash up front?" I asked. "Can we get it back?"

"That's already spent," he replied. "The hash is waiting for us in a house not far from our hotel."

"So now what?"

"So now we wait for the plane."

To prepare the hash for Simon's arrival, Shaun and I had to leave the relative comfort and security of the Intercontinental Hotel to travel to a small adobe dwelling a few miles from the hotel. Shaun had paid fifty grand up front for the hash while he was still in Montreal, and now I was to examine the product and complete the second payment. I would have liked to have seen our pilot and the DC-8 land in Lebanon before I committed to the purchase of the hash, but Simon was not due to arrive for a couple more days yet and we had to get everything ready before his arrival.

It was an eerie ride that night, as Shaun and I drove through the streets of Beirut with a low rolling fog and darkness setting in. Every street and every corner had machine-gun-toting soldiers on patrol but they ignored us for the most part while we drove past. The moment we stopped and parked at our destination, however, we were immediately questioned by two soldiers on foot patrol. We were on a narrow street beside a row of one story buildings made of stone and mud. As the soldiers spoke no English and we spoke no Lebanese, we pointed to the house where we were going and the soldiers examined our documents then bade us pass. Entering inside the adobe structure, I was ushered with Shaun into a small, dark room where I was surrounded by several men dressed in loose-fitting clothes. As I entered the dwelling, I looked quickly at the three or four men but I had little time to study their faces. There was a small wooden table with four chairs in the main room of the two-room house. A small portable stove was in the kitchen area, along with one or two pots and pans on the counter. A sheet hung over the one window facing the street. I was struck by the simplicity of the lifestyle these people were living. The entire dwelling and all of its contents would probably be worth less than the money I kept in my small change pocket. As we moved inside the house and the door closed behind us, I was thinking about the hundred grand in my jacket and how Shaun and I could disappear in Lebanon without leaving a trace. I was seriously wondering if my throat was going to be cut, when one of the Bedouins gestured to me to come into the next room. The room was dark and I could not see what or who was in there as he led the way and bade me to follow. I entered the small closed-in room with Shaun behind me and several men following behind him, thinking that if there was a rip-off coming this was where it would take place. The hairs on my neck began to stand up straight as I entered the windowless room, still thinking about a knife being pulled and my throat being cut. My fear was still present when the Bedouin bade me to come closer and I took another step into the bedroom. He pointed to the far wall and then walked over and pulled a wooden crate from beneath a cot like single bed. He lifted the lid from the crate and inside were four hundred and thirty-one slabs of fresh blond Lebanese bricks of hash, each wrapped in its own sackcloth and bearing the seal of the farmer who sold it. Another crate under the bed held an equal amount of hash, for a total of nine hundred and fifty pounds of hashish. After the Bedouin opened the crate for me, I broke off a piece of hash and smelled it. It was the finest gold Lebanese I had ever seen. It smelled like cinnamon and was so soft and malleable that it could be handled without it crumbling apart like blond Moroccan hash or Lebanese kief. At Shaun's signal, I handed a wad of one hundred Canadian one thousand dollar bills to the Bedouin. When the transaction was completed, we left the hash in the care of Shaun's Lebanese contacts, except for a small piece of personal that I brought back to the hotel.

Shaun and I returned to the Intercontinental Hotel for a toke and a late night drink on the balcony of my room where we discussed the day's events. I was glad to be out of there, I told him, when I finished rolling a joint of hash mixed with tobacco. I confided my fears to him but Shaun scoffed at the idea that his friends in war torn Beirut might have robbed and killed us. I believed his sincerity, but I thought him naive.

As the evening progressed I made a comment to him about the thunder in the hills.

"What a strange climate," I said as I inhaled a joint of our Lebanese hash and basked in the satisfaction of a scam that was coming together as planned. I gazed across the city from our seventh-floor balcony then looked over to Shaun.

"I hear thunder all the time and yet it never rains."

"That's not thunder," Shaun laughed. "That's the Israeli jets bombing the Lebanese positions in the hills just outside of Beirut."

It was a warm, beautiful night, in spite of the distant bombing, with a cloudless red sky that was melting into total darkness. My job here was almost over, I thought, as I felt the hashish calming my stomach. The cargo of hash was all ready to go and Shaun's Lebanese friends had even offered to drive the crates to the airport for us. In spite of the positive events, I found myself almost hoping that Simon would not show up with the plane. Without the services of Shaun's Captain, we would have to use stealth to get the hash through the city and onto the plane. And if anything went wrong in Lebanon, we would be royally fucked. This wasn't Jamaica with a rusty system of English justice. This was Beirut and a war was going on. Justice can come swiftly from the end of a gun barrel during wartime conditions and double-crosses can quickly become triple-crosses and worse when death is everyone's constant companion. How the hell were we going to drive through the streets of Beirut and breech airport security to load a plane with contraband hashish with a war going on?

The next morning I felt better after a good night's sleep and I attributed my earlier fears to the strong hash and not enough sleep. I had a job to do and somehow I would see it through. After a comfortable breakfast in the hotel restaurant overlooking the lobby, I wondered how I was going to stand another day in this boring hotel. I talked to Shaun about going to a famous Casino Resort Spa on the ocean a few miles outside of town, but Shaun looked into it and informed me that the resort had been bombed and destroyed.

It was my fifth day in Beirut and I was becoming impatient for the arrival of our pilot and plane. While sipping a cup of coffee at the coffee shop, I thought I saw a familiar figure at the front desk check-in. It was a short man with a full head of thick, wavy hair, dressed in an airline captain's uniform. Another slim nondescript European man in a gray suit was standing behind the man in the captain's uniform and I could barely believe my eyes as I gave Shaun a nudge. Shaun looked over and he was as surprised as I was. Neither of us was expecting Simon Steinberg for another twenty-four hours and there he was at the front desk of the Beirut Intercontinental Hotel, a full day ahead of schedule. Simon looked very official in his starched white Captain's shirt. I caught his eye as he finished checking in. I thought I was

SMUGGLER'S BLUES

going to owe the little Jew an apology for doubting him, as I waved him over to join Shaun and me at our breakfast table.

"Good flight?"

"Excellent flight."

"I wasn't sure you would make it."

"I told you I would be here, didn't I?"

"Is the DC-8 at the airport?"

"Not exactly."

"What do you mean not exactly?" I asked. "You're here. So where's the plane?"

"I flew in by BOAC."

"What do you mean you flew in by BOAC? Tell me you're joking and the plane is parked at the airport."

"Well no, not exactly," said Simon. "There's been a change of plans."

"What do you mean a change of plans?" I said with my blood pressure rising. "We have the hash all set up and ready to go and now you show up with no fucking plane!"

"Now, don't get excited," Simon insisted. "I have a plane coming. It will be here tomorrow."

"What the hell are you talking about?"

Simon went on to tell us that the DC-8 he was going to charter in London had become unavailable due to mechanical problems. As an alternate plan, he had commissioned a Lockheed Lodestar that he chartered out of New York. When he told me that, I immediately saw a problem. The propeller-driven cargo plane was coming all the way from New York to Beirut to supposedly pick up a load of fruit and vegetables to deliver to Montreal. Now anyone with even a limited knowledge of aircraft economics knows that the cost of flying a Lockheed Lodestar to Beirut was prohibitive. Flying a fuel-sucking old crate that far to pick up fruit would have required that the oranges sell for a hundred dollars apiece to make a profit on the trip.

"That's no fucking good," I whispered as a kind of panic began to set in. "The charter crew isn't even in on the deal. What's to stop them from calling the cops, or for that matter, taking our load of hash and throwing it in the ocean?"

"Don't worry," soothed Simon, bad breath dripping from every word. "Shaun and I will ride back on the plane with the flight crew to make sure they don't fuck with the cargo. I'll tell the crew that the shipment of fruit was unavailable because of the war and that we will be picking up some spare engine parts instead. We'll throw the two crates of hash onto the plane as engine spares and fly from Beirut straight to Preswick, Scotland. Then we fly on to Reykjavik, Iceland and over the salt chuck to Gander and then on to our hanger at Dorval. I'll sit on the crate all the way back so no one looks in it."

I looked over at Shaun, whose pug face was showing remarkably little surprise at these latest developments. Shaun was not a gangster, exactly. He was a salesman before the untimely death of his friend Jean Paul. But Shaun did look like a gangster with his short hair and heavy build. He had an Irish face that beamed and reddened with changing emotions, especially when he'd had a drink or two.

This is like a plot in a B movie, I thought, as I gloomed over the latest developments. I surveyed the bar area trying to separate the spies from the businessmen, to no avail. What would businessmen be doing here in the middle of a war anyways, I asked myself. Only people with high stakes at risk would chance a visit to Beirut at this time. People like us. I was just finishing my coffee and I was still digesting the new turn of events when the slim young man who had been standing behind Simon at the front desk approached our table.

"Hello," he said in a Cockney accent. "My name is Chip Jenkins."

I looked at his outstretched hand like it was contaminated and made no effort to respond to it.

"Chip is an old friend of mine," said Simon, breaking the ice to introduce the stranger. "He helped me charter the plane out of London and I brought him along to meet the New York crew and help us out."

I was visibly angry about having a new face sprung on me without warning. This entire deal was spinning out of control, I groused to myself, until some hours later when I realized a benefit. Simon and Chip could now take care of the tasks that Shaun and I had been obligated to look after, like delivering and loading the hash onto the plane. Shaun and I would act as countersurveillance to keep an eye on things. Seeing as he was already here, the Englishman named Chip could help Simon do some of the dangerous work.

After the introductions, Shaun left our meeting to return to his room for a nap and Chip went to his room to unpack, while Simon and I stayed in the coffee bar to talk shop. As soon as the others left the table, I read Simon the riot act. I told him I was going to hold him personally responsible for anything that went wrong with this scam due to his bullshit and incompetence. He tried to back out of flying back with the load, but I made it clear to him that he had damn well better. As far as I was concerned, he had lied about the DC-8 and when I got home I was certainly going to inform Irving. Simon left the table duly rebuked and I returned to what was left of my cold breakfast. Things were not exactly going as planned but they were moving forward, I was thinking, as I sipped my third cup of coffee. I decided to stop by my room to calm myself with a toke of hash and meditate on everything. I signed the breakfast bill and made my way to my room on the seventh floor. The elevator chanced to stop on the third floor and as the doors opened to let out another passenger, I happened to see Simon's English friend, Chip, going into a hotel room that was not his own. I continued on up to the seventh floor where I met with Shaun in his room and told him what I had seen.

Who was this Limey that Simon had brought into our midst, I wondered out loud. CIA? BNDD? RCMP? Interpol? The best course of action was to go down to the room on the third floor and knock on the door to find out. When Shaun and I did so, the door was opened by Chip who had a look of astonishment and guilt on his face.

"Who the hell is this?" I demanded as I pushed into the room past Chip to confront a medium-sized white male about thirty-five years of age. The man had dark wavy hair and a mustache and goatee and he was a complete stranger.

"He's a friend of mine," said Chip.

"What the fuck's he doing here?"

"When Simon asked me to help him with a dope deal in Lebanon I wasn't going to come alone. I brought along my friend Bob Chambers here as backup. He's my mate."

I interviewed Simon's friend Bob for a while before deciding he was on the up-and-up. His history appeared to be that of a petty London thief who had a criminal record for stealing some frozen rabbits from a butcher. Since he was there to help anyways, we gave Bob the job of helping to load the plane with Simon and Chip, with payment for their efforts promised later. Could things get any worse, I wondered, as I left the two Englishmen in the room and departed with Shaun.

That night I had a fitful sleep and the next morning I was grumpy as a bear. All morning and all afternoon were spent waiting for the arrival of our chartered cargo plane, which was supposed to arrive in Beirut around 4 p.m. At 3:30 p.m. Shaun and I were having a drink at the bar when several very rough-looking individuals entered the hotel.

"Look," I said to Shaun, making a joke. "There's our flight crew." The three men walked to the check-in counter looking like carbon copies of soldiers from the *Dirty Dozen*. The first man in line was tall, maybe six foot two or three, with the lanky athletic build of a proball player. He was wearing aviator-style sunglasses and a khaki shirt with loose-fitting military-style trousers. He was unshaven with a three-day growth of beard and carried himself with the easy lope of an athlete, as he strolled into the hotel and set his flight bag in front of the check-in counter. Behind him stood a bald-headed white man with a Fu Manchu mustache. He was wearing a cut-off T-shirt and stood at least six foot four and weighed an easy two hundred and eighty pounds of solid muscle. The bald man had an appearance that fell somewhere between Genghis Khan and Attila the Hun and he made tough-looking Shaun Palmer look like one of the seven dwarfs. There was one other man standing behind the first two men in line and as I recall, he looked capable of handling himself in a fight. The three men standing together made a formidable

SMUGGLER'S BLUES

appearance. Shaun saw it, too, as he leaned over to inform me in a whispered aside, "If that's the flight crew, there's no fucking way I'm flying back with the hash."

"I don't blame you," I answered, just as Chip and Simon appeared in the lobby and walked over to join the three men at the check-in counter.

Simon shook hands with the tall one who appeared to be the pilot, while Shaun and I stared at each other in disbelief. It really was our flight crew!

At this point, we had over a hundred and fifty grand invested in the scam and there were a host of problems. There was no Lebanese military captain to deliver the hash to the plane. There was no DC-8 with enough room inside to safely hide a half ton of hash. We no longer had a pilot of our own to fly the load home to Canada. Instead, we had a crew of mercenaries out of New York who we were trusting to fly our shit home. The question I was faced with, after all that had transpired, was: should I scrub the mission, or send the load with the chartered flight crew and cross my fingers? The hash was already purchased and I doubted that we could trust Shaun's Lebanese friends to hold on to it safely until we came back to Lebanon a few months later with another exporting scam. Whatever decision I made, I would be responsible for the outcome. I kept on trying to make this scam work, but each time I made a step forward, fate was pushing me two steps back. I thought of Irving and how disappointed he would be if I just junked the scam and returned home. This was entirely his idea, I told myself, as I thought about tossing aside a multimillion-dollar score. But the money invested in the scam belonged to me, John Miller and Irving. I had a responsibility to try to see the project through to completion.

That night, I drove with Shaun to the airport in a car I had rented and we scouted out the Lockheed Lodestar from New York. We parked by the hangar where the aircraft was stationed and walked inside the structure to check it out. Our chartered plane was sitting bathed in fluorescent light between two other flying relics from the past. I walked around the hangar and checked out the three aircraft. The Lodestar looked like an old piece of unpainted junk, as did the two other nondescript aircraft in the hangar. After walking around the plane a couple of times, I passed through the "man door" on the opposite side of the hangar and walked out onto the open airfield. A lone runway outside the hangar was shared by both civilian and military aircraft. Military helicopters and planes sat unprotected on the runway waiting for the call to arms, but I saw no one guarding them. If I had been an enemy spy I could have blown up half of the Lebanese air force with a few well-placed hand grenades. It was amazing that I had such unfettered access to a military airport during a war.

I returned to the Intercontinental Hotel with Shaun and informed everyone involved that we were going ahead with the plan. When we left the hotel around 10 p.m. the next evening to pick up the hash and transport it to the airport, Shaun and I were in one car and Simon, Chip and Bob were in their own rental vehicle. As it turned out, the Bedouins were able to transport the hash to the airport for us without any problems and we traveled with them in a three-car caravan to the hangar. Shaun and I waited outside the airport, keeping watch for trouble, as the other vehicles continued on inside the hangar to unload the hash. A few minutes later, the Bedouins in the pickup truck drove out of the hangar and waved to us as they left for the return trip to Beirut.

Several hours later, Shaun and I were still in place outside the airport, waiting for Simon and the two Englishmen to complete their task and drive out of the hangar. Shaun and I had both taken the precaution of bringing our passports and money, in case we needed them, and it was beginning to look like maybe we would. I was talking to Shaun about the nearest country we could drive to if our plan went bust and the boys in the hangar were arrested. We checked a map in the rented car's glove box. Syria was closest at eighty or so miles. If the three men did not come out of the hangar soon, I would fear the worst and we would start driving towards Syria.

In due course, our work crew did come out of the hangar and phase one of our mission was complete. We all met back at the hotel to make final arrangements before the shipment of hash left the next morning for Montreal. Our two crates had been placed on board the aircraft, but it took a long time to arrange as the full crates were too heavy to lift into the Lockheed by hand. In order to get the hash on the plane, Simon and his Limey friends had to empty the hash from the crates, carry it on board brick by brick and then repack the empty crates once they had both been lifted into the aircraft.

When we finally all returned to the hotel I was glad my work was over and that I was flying home to Montreal with Shaun the next day. Simon Steinberg did not know it yet, but his English friends were returning to England, while Simon was riding back with the crate to make certain no one interfered with it, just like he said he would. That responsibility was his punishment for fucking up the whole scam, and I was making sure that he did not back out, even if it meant Simon would be flying back to Montreal alone on the Lockheed. Much to Simon's relief, Chip Jenkins suddenly changed his mind about returning to England with his friend Bob and decided to hop a free flight to Montreal on the Lockheed Lodestar. I thought that was pretty ballsy of him, considering the nine hundred and fifty pounds of hash on board, but Simon was pretty happy about Chip's change in itinerary. As I saw it, our job was complete, and all that remained was for Shaun and me to fly home to meet the plane with the rest of our crew when the Lodestar arrived in Montreal. All we had to do then was take our cargo on a ten-minute drive to a safe house near Dorval Airport and prepare the hash for distribution. The final detail in our preparation would be the rental of additional safety deposit boxes to store all of the money that would soon be coming our way.

Chapter Six

No Longer Invisible

I was tired after flying fourteen hours straight, but there was little time for sleep when I arrived home in Montreal. The Lockheed Lodestar carrying our hash was following right behind me, flying at half the speed of a commercial carrier and taking the longer polar route around the top of Canada. It was late Wednesday when I finally got into Montreal and had a quick meeting with Irving. I told him of the problems I had faced in Beirut, expecting some accolades for managing to get the load off in spite of the difficulties. At the same time as I gave Irving the news of our hash scam, I included my disgust at Simon's lies and Shaun's bullshit stories. There was no fucking Lebanese captain, I told Irving, and no DC-8, either. I expected some praise for managing to keep the whole scam together, but when I complained to Irving, he complained back to me that I should have scrubbed the mission. I reminded him that we were already over one hundred and fifty grand in the hole by the time I found out that Simon was full of shit. I told him that if he wanted to scrub the mission, we could do it now and the loss would be no greater than if I'd scrubbed it earlier. But we both had too much greed to walk away from a potential two million dollar score. Within twenty-four hours, the hash would be in Montreal, and so, with no real choice in the matter, we prepared for its arrival.

The night before the Lockheed was to arrive, I stashed my passport in the air conditioning ducts that ran through the basement of my house and removed any signs of my trip to London and the Middle East. After my air ticket receipts were destroyed and I warned my wife of the potential for police visits, I spent a fitful night trying to sleep.

The next morning I discussed the coming day's events with Big John Miller and Irving over a breakfast of eggs and bacon at Ruby Foo's Restaurant. The plane with our hash would be arriving at Dorval Airport around noon. We had already arranged for executive rooms to be booked for the flight crew at a nearby Holiday Inn. When the phone call came in from Simon Steinberg that all was well, we would keep the flight crew occupied in their hotel room with three hookers while we went to the hangar and picked up our hash. Simon Steinberg and Myron Wiseman would unload the plane and put the hash into the trunk of Myron's Land Rover. John Miller, Shaun and I would keep watch from a distance in my car. The Lodestar plane would be in the domestic section of Dorval Airport. It would have already cleared customs in Gander, Newfoundland, so there was no concern about customs inspectors. There were plenty of parking spots for cars around the hangar where the plane was to be kept once it landed. Hundreds of cars were normally parked in that area of the parking lot, as it accommodated the needs of a thousand or more airport employees. After Myron's Land Rover was loaded with hash, he was to drive to a predetermined stash house within minutes of the airport and I would follow him in my car to provide escort support and protection from rip-offs.

The Lodestar arrived late in the afternoon on Thursday. The good news was that all went well in Gander and we were pleased to hear that the plane had successfully cleared customs without a hitch. The bad news was that the hangar we reserved was unavailable that night, due to a late-night snowfall that was blocking the hangar entrance. We were forced to park the plane on the tarmac just outside the hangar. I wanted to grab the load the same night the plane landed, but Simon Steinberg had held a meeting with Irving that afternoon and was adamant that he was too tired to make the pickup that same evening. He had kept his word and sat on the crate all the way home and he said he needed sleep in the worst way.

We made arrangements for the hookers to be at the flight crew's hotel room by noon the next day to guarantee that there would be no interference from them when we went for our hash. That day, I awoke early and fidgeted away the morning while I waited for the appointed hour to leave the house. It was Friday the thirteenth, which held no significance for me, until later in the day.

Our team met at noon sharp at Modern Motors and we prepared to depart in a convoy for the airport. Simon was driving a BMW. Myron drove his Land Rover. I followed in a nondescript one-year-old Chevrolet Caprice, with John Miller riding shotgun and Shaun sitting in back. Chip "the Limey" was not supposed to be with us that day, but he just so happened to appear at the car lot right when we were all leaving. He was invited to come along with us in the cover car. As we left the car lot, Irving drove off in a different direction towards the stash house to wait for the arrival of the hash.

It was snowing lightly outside of the garage and the streets were wet but not yet slippery. The snow came down in fluffy flakes while our fleet of cars negotiated its way to the domestic area of Dorval Airport. The Lockheed Lodestar was clearly visible, with a dusting of snow on the aluminum fuselage. I broke away from the procession as Simon and Myron disappeared into the aircraft hangar to park their cars. I parked in an area where we could see Myron and Simon as they walked from the hangar to unload the hash, but we could see only a portion of the plane through the frost fence that surrounded the runway. I kept moving the car to different parts of the parking lot because there was a four-storey airport office building with lots of windows that overlooked where we were waiting. I did not want any alarms raised because four unshaven men were sitting in the parking lot for a half hour or longer. I drove out of the parking area and went off down the service road, returning at measured intervals to check on the removal crew's progress. It was one of the few occasions that I can remember when I was uninterested in smoking any pot or hash, as my nerves were on high alert, and I preferred it that way.

We could see movement towards the rear of the plane as Simon and Myron removed the hash in suitcases, leaving the wooden packing crates on board the aircraft. I had a momentary rush of alarm as an airport security car came racing across the tarmac towards the plane at a high speed with its lights flashing orange. At the last minute, it turned and drove away with its lights turned off. Fifteen minutes later, Myron's black Land Rover sedan left the hangar with its tail dragging low, due to the nine hundred and fifty pounds of hash weighing down the back of the car. I was hoping the Land Rover's suspension could stand the load of all that hash and was imagining the hassles if the rear end collapsed. I pulled in behind Myron, keeping a safe distance away, as the black Land Rover rolled along at a sedate fifty miles per hour which was pretty much the same speed that Myron always drove. There were one or two other cars on the road that day, which was not unusual for a Friday at noon. I noticed one car, a rust-colored Pontiac Lemans, follow us for a mile or so and then turn off the highway we had driven in on. I felt a sense of relief as I watched it turn and disappear down a side road that led in another direction. We were barely a mile or two from the stash house and all was looking well, when a short distance further ahead, I noticed the same Pontiac Lemans waiting at a side street to pull onto the highway behind us again. Since we had no stop signs to contend with and he did, I figured the driver of the Pontiac must have taken side streets and driven like hell to keep up with us.

"That's the cops," I said to the others in my car, as I saw the Lemans pull in behind me. I knew we were about to be busted so I pulled around Myron's Land Rover and made a dash for it. I started to pass the Land Rover and I could see confusion in Myron's face as I burned past him with the Chevrolet going flat out. Then another car two car-lengths in front of me, slammed on its brakes. I spun the steering wheel hard to the right and missed that car, then swerved further to the right to avoid a third car that slammed on its brakes directly in front of me. I found myself momentarily bogged down in the snow at the side of the road as my tires screamed for traction. I could see Myron's car behind me in my rearview mirror, as the Pontiac Lemans ran into the Land Rover's front fender and drove the car into a snow-filled ditch.

My Chevrolet started to break free of the snow and the wheels found pavement once again. I was almost free and away when another ghost car pulled in front of me and slammed on its brakes, trying to force me off the side of the road. The next moments rolled by in slow motion as I hit the gas with the Chevrolet's rear wheels spinning wildly. A man jumped out of the car in front and pointed a handgun at me through my front windshield.

"Stop," he said.

"Hold on," I said to the others in my car as I punched the throttle and slipped low in my seat to present a smaller target. I made it past the cop without getting shot and was on my way to freedom when another car came out of nowhere and rammed me back into the ditch. The next moments were mayhem as guns were drawn and half a dozen or more plain-clothes police officers surrounded us. We were all pulled from the car and made to stand with our hands on the roof of the nearest cop car. There were six or more vehicles stopped all over the two-lane highway, some with red cherries flashing on top and others just parked there with lights left on and doors left open. I can remember the chill of my hands on the metal roof, as I stood looking at Big John Miller and Shaun standing in the same position on the opposite side of the police car.

When it came time to handcuff the five of us, there turned out to be only one pair of cuffs available amongst all of the cops on the scene. That told me that they had been totally unprepared for this bust. The one pair of handcuffs that they found were used on Big John Miller, or "le Gros Bubull" as they called him, making reference to John Miller's extra-large size. We were all taken to RCMP headquarters in downtown Montreal where the cops tried to sort us all out.

I was separated from the others and put into a room with Shaun, where two police officers interrogated us at opposite ends of a long maple conference table. Some pieces of ID, including my driver's licence, were sitting in a pile at the centre of the table. My licence was pushed towards me by my interrogating officer and he asked for confirmation of my identity. I refused to talk or give my name until I saw my lawyer. After several failed attempts to get me talking, the two police officers left the room.

"Tell them your name at least," Shaun whispered to me. "They're getting pissed off."

"I'm telling them nothing," I replied, remembering Irving's teachings.

"It can't hurt to give them your name."

"They can see my name right there on my driver's licence. It has my fucking picture on it."

"You better tell them something."

"Not a chance."

Our conversation was interrupted by the two police officers returning to the room.

"So, you don't want to talk," my interrogator said as he smiled down at me. "Take him outside," he said to the other officer, with a nod towards Shaun. "Then send in Tarzan," he said, with a wider smile while looking at me. His fellow officer scowled at me, then handcuffed Shaun, and took him from the room. Then they both disappeared along with my interrogating officer and I was left in the room alone. After a minute or two, the door opened and a man entered.

This must be Tarzan, I thought, as he came to the end of the table where I was seated and looked down at me. For several seconds he stood there saying nothing. Something in his expression made me ask, "Do I know you?"

"I know you," he said.

"From where?"

"I know you, that's all." I tried to place him, but to no avail.

SMUGGLER'S BLUES

Then I figured it out. He knew me, all right. He knew me like a brother from listening to three or four years of wire taps on my phone.

"They tell me you're not talking," Tarzan said, as he leaned slowly over the table and with both hands he carefully removed my glasses. I don't actually wear glasses, but in keeping with my desire to look more like a businessman when I was on the job, I had ordered a pair made up that looked like reading glasses but were fitted with zero ground lenses. At the time, I was wearing the glasses so as to separate myself from some of my accomplices who looked like career criminals. When the glasses came off, I recalled my experience in the washroom with the Montreal homicide detective.

"Is this where I get my beating?" I said in a calm voice, looking Tarzan squarely in the face. The question caught him off guard and removed his element of surprise.

"This is the RCMP," he said with feigned indignation as he threw my glasses back on the table. "We don't beat people," With that, he walked out of the room and that was the last I ever saw of Tarzan.

After my brief conversation with Tarzan, I was removed from the conference room and I was asked no more questions. I was subsequently taken to Parthenais Detention Centre where I was held on the seventh floor until my lawyer could spring me out on bail. I called on Sidney Goldman, of the same legal office that Jean Paul had introduced me to when I had had my problems in the U.S. I was a little disappointed that Sidney's underling, Steve Bloomberg, came to see me in jail, instead of the senior lawyer himself. But the advice he gave me was to prove prophetic.

"Don't talk to anyone in here," Steve Bloomberg said. "Stay quiet and keep to yourself until I can get you out of here."

A few days later, I was surprised to see a guy that I had worked with at my old printing machine company. Andre Dumont came strolling towards me on the seventh floor of Parthenais Detention Centre with his hand outstretched in greeting and a welcoming smile on his face.

"They're all talking about you," he said, carrying a newspaper with headlines referring to our nine hundred and fifty pound hash bust.

"What are you in for?" I asked him while shaking his hand.

"I robbed a store," he answered with a sheepish grin. "I was drunk."

I guess Andre must have forgotten that he had told me just before he left the printing machine company we worked at that he was intending to apply to the Rosemere Police for a job.

"No kidding," I said, with my lawyer's warning ringing in my ears. "What did you use?"

"I used a knife." It sounded weak. No one uses a knife to rob a store in Quebec, where there are more guns than people. I disclaimed any knowledge of the nine hundred and fifty pound hash bust and said it was all a mix-up before I said goodbye to Andre and went back to my cell for a nap. I stayed in my cell all that day and the next. When I finally emerged, after two days of ignoring Andre's attempts at conversation, my ex-workmate was gone. A jail-wise inmate named Joseph Lemiuex came up to me.

"Hey, you know that guy you were talking to yesterday? They released him last night at 12 o'clock midnight."

"So?"

"So, no one gets released from jail at night. They don't process you at that hour anywhere in the province of Quebec."

It didn't take much to figure out that my workmate was a plant and that he must have got that job with the Rosemere Police Department after all.

After that, I stayed in my cell continuously and studied the book on criminal law that Joseph Lemiuex had loaned me. I returned the book to him after I got out, but by the time it reached him, he no longer needed it. He died in a jailbreak that saw four inmates try to escape. One of them produced a handgun that had been smuggled into prison. Joseph killed a guard on the way out and then was gunned down himself as his three accomplices made good their escape to a waiting car.

Before I got halfway through the law book Joseph gave me, I was processed and released after my lawyer sprung me on a fifty thousand dollar bail bond. A fifty thousand dollar bail condition isn't as bad as it seems because the court accepted my house as surety and I did not have to come up with any cash. Irving put his house up for John Miller's bail and Shaun had an aunt who covered his bail with a surety on her house. Simon Steinberg had plenty of equity in his own home and was also granted bail. But as a foreign national, Chip the Limey required a fifty thousand dollar cash bail. That was put up for him from our cash kitty, in my name.

All of us were charged with conspiracy to import narcotics. Simon Steinberg had an additional charge of actually importing the drug. The next few years were a continuum of delays and post-ponements, as the two sides attempted to match the personal schedules of five suspects, four lawyers and several Crown counsels.

A depressing reality settled over me after the rug was pulled out from under us that Friday the thirteenth. I had a sentence hanging over my head and money for lawyers was draining my pocketbook. Irving, John Miller and I still had our Jamaican scam to fall back on, but now that the element of surprise was gone, I no longer had the comforting anonymity I used to.

One thing that I was proud of was the fact that no one in our group squealed. Nevertheless, I was furious at Simon, who in my mind caused us all of our problems with his lies and bullshit. At one point, I suggested to Irving that we kill him. I did not trust the little rich boy to keep his mouth shut in the face of a min-imum seven-year sentence. I wanted to see him dead and buried in the woods before he could cause us any more grief.

"His family is rich," Irving said in response. "If he disappears it will cause a lot of heat. It's not worth it right now."

I felt that Irving had some personal responsibility for our predicament and I guess I wanted to see him make it right.

"What if Steinberg opens up?" I continued. "You could go down, too."

"He won't open up."

That's when I realized that Irving actually liked Simon, in spite of his fuckups and bad breath. In hindsight, I'm glad that Irving did not follow through with my wishes, which would have made me an accessory to murder and would have added a mortal sin to my roster of others. Instead of killing Simon, Irving pulled him aside and warned him what he would do to him and his family if he talked. The little rich boy stayed solid as a rock after that, and my soul was once again spared.

However, Irving had no such qualms about killing anyone else, and for a while it looked like Shaun was going to be next on the hit list. Using his drug profits, Irving had purchased a small house with a large mortgage in his wife's name. Irving had virtually nothing in his own name for two reasons. The first was that he wanted to remain unseizable, so that whatever he did, no one could come back on him financially. The second reason had to do with his being a career criminal on parole. He had to show that he was a normal working guy, or his parole would be revoked in a second. If it could be shown that he owned more assets than he could prove he'd earned, that would be enough reason to send him back to jail.

Instead of moving his ex-wife into the house as he had planned, Irving rented it to Shaun who, with his wife and two young children, needed a place to live. Because Shaun was moving our weed, he got a break on the rent with just one provision: that he should never be late with the rent. It did not matter that Shaun was handing over thousands of dollars a day for our weed that he was selling, Irving went absolutely berserk when Shaun started to stiff him on his rent. Perhaps it was because Irving had been such a troublesome renter himself that he had this unreasonable concern about Shaun stiffing him. It was as if he knew from the start that Shaun would fuck him but he rented the house to him anyway. Irv was so worked up after six months of expecting it, that when it happened he blew his top. Every day for months I heard Irving tell me and Big John Miller how he was going to go over to Shaun's house and, if the rent wasn't brought up to date, he was going to kill him. At first we thought he was letting off steam, but when he purchased a handgun and silencer to do the job, John Miller and I were convinced that he was serious. Of course neither of us could dissuade him from his plans, and day after day I expected to hear the bad news. It bothered me immensely to have Shaun come by and rap with us like nothing was wrong, knowing that any day now he could wind up dead. John Miller and I finally pulled him aside and warned him about fucking with Irving's rent money, and Shaun eventually got the message and paid up in full.

With all the expenses caused by the blown hash scam, Irving and John Miller and I needed more income quickly. The boys on the docks agreed to pull off another load for us and I returned to Jamaica a few months later when the heat from the hash bust died down. Before that could happen, I came to realize that I was no longer invisible to the Man.

It was a month or so after my arrest and it was Christmas Eve. It was snowing lightly as Barbara and I drove in my Corvette along the service road beside the Trans-Canada Highway which led to my parent's home. The night was still and silent, with snowflakes tumbling from a cloudy sky. I was looking forward to a few hours of a family get-together with my parents when I saw a red light in my rearview mirror. It was a QPP cop car and he was pulling me over. I was packing nothing more than a small piece of hash, which I slipped to my wife to conceal on her person because they had no probable cause to search her. There was no need to be quick about it, because instead of getting out of his car and coming to my driver's window, the police officer began hailing me through his vehicle's bullhorn.

"This is the police. Do not get out of the car. Drive slowly straight ahead and turn right at the next street."

I followed the instructions from the bullhorn and we tossed the hash a short distance later. I continued driving until I was ordered by bullhorn to pull into a large garage bay door with QPP written on the adjacent wall. It was a substation office of the branch of police that took care of the province's highways. After I drove into the garage, my wife and I were ordered out of the car. We were both going to be given a pat-down search, although at that time, there were no female cops on duty and the male officers could only search my wife's purse. They started working on my car, taking off the door panels and removing the spare tire.

"Do you think I'm out delivering drugs on Christmas Eve?" I protested.

The QPP officers took no mind of my sarcasm and looked everywhere in the car until they finally opened all of our carefully wrapped Christmas presents. The cops were waiting for a female officer to come to the station to search Barbara, but after a couple of hours of fruitless waiting, they finally let us go. The police mechanics reassembled and replaced my car parts before returning our Christmas presents to us in tattered wrappings. I didn't care much for the inconvenience, but from that point on, I realized that fame came with the territory.

The next time I went to Jamaica I decided to travel on false ID. At that time, Jamaica and Canada were both crown colonies and travel between the two required only a driver's licence. Myron Wiseman had provided Irving with a brand new credit card that was stolen from the mail. The credit card was never to be used, Irving told me, and he gave it to me as the focal point of my ID kit. Myron then provided a blank driver's licence and birth certificate that I filled out with a typewriter, using my photo and the credit card's name of Murray MacDonald. I added a library card and a few other easily obtainable club cards to the package and my fake ID kit was complete.

I booked my air tickets in my alias name of Murray MacDonald and headed down to Jamaica. I did not care who followed me around in Montreal, but I did not want to be followed to Jamaica. I would travel to my destination and do my work. On the way back, I did not need to use my fake ID and I would fly home in my own name. Once I had done my end in Jamaica, I never went near the weed in Montreal and the authorities could watch me all they wanted.

On one occasion, I came through Canadian Immigration in Toronto while traveling with a long-legged blond who I had met on the plane. I was traveling as Murray MacDonald, and not wanting the blond to see my real name, I passed through Toronto on my fake ID. The immigration officer checked my ID and asked me some questions as my blond showgirl companion looked on.

"Where is your passport?" he asked me.

"You don't need a passport to go to Jamaica," I answered, as

I presented my fake driver's licence and birth certificate.

The immigration agent barely glanced at the ID before directing me to a small room filled mainly with blacks from the Caribbean and Indians from South Asia. A sign over the glassed-in room read "Immigration Security." After the immigration booths, the Immigration Security room was the next level of interrogation before entering Canada.

"Nice meeting you," I told the blond.

I stood still for a few moments contemplating my next move as I looked around the crowded immigration room. I made no attempt to find a line to stand in. Instead, I quickly collared a white Canadian immigration officer who was pushing his way through the crowd. He saw from my appearance that I looked out of place and when I hailed him, he immediately stopped.

"Excuse me, can you tell me why I was sent here?"

"This is Immigration."

"Do I look like an immigrant?" I raised my eyebrows as I showed him my false ID in the name of Murray MacDonald.

"Your buddy out there asked me for a passport and I told him you don't need one to fly to Jamaica." I pointed out through the glass doors at the officer who had sent me to Immigration. "I don't think he liked my answer."

The harried and overworked immigration officer scanned my ID. "Where do you live, Mr. MacDonald?"

I gave him the address that I had memorized from my fake ID and threw in a little Quebecois-accented French to complete the picture for him.

"Go on through," the officer said after handing me back my ID.

That was the last time I ever traveled back to Canada on fake ID.

The loads I sent up from Jamaica came through like clockwork, as usual, and money began to pour back into our coffers. Even when bad weather sent one of our containers to Halifax instead of Montreal, the boys on the dock came through for us.

It was about this time that Irving, John Miller and I purchased new houses. Irving purchased a house near the water and then sold it to me before he even took possession of it. He had found another house he liked even better that was right on the water. His new house was made of stone and brick and came with wrought iron security grills. I wondered how Irving could live in a house covered with iron bars after all his years in jail. The house sale that I completed in his place was for a long, two-level bungalow that was fronted with Adirondack stone and featured two fireplaces, central air, an above-ground pool and four bathrooms. It was more house than Barbara and I needed at the time but it was a way of sucking some money out of the partnership holding fund. The house that John Miller purchased was a modest split level in the nearby community of Kirkland in the West Island, while Irving's house and my house were a block apart from each other in Beaconsfield

Even though I did nothing to expose myself to the police in Montreal, I was always on the lookout when I moved around my hometown. My eyes never left the rearview mirror as I checked sidestreets for parallel covers. I checked out suspicious licence plates through a crooked cop Irving knew. One time my neighbour came by my house to talk to me. She told me of a car that was parking in front of my house late at night, with two people sitting in it. Irving ran the plate through his cop friend, Luc Lavoie, and traced the car to an apartment in Montreal. The plate belonged to a Volkswagen Beetle. Irving and I drove to the apartment listed in the Department of Motor Vehicles records as the address of the Beetle and located the car parked underground. Irving waited outside while I went inside to check out the car. The Volkswagen was locked. I pried open the vent window and opened the passenger door and then I went through a briefcase in the back seat. It belonged to a schoolteacher. A woman schoolteacher. A teacher and a Volkswagen Beetle. Not exactly a dangerous combination. We figured the teacher was probably having a make-out session with her boyfriend at the end of my dark dead-end street. Case closed.

I never talked shop on the phone. If I needed to attend an important meeting in secret, I would have a buddy rent me a car and park it downtown in the underground parking at Place Ville Marie. I would have another buddy drive me to nearby Saint

Catherine's Street, where I would jump from his car and run the wrong way down a one-way side street so that no car could follow me. I would stop and turn to see if anyone was running after me on foot, then duck into the Hudson's Bay department store and run to the elevators that led to the underground floors. At the lowest level, I would jog through a tunnel connecting the Bay with the Place Ville Marie parking arcade that was as large as a small city. Once in the parking arcade, I would slip into the car that had been parked there for me. Then I would slip on a hat for a disguise and calmly drive away to my meeting.

While others watched soap operas and movies, I was hooked on the show trials playing on TV about the Quebec government looking into organized crime. It was interesting to see the tactics used by both sides of the law, and the show was very informative to a person like me. If I happened to suspect a tail was on me when I was driving, I would stop for gas and go into the washroom to stash any personal drugs or other contraband I might have on me. A plastic bag placed in the toilet tank was a good place to hide stuff when there was nowhere else. I would come back for the goods later when the tail was gone.

In those days, I felt above the law and without any connection to the regular world. When I was stopped in my Mercedes for speeding and the cop started to explain why he was writing me a ticket, I rudely pushed the power window button to close him out.

Meanwhile people were coming in and out of our place of business with offers of scams and business ventures on a daily basis. Old man Laviolette, who sublet the office space to us, still had a paint and body shop on the fifth floor of the garage. He did all of our body work and painting. At one time, the old man had operated the entire garage when his business was flourishing, but now he was content to work for us and take in the odd private body work job. Laviolette had a prior relationship with Irving, although I never found out what it was. One thing I knew was that Irving trusted him, so the old man must have been a scammer at one point in his life.

Freddie Peters would come by on a regular basis, selling articles he had boosted from high-end department stores. Irving told me once that Freddie was such a good shoplifter that you could put several objects on a table and Freddie could steal them right in front of you, without you seeing him do it. Freddie brought in Inuit soapstone carvings and ivory figurines and Royal Doulton china. Irving had a large collection of Royal Doulton figurines, which I found peculiar for a man with no social graces whatsoever. Irving lived in his bathrobe until 10 a.m. and after 4 in the afternoon, and he ate most of his meals standing up at the kitchen counter.

When Irving came across some hot diamonds, he offered an unmounted five carat clear stone to my pal, Bishop, at only five thousand dollars. I could not believe that my buddy passed on the deal, but Bishop told me later that he did not want to start his marriage off with a hot wedding ring. If he'd had a crystal ball and could have looked twenty years into his future, he might have given his now ex-wife that hot diamond.

One time Irving bought some meat that "had fallen off a truck" and he gave me a good deal on some of it. I put it in my freezer and when I finally tried it out, the prime filet mignon steaks tasted like cardboard and had the texture of leather. I found out later that Irving bought the "hot" steaks from Marvin Abrams who became famous for selling rendered meat to the patrons of Montreal's Expo.

Lots of people came around our office at Modern Motors hoping to catch a ride on our gravy train. There was one friend of mine named Izzy who came around on a regular basis. He would always leave his big pig of a Chrysler parked in the middle of the floor, blocking everyone from going up or down the ramps. Invariably Irving would come by and freak out over Izzy's lack of manners and the car would quickly be relocated elsewhere. The last time it happened, Irving got so mad he punched a hole in the office wall a foot or two above my head. Izzy jumped up from the card game and left our car lot never to return. When Irving left, John Miller laughed and said, "That's you he was hitting when he hit that wall because it's your fucking friend who keeps parking in his way." I hoped John Miller was wrong because if Irving ever hit me that would be the end of Irving and me. Money or no money. Scam or no scam.

As time progressed, I was starting to tire of Irving's constant bad moods and many a time I found solace in Big John Miller, who was Irving's age and who had known him longer than I had. "Just ignore the old Jew," John Miller told me. Only John Miller could ever have called Irving an old Jew to his face. John Miller had a way with Irving that allowed him to snort out an insult yet not offend him. I, on the other hand, gave Irving as much respect as I wanted him to show me and I was careful not to bridge the gap in the way that John Miller had.

Myron Wiseman was always quick to jump to the pump when Irving was around. Myron had shared a cell with Irving and when he was released or "rehabilitated" as he liked to say with a smirk, he came over to Modern Motors as a general helper and car washer. In reality, he became part of our crew and he was useful in many other ways. Myron used to laughingly refer to Irving as "the Fuhrer," in reference to Irving's renowned lack of patience. But even Myron was getting a little perturbed at Irving's imperious attitude, and from time to time he would disappear for days, either sulking over a remark Irving made or off with his own crew of shysters hanging paper across Canada.

Inflation was starting to hurt the Canadian economy at the time, but as a fellow smuggler once said, ours was a recession-proof business. A couple of times Irving considered the wisdom of trying to move some coke, but I was adamant about not going there. Not only did I feel that coke dealers were bad karma, but I also thought that they were dangerously schitzo. Weed people were far more even-keeled, even when you reached the multi-ton level. Besides, I argued, we have a market for weed, not coke. It seemed to me that my arguments were carrying a little more weight now that I had been busted and Irving never brought up cocaine again.

We had great things going on before Irving and I got greedy. I was angry with myself for not following my initial reservations about going to Lebanon. Inside, I held Irving largely responsible for my getting busted because of that fucking Simon Steinberg he brought into our crew. So when Irving propositioned me several months after my bust with another scheme to smuggle hash into the country, I was clear on my position:

"No fucking way."

Irving's friend in Ottawa, who had provided him refuge during the trouble with Charlie "the Weasel" Wilson, had been released from jail. He had called Irving to say that he had a son who was involved in dealing hash. Irving's friend said that his son could provide a ton of good Moroccan hash at the source and he was even prepared to sail it from Morocco to the Bahamas in his boat. Then, on a small, remote island in the Caribbean, the sailboat would off-load the hash. Then it would be brought to an airfield where Irving and Simon Steinberg would fly in to make the pickup. Using a long-range aircraft that could reach Canada without landing in the States, the hash would then be flown north to a small airfield north of Montreal. John Miller and a few of our Montreal cronies even volunteered to unload the plane. All that was needed was to buy a plane with enough range and durability to make the journey from Montreal to the Bahamas without landing. The plane Irving and Simon decided on was a Douglas Dakota.

I reminded Irving that I already faced up to seven years in jail for smuggling and I was already bailed out on that. But there was no way I could stand being jailed for twelve years or more, as I would have been if I were caught doing back-to-back hash runs. My ace in the hole for backing out of Irving's score with no ill feelings was my American beef. I could not travel to the States, or the Bahamas, because of my earlier deportation from New York. All the pressure in the world could not move me to go anywhere near the Americans, and so, as far as Irving was concerned I was off the hook. Instead, Irving offered me the right to sell the hash once it was landed in Canada, which left me with a stake in Irving's hash deal and still kept me safe to continue the weed scam if the hash scam failed a second time. I did my best to convince John Miller that he did not have to go on the new score. At first, he agreed with me.

With everything to gain and nothing to lose, I helped Irving with the mechanics of making his plan work. Simon Steinberg flew to England to put an option on ten aircraft that had been recently retired from the military. The Hawk T-1 was a solid aircraft capable of seven G landings, but with twin 340 horsepower turbocharged engines, it was expensive to fly commercially. The plan was to use the planes for future importing missions, but the procedure to get them civilian airworthy certificates turned out to be a long one.

The Hawk T-1s were bought, in part, as cover for the purchase of the American Douglas Dakota that was actually going to do the Bahamas run. The Dakota would be registered and picked up in the States. It would then be flown to the Bahamas to pick up the hash and then north to Canada, nonstop. There was no interest in making any money from the plane itself. When they were finished with it, the plane could be torched and no one would even miss it.

All of this preparation costs money. Lots of money. Including the purchase of the hash itself, the investment on Irving's scam was in the hundreds of thousands of dollars. His true gambling spirit came out, as Irving withheld payments to the boys on the docks as well as to me and John Miller while he shopped around town for other investors. He used one hundred thousand dollars belonging to a friend of his from out west who had begun buying high-end cars from us to ship to Vancouver. Irving took his friend's money for a 1979 Rolls-Royce and substituted a 1963 Rolls-Royce worth a third of the value. The Rolls-Royce was supposed to be the start of a new importing venture, after Irving sent Chip the Limey to London to buy it. When the car arrived in Canada, Irving took one look at the body, which was full of Bondo, and gave up on the idea of importing cars from England for good.

Irv got his cop pal Luc Lavois involved, by getting a fifty thousand dollar investment out of him. That gave Luc the rights to a share in the profits and a place on the squad that was going to meet the plane and unload it in Canada. Simon Steinberg put money into the scam, too. Irving approached so many people to invest in the scam that security went from lax to nil, and the only secret left was the schedule of the run.

Irving arranged to purchase a speedboat in the Bahamas which could then be used to run out to the surrounding islands to find a good location for the drop. Freddie Peters looked after the Bahamas logistics, including finding the drop site, paying for the speedboat and meeting the sailboat full of hash when it arrived from Morocco. The word was that the crew of the sailboat had changed the name and painted the vessel twice on the way across the ocean in order to conceal its movements from the authorities.

A large black truck with tandem back axles and double back wheels was purchased brand new in Montreal to handle the weight of the two thousand pounds of hash that would be picked up at the airstrip. Irving's ex-partner, Little Irving, from his first robbery conviction, was drawn into the plan. He had turned his life around at this point, with a good job and a future in the computer industry. His live-in girlfriend happened to be Big Irving's twenty-three-year-old daughter, Donna. Little Irving was hired on to meet the plane with the pickup crew and unload the hash when it arrived in Canada. Ziggy Epstein was given the responsibility of driving the pickup vehicle to the airfield and having the canopy windows tinted black beforehand. Big Irving was going to call Ziggy with a coded message, giving the time and location of the airfield to be used for the drop.

The day before Irving was to leave for the mission, my wife drove past him while he was walking his dog, Nitro, at the side of the road.

"He looked so lonely and forlorn," said Barbara. "He was walking with his head hung down and his hands in his pockets, looking like he had lost his last friend."

The day after Barbara painted this ominous portrait of Irving, he and Simon left for the States to pick up the Douglas Dakota. They waited in the States for a few days until they received a phone call from Freddie in the Bahamas telling them that the hash was stashed on the island and ready for pickup. When that call came through, Irving made one last unscheduled phone call to Ziggy Epstein in Montreal, asking him if he had tinted the windows on the "black garbage can" yet, which was the stupidest code word for a truck I had ever heard of. Then they left for the Bahamas to pick up the hash.

While Freddie the Booster made contact with the sailboat and arranged to meet it at a small island a few miles north of Freeport in the Bahamas, an unnerving incident occurred. Just as Freddie and the boat crew were meeting and unloading the hash to hide it on the island, a U.S. Coast Guard plane made a pass and swooped low overhead.

"The jig's up," shouted Freddie to the others as the plane made its pass and flew off into the distance.

But there were no other disturbances, until a day or so later, when the giant Douglas Dakota thundered down from the clouds to make a perfect landing on a dirt runway that must have looked like a postage stamp from the air. Simon was vibrating, and Irving's hands were shaking so badly he couldn't light his cigarette when the big bird rolled to a stop at the end of the island's small runway. However, there was little time for conversation as the sailboat crew and Freddie loaded the plane with the hash. It was only a matter of minutes before the plane was fueled and loaded. It took off again, sailing towards a lonely airfield in Canada some two thousand miles away.

After loading the plane, Freddie drove the speedboat back to the Freeport Marina where it remained until some months later. He then hopped a commercial air carrier back to Montreal. He arrived just in time to drive over to Irving's house, where he waited with Irving's girlfriend, Jane, for news of the plane's successful arrival in Canada.

Once the hash was safely unloaded in Canada and placed into the bed of the black tandem-axle pickup with the tinted window canopy, it was supposed to be driven to a safe house in Montreal's West Island that was known only to Irving, John Miller and me. The airfield pickup crew was composed of Ziggy in the black truck, Luc Lavoie driving his own car and Little Irving riding shotgun with Big John Miller, who had changed his mind at the last moment about going to work on the scam. John had agreed to help unload the plane and ride shotgun in the pickup when it headed back to the stash house with Big Irving and the hash.

It was snowing lightly when the pickup crew met at the Holiday Inn in Montreal. They were there to meet with Ziggy in the heavy-duty pick up and to follow him to the airport, which only he knew the whereabouts of. He gave the work crew last-minute instructions of where they were going, and the procession traveled in a loose-knit caravan to the airport that had been preselected and was in the remote hills of Quebec. There was a surprising amount of traffic on the road for an early morning drive in the country, but only Ziggy felt uncomfortable about it. He had remarked earlier to Big John Miller that he had noticed a couple of suspicious-looking guys in the parking lot of the Holiday Inn reading a map in their car, but was told to stop being paranoid.

The snow began to fall harder as the procession of cars picked its way through the countryside. An hour or so later, they arrived at a private airstrip that was covered in a foot of snow. Luc Lavoie used bolt cutters to snap the chain barring access to the deserted airfield, while Little Irving ran over to check out the snow-covered runway tower, brandishing a loaded .45 for all to see. There was no one in the tower, but if any police agents had been in pursuit, they would certainly have been concerned to see that guns were being carried around openly.

John Miller and Irving were also packing heat as protection from any rip-offs that the multimillion-dollar cargo might attract. Irving had committed himself to going for broke on this one, and he swore he would not be taken to jail again. He said he was prepared to shoot it out, if necessary, to protect what he had worked so hard for, and John Miller stood solidly beside him.

Luc Lavoie thought that I was going in on the scam, right up until the day before he left for the airfield. I told him when it was all over that Irving had asked me not to tell anyone that I was not in on the scam, in case it demoralized the others. The reason Irving was so actively involved in this score had little to do with his thirst for adventure. Irving had to go along on this one in order to convince everyone else that it was safe to do so. If everyone had known that I was not going to be involved, it might have soured their willingness to help Irving with the mechanics of the plan.

As it turned out, the plane came in as expected and the hash was unloaded without any complications.

When the plane landed safely, Irving jumped out of the cockpit to embrace everyone on the ground and to tell them that they were all rich. He told them that the plane ran out of oil on the way to Canada and they had to stop in the States. When Simon tried to call in a mayday, Irving pointed his gun at him and told Simon that he would shoot him and fly the plane himself if Simon touched that radio again. In the end, there was no choice but to land and Irving hid the hash in the rear toilets as the plane flew into Connecticut where it faced customs clearance before it took on oil. When they landed, one solitary customs inspector stuck his head inside the plane to see that it was empty and gave the plane official clearance to take on fuel and leave again.

It is somewhat ironic that after they took off again, Irving and Simon Steinberg were legally cleared to land anywhere in the USA, where their load of hash would have been even more valuable than it was in Canada.

The snow was coming down in buckets at the Quebec airfield when the plane landed, and kept falling during and after the hash unloading. The most immediate concern after the hash was unloaded was whether Simon would be able to take off again through the deepening snow on the runway. Simon Steinberg was heading back south intending to land the Douglas Dakota as a domestic flight arriving in Dorval Airport, and Ziggy Epstein went along with him to sweep up any debris left by the hash. The plane made it into the air with a deafening roar for the short twenty-minute flight to Dorval, while John Miller and Irving drove the truck full of hash towards the stash house in the West Island.

As the snowstorm worsened, Irving and John Miller headed home, followed from the airstrip by a happy crew of partners who looked forward to a life of ease and wealth to go along with their own special days in the sun.

Chapter Seven

I'm in Sales,
So I'm Always a Little Stressed

The call came at 8 a.m. It was from Louise Miller. Had I heard from John? Upon hearing her question, my heart sank. I had been awake since 6 a.m. and I, too, was wondering why no one had called me yet. I was starting to feel somewhere between a little concerned and a little pissed off.

"No, I have not heard from John," I told Louise "But I'll look into it right away."

I called Irving's house. No answer. That was impossible. I knew for a fact that Jane was there waiting for Irving's return. A few hours later, a news flash came on the radio. Several people had been arrested on a charge of importing hashish in an airplane. The final confirmation of the disaster came when Barbara got a phone call from Jane, a few hours after the newscast, asking her to feed and walk Nitro. Jane was in jail but was expected to be released soon. John Miller and Irving and everyone involved in the Bahamas scam were in jail, Jane said. She could not tell us any more at the time but the bad news kept coming. Freddie Peters and Little Irving had been picked up by the police while waiting with Jane for Big Irving to return home. The cops came to Irving's house in force and threatened to shoot the dog through the glass if Jane did not put Nitro away and open the security grilled front door. Freddie had managed to flush his air tickets to the Bahamas down the toilet before the police gained entrance, but he was brought downtown and charged with conspiracy anyway. Little Irving's involvement in the scam had been documented by the RCMP surveillance team, and so he, too, was arrested. I am certain it didn't help that he was running around at the deserted airfield waving a gun.

When the police team came in to Irving's house, they arrested everyone there and took them downtown to sort it all out. Luc Lavoie slipped the net because he said he could not find his way back to Irving's house for the final celebrations, after unloading the plane at the airfield. Personally, I think he was too smart to find his way back. I never really knew Luc that well, although we hung out for a period of time. Luc was an ex-Montreal Police Force cop who was thrown off the force for fixing tickets or some other petty infraction. The only problem I had with Luc was that he was too well-mannered and cultured to be a criminal. With my paranoia about cops, I never quite let my guard down around Luc. I did, however, at his insistence, keep a bottle of his favourite Scotch on hand in case he came by my house for a drink.

As far as the hash importation and possession charges were concerned, John Miller and Irving were dead bang gone, to use the terminology of the joint. They were arrested at gunpoint in front of the stash house, with a truck full of hash and loaded guns sitting on the dash of their truck. I found out later that the entire operation had been under surveillance, just as little Ziggy had suspected. The black pickup truck with the tinted windows was followed from the Holiday Inn to the airport up north, and all of the other traffic on the road that day was almost exclusively RCMP surveillance vehicles. It came out in the pretrial that the RCMP had allowed the plane to be unloaded of its cargo thanks to a shortage of preparation time to plan a raid and because of the inclement weather. A decision was made, at the last minute, by the Mounties to follow Irving and John Miller back to the stash house rather than try to take the entire crew down at the airstrip. The RCMP chase team lost the truck in the bad weather when it turned off from the Trans Canada into a subdivision. Irving and John Miller were almost home free when they pulled up to the stash house and stopped the truck in the driveway and prepared to drive it to safety inside the garage. There was only one small problem. With the addition of several inches of fresh snow on the driveway, the pickup no longer fit into the garage. The truck was several inches too high to pass under the garage door. Irving and John were still scratching their heads about how to deal with the problem when the cops pulled up and arrested them. One solitary police vehicle took them down, without either one of them ever pulling their guns.

So much for Irving's promises of do or die.

The next few weeks were nothing but tears and problems as I ran around consoling the wives while preparing defence lawyers for the jailed crew. But there was no defending anyone after Little Irving flopped over, with his legs in the air like a bitch in heat. He confessed everything to the cops in the hope they would show leniency. In spite of his evidence, he was sentenced to seven years in jail, which is the minimum sentence for a major importation charge even if you rat on your partners.

There were no bail possibilities for Big Irving or John Miller who were both ineligible for release since Irving was on parole and John Miller out on bail, like I was, for the previous importation offense. I went to the bail hearing to hear the charges read out, but my lawyer Sidney saw me before I entered the courtroom and shooed me away. I told him not to worry, that I was not directly involved in the Bahamas caper, but he told me to leave immediately anyways, which I did. I ended up reading through the transcripts at a later date, but there was nothing much there. Once Little Irving fingered everyone, the transcripts ignored many of the material facts and were all about legal precedents. There was no information that came out about how everyone was caught because they all avoided trial and went straight to plea-bargaining.

Freddie Peters' home was searched while he was in Parthenais Detention Centre. His wife Helen came by my house with a magnet that she had seen the police surreptitiously place under her phone before they left her house. I looked at the small object, which was a half inch square in shape and about one sixteenth of an inch thick. I broke it open and saw what looked like a black carbon material in the centre. The carbon material was covered with an orange layer of ceramic coating. I showed the object to Ziggy Epstein, who was keeping a low profile since slipping the net on the Bahamas scam. He agreed with me that what Helen had found in her house was some kind of ceramic magnet. Placed under a telephone or beside a window, the magnet was capable of acting like an amplifier, turning a phone or window into a speaker. With the right receiving equipment, it would be possible to hear every word spoken in the vicinity of the ceramic magnet. The disturbing part of this news was that I had similar orange ceramic magnets stuck to the latch mechanisms of every window in my new house. Barbara had been lifting and cleaning the window sills beneath the magnets before replacing them. We both thought the former homeowners had placed the magnets in the window latches as a security method to prevent the locking mechanisms from being picked or pried open.

After Helen Peters' visit, I tried to mentally review the hundreds of conversations I had had on my own phone. I never discussed business on my phone, but many incoming callers did, and I was always stopping them mid-sentence, especially Irving who used to find my paranoia amusing. Now I was on the hook for every conversation that I had ever had.

No trial date was set for the perpetrators of the Bahamas hash scam. After Little Irving turned rat, all that was left to determine was how much time everyone would get, before they copped a plea and turned themselves in for a ride on the bus with no windows. After months of negotiations between defence lawyers and crown prosecutors, John Miller and Irving were sentenced to twelve years in jail. Simon Steinberg received eighteen years as the supposed leader of two hash conspiracies, but only after the Crown had great fun questioning him about his borrowed captain's uniform during the Lebanon scam. Freddie Peters copped to two years on conspiracy. Luc Lavoie should count his lucky stars that he did not remember the directions to Big Irving's house and that Little Irving did not know him by name. Luc walked, while Ziggy Epstein turned himself in at a later date, after the cops had come looking for him.

During the drawn-out negotiations in the plea bargains of both Irving and John Miller, I pretty much spent all of our remaining assets to cover lawyer's fees. It cost fifty grand for Irving's lawyer alone. Irving's lawyer was Morris Shipman who is now a Chief Justice of the Supreme Court. Then John Miller changed from Sidney Goldman's office to the same office as Irving's lawyer. That was another fifty grand, on top of five grand that I had already paid on his behalf to Sidney. The other guys in our Bahamas crew spared themselves the expense of a lawyer and worked a deal directly with the Crown.

When it was all over, I was nearly broke and our gang was decimated, with everyone in prison or on the lam. I sold off all of the cars at Modern Motors to cover the bills, but old man Laviolette scooped a good portion of that money to cover our business overdraft expenses. He claimed it was all aboveboard, but he was shaking like a leaf when I confronted him over the figures. I felt bad for the spunky little old man, who could see as I did that our world had changed forever.

I still had fifteen hundred pounds of weed left to sell, which was removed from Bishop's care and hidden behind a false wall in Big Johnny Lakeburn's townhouse. But the weed was going rotten, and the only mover I had left who would touch it was Brian Kholder. He had local people in Montreal who were buying our shit weed for one hundred and thirty dollars a pound to be used as a filler for good weed that had been imported by others. When that market dried up, Brian had to go all the way to Edmonton to find a market for the rest of our weed. When he did, he was subsequently busted with two hundred pounds of low-quality Jamaican coli weed in a steamer trunk that he had loaded onto a train. His wife Karen was with him at the time and she was also charged. To spring her from jail, Brian had to cop a plea and he ended up getting three years in the slammer for that shit weed. The saddest part of all was that the jail term destroyed what was left of their storybook marriage.

I sold off a third of the low-grade coli weed, which was enough to cover our debts and expenses for a while. In my mind, the remaining thousand pounds of weed belonged to the boys on the dock, but when I visited Irving in jail, he said to pay that no mind. He wanted me to sell off the weed as quickly as possible. I asked Irving where the remainder of my end was coming from and he offered me the ten Hawk T-1 planes that he still had title to in England. I was owed at least two hundred and fifty thousand at that point and it sounded like an almost fair deal, under the circumstances.

A year and a half later, I was still no closer to getting the planes certified for sale and I questioned whether the cost of the certification program was draining more out of me financially than I could expect to recoup. Irving told me to sell the speedboat in Nassau. But when I looked into it, I was informed that the cigarette boat had sunk months ago while docked and no one at the marina was taking any responsibility for it. I had no interest in pursuing our claim in the Bahamas over a fifty thousand dollar item. I also looked into the possibility of selling off the Douglas Dakota which was still parked at Dorval Airport, but before I could have my lawyer check into the process, an airport snowplow accidentally broke the tail off the Dakota, rendering the plane useless. I could have instigated a suit against the federal authority responsible for the snowplow, but seeing as the plane had been used in a criminal case, my lawyer suggested I do nothing. The hash was gone. The money was gone. The assets were gone. I had no income other than a trickle of money from weed that was so bad the buyers were using it for fill.

I was sorry for Irving, but I had to get on with my life. If the truth be told, I blamed him for all of our losses. He was an inveterate gambler, I now realized, and what I saw before as balls or "chutzpah" was really just a sickness. John Miller was easier to visit than Irving because he was in a medium security prison. To visit Irving, who was in a maximum security facility, I needed the services of a civil lawyer. The lawyer made application for me to have special access to Irving for business reasons relating to the dissolving of Modern Motors.

I disliked going to visit either Irving or John Miller in the can but I felt it was my duty. I did favours for both of them. At his request, I sent Irving a typewriter filled with hash and mescaline that I had hidden in the roller. That made Irving king of the maximum-security prison for a little while. I made sure John Miller had his lawyers and his immediate needs covered, too.

Of course, the boys on the docks eventually contacted me, as I expected they would. The message came to me through Bob Robertson, who, along with his brothers, was a major player in the west end underworld. The boys on the docks wanted to know where their money was. I told him their money was all spent by Irving on the Bahamas hash scam, but I offered to give them the thousand pounds of shitty weed that was left.

I insisted on actually meeting with the boys before I handed off the weed to Bob Robertson. I met with Bob downtown in Old Montreal, and he introduced me to one of the boys on the docks at a bar near the port where the stevedores hang out. I had never met the guy before and Bob could have passed off any old wino on me, but when I met him, I knew the guy was the real McCoy. The meeting lasted less than a minute and the guy who introduced himself to me looked like he wanted to be anywhere else but where he was. He told me to give the weed to Bob Robertson, so I did.

I arranged for my buddy Joe Dudley to drive the thousand pounds of weed to a parking arcade downtown and I gave the keys for the rental van to Bob. There was no problem getting the van up to the third level of the parking arcade, but on the way down the ramps, Bob told me later that the van scraped the ceiling at every level. The transfer was made without further difficulty and I prided myself on being able to call upon Bob Robertson if I ever needed to. His brothers were well-known heavies in town, and from what Bob told me, they wanted him to go straight and become a lawyer. When I first met Bob, it was in a bar that catered to stockbrokers and he was dressed like they were, in a three-piece suit. He told me he dressed that way so that he could fit in with all levels of society. He told me after the delivery that the weed was shit, which I already knew.

I experimented with making oil out of some of the low-grade weed and came up with a passable product, which I offered to provide to Bob and the boys down on the docks. He did not take me up on the offer and instead, gave me an ounce of blow to move on a front. I passed the blow on to my card-playing friend, Izzy Solomon, with a warning that he could have it on a front as long as he did not front it out himself. I told him I was on the hook to a major heavy and I didn't want any fuck-ups. He ignored my warnings and I eventually had to hire Joe Dudley and Bishop to watch for Izzy who lived at his parent's house. I paid them to park in front of his house for several weeks, until I finally received a phone call from Joe that he had spotted Izzy moving around in his bedroom. I paid Izzy a visit.

He was pretty cool at first. "I saw your guy watching me out there," he said, looking out his bedroom window with a weak smile. "He's been there for days."

"He's been there for weeks," I told him. "Where have you been?"

"I was out of town for a while. I just got back."

"Where's my money?"

"I don't have it right now."

"Fuck you, it's been three fucking weeks and you haven't called me."

"Take it easy. I'm expecting to get some money tonight."

"How much money?"

"A couple of hundred maybe."

"You owe me eighteen hundred. Where's the rest?"

"I'll get it."

"You fronted the ounce, didn't you?"

"No, I didn't."

"If you don't have my money then give me back the rest of my ounce."

"I can't."

"You fronted it out."

"Okay. I fronted it and the fucking guy won't pay. I thought maybe you'd help me collect."

"Like shit I'll help you collect, you little prick!"

I threatened to beat his ass and destroy his parent's house, starting with a beautiful glass credenza in the living room. I gave the credenza a nudge, and before it leaned too far over, Izzy agreed to cover the debt. I walked away with a Fender guitar, some gold jewelry, a couple of hundred bucks and a few other trinkets. I paid Bob Robertson for the blow out of my own pocket and sold off Izzy's possessions to cover my losses. After that I gave up on blow and never saw Bob Robertson or Izzy again.

Other opportunities presented themselves to me during the years that followed the Bahamas bust, but none of them panned out. A friend of Little Joe's named Gary Martin had another friend with a printing press and a small business that was feeling the pinch of recession. The friend wanted to print up some funny money and I looked into it for him. The hardest part of counterfeiting money is getting the paper. Paper that feels like money is only made at special places on special presses and the closest source at the time was in Germany.

I passed on the scam because of something Irving had told me about years earlier. One of Irving's friends, named Frankie Romano, was very successful at forging money, having printed off millions of phony Canadian hundred dollar bills. Frankie did so well that he ended up owning a small regional airline that served northern Quebec. He never got caught at counterfeiting and the only reason that he stopped was because the Canadian equivalent of the Secret Service paid him a visit and gave him a warning. They more or less told him that they knew what he was doing and that it was equivalent to treason. They said that even if they could not prove his counterfeiting, they were going to make him pay if he did not stop. Frankie took that as a death threat and immediately ceased hanging paper.

That told me that certain police agencies will go to great lengths to stop certain crimes. Even some smaller forces will take justice into their own hands. Irving's story about Frankie reminded me of the story told by Jean Paul LaPierre about why he did not kill his partner for ratting on him about some bank robberies they did together. After one robbery, Jean Paul and the partner were driving away down a rural highway with a QPP car in hot pursuit. They rounded a curve and then stopped and positioned the getaway car across the road. When the QPP car rounded the curve, Jean Paul and his buddy ambushed the cop with automatic weapons fire from M-I carbines as they stood behind their getaway car. It was either good shooting or a miracle that the bullets punctured the engine compartment and did not kill the lone officer. The local detachment of the Laval Police Force caught up to his partner before they found Jean Paul. The partner told Jean Paul that the Laval police had taken him for a ride into the woods and made him dig his own grave. Then the cops told him they would kill him and leave him there if he did not provide the missing information they needed to convict both himself and Jean Paul. There was no doubt in Jean Paul's mind that the story was true and he forgave his partner for ratting. He also made certain that when he turned himself in he was with his lawyer. In the end, Jean Paul died before he could face trial on that charge and several others, but the point is well made that some crimes are not worth the risk.

Other scams were offered to me, and some were pretty good, but the truth is, by that point in my life, I was becoming a little gun-shy. Otherwise I would have followed up the offer made by Bobby Mayweather, whose family owned a moving and transport firm in Montreal, Toronto and Ottawa. The older Mayweather brother managed the Ottawa branch of the firm and he offered to receive a container from Jamaica full of weed if I could send it up safely. The brother agreed that he would tip me off if the container came in hot, but he would not agree to help me rip off the container from the in-bond section of his warehouse if it came in with a "hold for inspection" label. I passed on the idea but not because I always suspected Bobby of working with the Man. If he was feeding the Man names, it was only to get himself off drug charges. But I knew that even if he was a rat, Bobby was unlikely to involve his own family in a deal and then bust them. The real reason I passed on the deal was that I could not afford to send up a container load of weed on my own, nor could I afford a loss like that if the container came in hot. Not to mention I was as hot as a firecracker. I might have just as well been walking around with the word "smuggler" tattooed on my forehead. I passed on the scam and looked elsewhere for new opportunities.

It was around this time that I received a message from Jane, who faithfully visited Irving in jail every single week. She wanted me to arrange a visit with my friend Derrick who had a small medical practice in Montreal. If Derrick would agree to register as Irving's doctor, Jane had a way of arranging for an outside visit through the prison. Then if Derrick didn't mind, Jane was planning to dress up as his nurse and Irving and she could spend some time together while he was in the examining room.

In the first place, there was no way I trusted Irving not to pull a jailbreak after only a year or so in prison. In the second place, I did not want to impose on Derrick a handcuffed and legcuffed prisoner coming into his medical practice with armed guards. I told Jane that Derrick would not do it, without ever asking him if he would. Irving had already pulled one jailbreak in his life, and after only eighteen months into a twelve-year sentence, I knew he would bust out of jail the first chance he got.

After I nixed the caper, Jane came with another message from Irving. He had somehow set up a deal to sell two hundred pounds of the low-grade weed we still had stored at Big Johnny Lakeburn's. He wanted me to personally arrange the drop, after meeting with two of his jailhouse contacts from Archambault Prison, a couple of miles down the road from the jail.

I couldn't fucking believe it. As if I would ever go to a rendezvous on a dark road, within spitting distance of the most dangerous and well-patrolled jail in Canada, to meet two people I had never met in my life and do a dope deal. He even wanted me to handle my own weed delivery because his friends were paranoid and did not want to meet anyone else but me.

I was polite to Jane but I avoided the subject for as long as I could. I didn't want to say no to Irving, who was obviously trying to help with our money problems, but I was not going to meet his jailhouse connections no matter what he said. I wondered if the clowns he was arranging to meet me were on a day pass.

A few weeks later, I was at my desk at Modern Motors when I had the most unusual visit from a legend in the underworld. It was in the dying days of the Modern Motors dealership when Sam Andrews walked into my office, fresh out of jail. Sam was a friend and partner of the late Simon Epstein, Little Ziggy's older brother. Sam had just been released from Archambault Prison, where Irving was serving his time and I got the feeling that Sam did not socialize much with Irving in stir. But he knew of the connection between Irving, me and his friend Ziggy and he came to my place of business with a message. As I sat down with this soft-spoken man some ten years my senior, he told me a story that was difficult if not impossible to believe.

"Be careful. Be very careful," Sam said, after taking me to a quiet area of the garage. "I heard some guards talking before I was sprung from the joint and they were talking about setting someone up on the outside. I found out later that the person being set up was you. Now listen to me. I can't tell you any more than I told you and I know it sounds crazy, but you better believe me. You're a friend of Ziggy's so I came to see you. Don't deal with anyone new, because I know for sure that you are being targeted for arrest. Someone is trying to set you up. So watch it."

Sam Andrews stayed for a while chatting with the other rounders hanging about the office and then he left. As soon as he did, I immediately began thinking about Irving's deal that he was trying to set up for me just outside of his prison.

Were the guards setting me up? I had never heard of such a thing. The cops sure, but not the guards. I was positive that Irving would not have been in on any setup. Not the way he detested rats. But I was starting to feel that Irv was more than just a stupid man. He was fucking insane. I passed a message on through Jane that I was not going to see his prison contacts. I said I was too hot to handle a dope deal right then but I did not mention the visit from Sam Andrews.

After that, my attentions went to my own trial that was coming up, for conspiracy to import the nine hundred and fifty pounds of hash. Before you can have a trial in Canada, you must go through a preliminary hearing. In the beginning, our preliminary hearing was full of laughter, with Big John Miller and Shaun Palmer swapping jokes in the corridors outside the courtroom. The rest of our crew were circled around them and if you didn't know better, you would think we were all at a nightclub instead of at a trial. Shaun even had the cops and the Crown prosecutors laughing with his quick repertoire of one liners. They were old jokes of the Rodney Dangerfield type like, "The judge said order· in the court, so I asked for a rum and coke." Shaun was a born showman and his delivery had us all in stitches. It took some of the sting out of the proceedings, which had butterflies fluttering in everyone's stomachs.

The preliminary took months to complete and stretched even longer after the Bahamas bust. At that point, the preliminary was halted several times, while the Crown negotiated with John Miller and Simon Steinberg, who were both up on separate charges for the Bahamas and Lebanon scams. From that point forward, John Miller was seated in the glassed in box reserved for people held without bail, while Simon Steinberg remained free on bail.

All of the little details about the Lebanon caper came out in court. The Crown was constantly making reference to Simon Steinberg wearing a pilot's uniform, which he never should have had. They cited him wearing the uniform in London and in Beirut. Simon's father sat in the court room gallery with his head hung low throughout the proceedings, and Simon's mother sat at his side. Simon's father never looked over at the group in the defendants' box, as though embarrassed to be associated through his son with the rest of us. It came out that Simon had borrowed the uniform from a BOAC pilot for a fee.

When the flight crew from the chartered Lockheed Lodestar was brought into court, I was certain some of them would recognize me from the hotel lobby and restaurant in Beirut. I have the kind of face that people do not forget. I once returned to my old childhood neighbourhood, and fifteen years later, the owner of the local candy store recognized me when I came in to visit.

The flight crew had to have noticed Shaun and me talking and drinking with Simon in the hotel bar in Beirut. Shaun, like me, also has the kind of face that you don't forget. But when each member of the flight crew was asked to look around the court-room and point out faces they recognized, they looked right past Shaun and me and pointed to Simon Steinberg. Simon had two of the best lawyers that money could buy, but he ended up cop-ping a plea because of his back-to-back doubleheader charges. The same thing happened with my sidekick, Big John Miller.

My lawyer, Sidney, who also represented Shaun and the Limey, started to behave like a clown and pretended to snooze during the proceedings. With his courtroom shenanigans, Sidney was an even bigger showman than Shaun. Myron Wiseman, who was driving the Land Rover full of hash, was a no-show at the trial. He absconded while on bail and changed his name and appearance, never to be seen again. Shaun copped a two-year plea that was tied into an earlier beef for possession of the four hundred pounds of our weed that he lost in a motel room. Chip the Limey and I were released as free men and the judge gave special instructions to the Crown not to attempt to retry us.

"You were in the wrong place at the wrong time," the judge chided the Limey and me. "Make certain it doesn't happen again."

At this point, I took some time off and enjoyed a much deserved rest from all things criminal. My wife gave birth to our first child, Allison, after my acquittal and I began to crave a dif-ferent lifestyle. I spent almost two years of nonstop work to get the Hawk T-1s through their certification program. Of the ten Hawk T-1s I lost five because I did not have the money to pay out the options on them, and then I lost one more when I had to sell it to keep the rest of the certification program afloat.

You have to understand that these planes were not just sitting for free in some field in England. They required constant main-tenance and a place to stay, all of which costs money. I had to take several trips to England before the Hawk T-1s completed their certification process. The process involved mechanical con-versions to the aircraft as well as conversions of flight manuals from military to civilian status. The problem was that the military had to decertify and release the flight manuals before they could be translated into civilian language. Before the process was completed, two years had passed and I ended up having to borrow ten thousand dollars from Barbara's sister. I gave her my Corvette as collateral which she promptly smashed up while driving home drunk.

Chip the Limey was of some help to me, as he had friends and family in England where the planes were stationed. Those friends helped with errands and deliveries of paperwork and so forth that passed between the mechanical shop certifying my aircraft and myself representing the various authorities in Canada and the U.S. who were involved in the certification process.

I visited Chip's buddy, Bob Chambers in London, who I first met on the Lebanon scam in Beirut. Bob got me a piece of hash and showed me the sights around London. It was springtime and it was the first time I ever enjoyed England. I rented a car and Bob and I drove down to the forested countryside of Kent. I was surprised to see that the trees in Kent were well spaced and looked manicured, as compared to our northern Canadian forests full of tangled underbrush and evergreens. The English forest, like all things British, was neat and tidy, with no need of walking trails because the space between the trees was open and carpeted with pine needles.

When I returned to Canada from my last trip to England on the Hawk T-1 certification program, I took a job selling computerized word processors which were new to the marketplace. I needed the income until the Hawk T-1s were sold and I was not interested in trying to maintain my criminal status any longer. A change was brewing, as I hung out with mainly straight friends, except for Luc Lavoie and Pierre Allard who owned a car lot near Decarie Boulevard. Pierre Allard was an interesting character, with a combination of straight and criminal tendencies. Pierre was as charming and polite a person you could find, but when he was doing poorly in the car business, he would supplement his meager income with the occasional bank holdup.

"I have to do it," Pierre said to me, as his bank robbing partner Ti-Lou looked on with hooded eyes. "I opened the freezer last week and I found all of the Mastercard statements that I gave my wife money to pay. She'd spent the money on clothes and makeup. When I tried to explain to my wife that she had to stop doing this she threatened to jump from the overpass onto the Decarie Expressway. What can I do? She's crazy, but I love her."

Ti-Lou was the smallest bank robber I ever met. He stood about five foot six and weighed barely one hundred and fifty pounds. He looked like a kid, until you looked into his soulless eyes which were gray and without life. Stone-cold killer Randy Segouin also had dangerous eyes, but his eyes sometimes had sparkle. Ti-Lou's eyes were dead. He used cocaine which he loved, and prostitutes which he despised. He was a woman hater and a serial killer, which I knew nothing about at the time of our meeting. After he left the shack that served as a sales office, Pierre told me a little about Ti-Lou, starting with an apology for having him around.

"He's not my friend," he said, when his bank robbery partner was absent. "We just do holdups together."

A Jewish prostitute named Sarah would stop by Pierre's place from time to time to chat and complain about the difficulties of her profession. She was a pretty brunette with a slim figure and a whiny voice. When I had not seen her for a few weeks I asked Pierre about her.

"He killed her," said Pierre, referring to Ti-Lou. "He took her to Quebec City, and on the way, she tried to steal his coke. He said he gave her as much coke as she wanted, but when he saw her trying to steal some from his bag, he pulled out his gun. He was going to shoot her on the spot but just then, they came up to a tollbooth."

Pierre went on to tell me that, fearing for her life, the prostitute started screaming hysterically and tried to jump out of the two-seater Corvette as they slowed down for the tollbooth. Ti-Lou immediately put the gun away and calmed her down. When they left the tollbooth, he took his gun out again and, without another word, he shot her three times in the head.

"I buried her in a special place where they will never find her," Ti-Lou told Pierre. He said he had used the burial site many times before, without anyone ever discovering its secrets. I thought the story was bullshit until I realized that Sarah wasn't coming around anymore.

After that, I was uncomfortable around Ti-Lou but since I knew that he was always armed and was most probably a serial killer, I did not reveal the disgust I felt for him. Ti-Lou was eventually sentenced to life in prison for one of several other murders he was charged with. All of the murders involved women. I was not exactly sad to hear that he was in prison, and I laughed along with Pierre once we'd read his penciled note sent from Parthenais holding cells asking Pierre for an alibi.

While in prison Ti-Lou got his just rewards. He was killed by the boyfriend of one of the murdered women, who happened to be in the same prison as Ti-Lou. The boyfriend stabbed the little murderer so many times in the head that he was forever after referred to as "Eye picker."

My new job selling word processors went well through my three-month training period, at which point I was assigned a sales territory and a quota. I found myself under the supervision of a young woman, which was a first for me. The printing business had always been the almost exclusive domain of men and this experience with a woman supervisor was troubling. I was still expounding the female-bashing opinions of my chauvinistic friends in the underworld when suddenly I was subservient to a woman. And she was a bitch. A sarcastic, ball-busting bitch of a woman, who turned me off sales completely. She accompanied me on my rounds like I was a junior and on the first call I made, I went into a meltdown and broke out into a sweat that ran down my face and turned my ears red. I couldn't wait to get out of there. A few days later I found another job and handed in my notice.

At this point, my lifestyle was starting to catch up with me and I found myself sleeping poorly and I began suffering chest pains. I started to imagine voices in my head with conflicting ideas. Do this. Do that. Kill him. Don't kill him. Find a new job. Find a new score. All of the voices had a different character and voice. It was like being in the middle of a discussion group and not being able to offer an opinion.

I went to see a doctor.

"Are you nervous?" he asked.

"Me, nervous? You gotta be kidding.

"What about stress in your life?"

"Stress? No. Not really. I'm in sales, so I'm always a little stressed."

"Are you sure you don't have any personal problems?"

"No more than most people."

He gave me some pills. I used them for a while, but when I sold the three Hawk T-1 planes and got one hundred and fifty thousand dollars U.S. I felt I no longer needed them. I paid back all of my loans to my sister-in-law and to the bank and I totaled up the expenses paid to complete the Hawk T-1 aircraft certification project.

After I deducted the cost of completing the purchase and certification of the Hawk T-1 aircraft and calculated my profits, I went for a final visit to jail to explain the bookkeeping to Irving. I knew it was going to be a difficult meeting. Irving thought he had paid my debt with the planes and he was certain to be disappointed to learn otherwise. The documents detailing my expenses showed nothing in the way of salary for me, although I had put years into the program. The net return, after everything, was about seventy five thousand. No matter how you sliced it, that was nowhere near the money that was owed to me. There was only one asset left from our group fund and that was the fifty thousand dollar cash bail that was put up in my name for Chip the Limey.

When Irving came to the security window in the visiting room and picked up the telephone to speak, I could see that he had been working out. His shoulders were broader and he had grown a beard that obscured the softness of his unshaven face.

"You look like shit," he said to me.

"I got a cold." The truth was I was taking coke and the doctor's pills and I was dreading this meeting.

I told Irving that the Hawk T-1s did not cover what he owed me. I felt I was owed the fifty grand cash bail for Chip the Limey that was put up in my name. Irving disagreed. I showed him the expense sheet I had drawn up, but he paid no attention to the figures. Irv said that he should have the bail money. His logic was simple: "I'm in here and you're out there."

I said that it was not fair and that I did not agree. He penned me a note and held it to the security window. The note was simple.

"Buy life insurance."

I was furious. "This is the way you treat me, after all I've done for you?"

He shrugged. I collected my papers and stood up to leave.

"Don't think I'm joking," he warned. "And don't think I'm broke either. I got lots of money put away and lots of friends."

I left without looking back. On the ride home, I thought about Irving's threat and where I was in life and where I was going. I no longer felt any high or rush in my lifestyle. It had all turned to shit. I was almost broke. I had no income, save the chicken feed I was earning selling word processors. I hated my boss. I hated my job. I hated Irving. I hated my life.

I stopped on the way home to have a drink with some of my friends who I had left behind in the straight world. It was Friday, and a regular meeting place for some of the guys I used to work with in the printing business was at a small tavern in Lachine. I sat down beside Ed Johnson and tried to join in the raucous conversation he was having with some others. But my mind would not let go of the meeting with Irving. Irving had been my friend. He had been like a father to me. But I felt as though I had grown smarter since I met him. I no longer needed or wanted a mentor, and if I did, it would not be Irving. And now it had come to this . . . death threats.

"Where've you been keeping?" said Ed.

"I been around."

"What's wrong?" he asked.

"Nothing."

"Come on. I can see you have a problem."

"Nah, it's nothing."

"You can tell me."

"There's nothing to tell."

"Looks to me like you've forgotten how to talk to your friends."

I left without explaining my problems to Ed. How could I? I had tried to go straight, but my old life was still holding firmly on to me. I could have let go of the bail money and let Irving have it, but I was not going to be bullied into it. If I had been allowed a little more time to think things over, I might have done things differently. If I'd had a crystal ball to show me the future, I certainly would have turned loose the bail money and let Irv have it.

Instead, I went to Irving's house and conned Jane into giving me the bail ticket that was hidden in the stone crawl space beneath their house. I knew that Irving would be furious, but as far as I was concerned, it was check and mate. Once I held the bail ticket that was in my name, I had the bail money. I knew that Irving's screams of anger would be heard for miles outside his jail cell when he found out, but too bad. It would be years before he was out of prison and by then . . . well, who knew what would happen between now and then?

After I secured the bail ticket, I did what Irving had advised me to do in his three-word note. I bought some life insurance. My friend Gary Martin found it for me. It was the cutest little .32 automatic you ever saw and it was made by Savage. I purchased a shoulder harness, and from then on, I wore the gun twenty-four seven.

Over the next six months I lived a double life as I continued to go to work selling word processors while armed to the teeth. I was cautious in my movements and arranged certain codes with Barbara so that she would know where I was and what I was doing at all times.

I stopped into my old stomping grounds at Modern Motors which had been taken over by friends of Luc Lavoie. Ziggy Epstein was there on a weekend pass from prison and he pulled me aside with a warning about Irving. Irving was telling everyone he knew how he was going to get me. Freddie Peters who was on a day pass also pulled me aside and warned me to make up with Irving.

"If you don't, he'll pick you off with a .30–06 from the end of your street," he warned.

I knew my dispute with Irving was getting serious but I would not give in. It was about much more than the money. In my mind, I had been used and double-crossed. I had backed him up with weapons. I ended up on trial because of him. I went to Lebanon during a war because of him. I went to Jamaica countless times that could have landed me in prison because of him. And what did I have left to show for it? Nothing. And on top of that, Irving was trying to cheat me out of the money I was owed. Why was he after the bail money so badly if he still had lots of cash stashed away like he said he had? Was he pissed off that I wasn't in jail with him, or was he just letting the animal side of him take over now that he was in jail again?

My pal Bishop offered to broker a peace between us.

"I've seen this before," Bishop said. "I can arrange a meeting between you and Irving so you can work it out."

"Fuck him." I said "He's a fucking cheat and I don't care if we work it out."

It was only a matter of time before Irving was given a day pass, which he used to come by the old car lot and tell everyone within hearing distance how he was going to get me. He said he was going to take my house. Take my car. Take my money. And waste me. I came into the garage only minutes after Irving had left one day, and the place was buzzing.

"You just missed him," said Ziggy, "And man is he mad! You're lucky you didn't come in a few minutes ago. He's been looking for you."

"I live down the fucking street from him," I told Ziggy. "If he wants to see me he can come over anytime."

I was concerned, but I was not smart enough to be afraid. Irving was ten years older than me, and with his bad back the way it was, all the weightlifting in the world would not help him in a fight. I felt I could probably hold my own with him in a scuffle. And if it came to more than that, I was packing my .32 Savage. I kept it fully loaded with one in the chamber so that I could pull it and cock it in a second and it would be ready to fire.

Now that he was getting day passes, I was expecting Irving to come to my house and confront me on the bail issue, and I was ready. I slept with a loaded shotgun beside the bed and kept a constant vigil that had me waking several times a night. One night, the cat jumped up on the hall shelf and broke it free from the wall with a loud crash. It sounded like the front door was crashing in and I jumped up and grabbed my loaded shotgun beside the bed.

"Don't come any closer! I got a gun!" I yelled into the pitch black night.

That it turned out to be nothing did little to help my peace of mind. During the day I kept a regular routine, leaving in the morning for work and coming home around three or four in the afternoon. I put our house on the market, without a sign on the lawn. My conditions to the realtor were that the house could be seen by appointment only.

One Saturday morning, Barbara and I were doing yard work in the front of the house when a white Corvette turned slowly onto our street. The Corvette suddenly sped towards us and I had a vibe that went through me like an electric charge. I told Barbara to get in the house right away. I turned my back on the approaching car as I followed Barbara inside. The Corvette slowed down in front of our house and pulled into our drive-way. A tall, well-built young man of about thirty stepped out of the car and began walking towards me. I was standing in the doorway inside my garage with the garage door open and a loaded shotgun just behind the door. The stranger said he was interested in the house and asked if he could have a tour. With the situation in Quebec the way it was and the Separatist movement stifling house sales, you might have expected me to jump at the opportunity to show my house. I looked him over as he approached with both of his hands in the pockets of his wind-breaker. He did not fit the profile of a guy who'd want my house. He was young and had no children, judging by his two-seat Corvette. He had the same gray eyes I had seen in others of his ilk. If I was casting for the part of a contract killer, I would have picked him in an instant. I told him to stop where he was

SMUGGLER'S BLUES

and I told him in no uncertain terms that I would not permit him to tour the house.

"Call the agent and make an appointment," I said.

He paused a moment, and I thought he might make a move to pull a gun from his jacket as my hand rested on the barrel of my shotgun. He stood for a moment, looking me over, before turning away with a resigned shrug of his shoulders. I was not surprised to find out from our agent later that she knew nothing about him, and he never followed up with her after his visit. I took down his licence plate number and checked it out with Luc Lavoie, who still had contacts on the police force. The licence plate was registered to a roofing company and I wondered if it was just a front. I never found out if the guy was on the level, but in retrospect, I am glad that I did not let him into my house.

I phoned Barbara several times a day to touch base after that. I was concerned about her safety, although it was unheard of at that time for underworld settlings of accounts to involve family members. Even vendetta murders were planned to occur away from a victim's family. I visited my friend Hoss at his car dealership and he warned me to be very careful. He had heard through his underworld friends, Solly Cohen and Allan "Hawkeye" Stone, that a contract was out on me. I showed him my shoulder rig setup but he laughed out loud. "What . . . do you think they're going to say "draw?" Hoss warned me to stay out of nightclubs and keep my eyes open at all times. "Stay away from downtown and the east end," he said. "It might be a good idea to move or at least change your phone number."

I did not need to hear his warning about nightclubs. With a full-time job and a new baby daughter, I had no interest in going to nightclubs anyway. I could have listened to him about moving and changing my number, but that would have looked like running away. Instead, I made certain preparations to protect myself. And the day soon came when my preparations were put to the test.

It was a typical workday and I had dropped my guard a little. Irving had not phoned or visited me, even though he had been out on several day passes, which I took as a sign of his unwill-ingness to take a run at me head on. I still carried my .32 automatic everywhere. The weapon gave me confidence and I enjoyed the feeling of power it gave me. I strutted a cocky walk when I sauntered around town, heeled with a gun.

I even found enough confidence within myself to get a dif-ferent job with a company selling copiers. The manager who hired me was a friend from the printing supply days and he must have known about my importing charges from all of the public-ity. He asked me about my criminal charges, which I explained were far behind me, and he hired me on as the photocopier divi-sion sales manager. We both had high expectations for my future with the internationally known firm, and I was pleased as punch to quit my job at the word processing firm.

It was an exciting and mood-lifting week at the copier com-pany and even though I still wore the .32 under my jacket, I felt I was finally making some progress away from my life of crime. At the end of that week, I headed off to meet my friend Mouse, who had placed me at my new job through his career agency. I knew Mouse through his drug dealing past and I knew that the owner of his job placement business was a member of a famous Montreal crime family. The crime family bore the surname of McDonald and the youngest of several brothers was Mouse's boss, who was making an effort to go straight, just like I was. I remember Mouse counselling me after my first few unsuccess-ful job interviews, "Come on, man. It's an interview. You have to at least appear to want the job."

Towards the end of my first week, I drove out to Lachine to buy a chunk of hash from Mouse and celebrate my new job. I reached Mouse's house at about five o'clock in the evening and stayed until almost seven, smoking hash with him and his wife. I knew Barbara had gone shopping with her sister and I expected her to be home later than usual. I called home every thirty min-utes or so from Mouse's house and received no answer.

At about seven, with still no answer from home, my radar went off and the hairs on the back of my neck started tingling. I called my brother-in-law, Pierre, at home and he too was waiting to hear from Barbara or his wife Brandi. I toyed with the idea of having Pierre go over to my house and check if our wives were there, but I thought better of it. I finished my drink and my pipe full of hash and thanked Mouse for his hospitality before I drove off into the night with a premonition of danger.

I thought of calling the police and having them check on my house but decided against that. I was only a few minutes from home and I could get there faster than any police vehicle. The night was dark and still with freshly fallen snow on the roadsides as I made my way through the quiet streets of the West Island of Montreal to my home. The snow was melting as it hit the ground and the winter tires on my big Lincoln made a squishing sound on the bare, wet pavement. The radio was off and my senses were on keen alert as I pulled into my driveway. I stopped and waited. The sensor-driven coach lights at the end of the driveway were on, but the house lights were off. It was seven o'clock. By this time of night, the house lights should have been on. The dog was not barking and Barbara was nowhere to be seen.

Chapter Eight

The Great Escape

I held my position for one or two minutes and then backed my car down the driveway as if I were leaving. I was looking for a reaction. If it was an ambush, my leaving might provoke a move. I stopped at the end of my driveway and looked around. Nothing moved but I could sense by the hairs on the back of my neck that something was definitely not right. I thought again about calling in the cops, but I was already there at that point. I took my handgun out of its shoulder holster, cocked it and then pushed the remote garage door opener. When the double garage door creaked open, the overhead light clicked on and I saw nothing out of sorts inside the garage. I scurried on all fours around the front end of my Lincoln, which I left idling at the end of the driveway. The Lincoln was bathed in the amber glow of the coach lights, as I took a breath and quickly ran up to the house in a running crouch. I entered the garage and cat-walked through it to the inside door entrance to the house. I opened the door, half expecting to be shot in the face as I peered into the darkened hallway with my gun cocked and at the ready. I cursed the little gun I was carrying and I was hoping the Savage automatic wouldn't jam on me, as it had in practice after every three or four shots. But three or four shots might be all it would take if I could get them off quickly and accurately.

I looked to the left first, towards the bathroom at the closest end of the hall, which is where I would have hidden if I had wanted to pull off an ambush. When I saw that no one was there, I crept to the right and Indian crawled into the darkened kitchen.

"Hello? Is anybody here?"

"We're downstairs."

I recognized the voices of Barbara and her sister speaking in unison.

"Come upstairs," I called back.

"We can't. We're handcuffed to the post."

"Handcuffed? Who handcuffed you?"

"Two men," answered Barbara "They're gone now. We heard them leave. They stole Brandi's car from the garage."

"Hang on. I'm going to check around upstairs."

"No, please come and free us from these handcuffs. I have to pee so badly." It was Brandi speaking.

"I'll get my handcuff key and I'll be right down."

As I spoke, I retrieved a loaded .45 caliber handgun that I had hidden in the hall cupboard next to the garage and added it to my weaponry. With a cocked and loaded gun in each hand, I made my way through the darkened upper level of my house, checking for intruders. I let our young dog Tania out of the upstairs bathroom, where she had been locked up by the home invaders. I remember wishing I still had my last Doberman, Max, who had died after a dogfight with a neighbour's Malamute. No one could have come into our house and locked Max in a bathroom. I checked each room and saw that the upper level of the home was clear.

"Where are you?" came an impatient voice from downstairs. "My bladder's going to burst!"

"Let me talk to Barbara," I called down from the top of the stairs.

"I'm here," she replied

"Are you alright?"

"Yes, I'm alright."

"No one has a gun on you?"

"No. I already told you. They've left."

I found in Barbara's voice the tone I was looking for, which told me no one was prompting her with a gun. Nevertheless, I peeked around the corner of the top of the stairwell, with both hands holding a cocked and loaded weapon. I slowly walked down the flight of stairs and peered around the corner at the bottom of the stairwell.

I saw that the playroom was just as I had left it. The basement was pretty much empty except for a couch, a chair, and a coffee table with a ping-pong table in the centre. The ping-pong table stood beside a carpeted structural support pole in the middle of the spacious basement. My wife and her sister, Brandi, were handcuffed to that pole, while our one-year-old baby daughter played innocently at their feet.

"Get me out of these handcuffs," Brandi groaned. I checked the rest of the basement rooms for intruders before I came back to the issue of the handcuffs. When I returned to the support pole, I stood staring helplessly at the handcuffs, my mind clouding with anger and rage. I was momentarily numb as my mind went blank.

"I don't have a handcuff key," I said helplessly. "The police took my handcuffs and keys when they raided the house last year."

"Use a bobby pin," Barbara said, reminding me of a trick I had once shown her that I was too adrenalin-rushed to remember. I quickly ran upstairs and found a bobby pin in our bedroom. I returned downstairs and opened up the bobby pin, then slid the pin up and along the handcuff ratchet of Brandi's restraints until the handcuffs slipped open. Brandi bolted for the washroom while I repeated the same process with Barbara, who immediately picked up our baby daughter and held her close.

When Brandi returned from the washroom, we all went up to the kitchen where the story came out in breath-filled rushes that were mixed with sighs of relief. As I stood in the kitchen listening to their story, I could feel my blood warming to a boil. From what I could gather, Brandi and Barbara had returned home from a shopping trip and parked Brandi's Volkswagen in our heated garage. When they came into the house for a glass of wine and some further conversation, Barbara noticed right away that something was amiss. All of our suitcases were sitting packed in the hallway and, at first, she thought that maybe I was preparing to leave on a trip somewhere. When Barbara realized that the dog was missing, she made an immediate attempt to flee the house.

"Brandi, let's get out of here!" she said, but it was too late.

Before the girls could get out, two men in masks stepped from around the corner of the kitchen and pointed guns at them. Both of the gunmen wore hoods. One man was about five foot ten and slender. That man was mean and threatening while the other man, who was about six feet tall, seemed to be less aggressive.

"Is your husband nervous?" asked the mean one from beneath his mask. I found out later that he was an old associate and ex-partner of Irving's named Roger Ouimet. Ouimet was a contract killer who had worked with the infamous Jacques "Apache" Francois, the most prolific hit man the Montreal Hells Angels ever had in their ranks.

"No, my husband's not nervous," replied Barbara holding tightly to the baby. She was taken downstairs with her sister and the baby and then the two women were handcuffed around the support pole in the centre of the basement.

Roger Ouimet's partner, Ronny McGuire, was a recently released jailhouse con who had served time with Ouimet. He appeared to have little interest in the questions his partner was asking and he was basically along on the ride as backup. Ronny McGuire escorted the girls to the bathroom when they needed to go and passed Barbara the baby's bottle when our daughter started crying. Although he was along on the home invasion, Ronny seemed kinder and more sensitive than his partner.

Roger Ouimet pointed his gun at Barbara and demanded the bail document that I had manipulated away from Irving's girl-friend, Jane. When he was told that the bail ticket was with my lawyer, he placed the baby at Barbara's feet in the basement and went upstairs to wait for me to return home. The telephone rang several times throughout the hours that the two men waited in darkness for me. Barbara told me the men were upset by the phone calls. When my expected arrival time came and expired and more hours began to drag by, the two men became nervous. They were careful to flush the butts of their chain-smoked cigarettes down the toilet to avoid DNA printing. That indicated to me that they were well-schooled professionals. After several hours of fruitless waiting the two men gave up the hunt and helped themselves to everything of value that I owned. They took my stereo and my shotgun and they also took my wife's jewelry and loaded it all into suitcases which they put into Brandi's Volkswagen. In a curious twist of behaviour, they left my wife's wedding rings on her fingers while stealing her gold watch and gold chain and gold bracelets.

After the girls finished their story, I began absorbing the gravity of the situation until I came to a realization. The gloves were off in the battle of wills between Irving and me and the rules of engagement had now been made clear.

There were no rules.

Irving had sent two men into my home and terrorized my wife and I didn't care about what anyone said, I was going to make him pay.

I hid my guns and my pot in the air conditioning ducts in the basement and I called the police and told them we had had a home invasion. I told the police that the robbers had already left. Ten minutes later, two cops slowly came up to the front door. I was disgusted by their caution, as I watched through the living room window as the two police officers crept up the front walk. I opened the door before they rang the bell and advised them in sarcastic tones that their concern was unnecessary and that the gunmen had left a long time ago. The two uniformed policemen entered the house and then waved in a dozen more policemen who were hiding outside behind their squad cars.

When the first two cops came inside to take my report, I told them that the gunmen who had come to my house were sent by my ex-partner from Modern Motors to collect the bail stub that I was holding onto for Chip the Limey. I told them that my ex-partner was in jail and that we had had a disagreement over the bail money that had turned into an extortion attempt and a home invasion robbery.

The police were skeptical of my story until the telephone rang while they were standing and milling about searching for clues. One of the police officers motioned for me to take the phone, while he listened in on another line. His partner listened in beside my ear. It was one of the gunmen who had invaded our home and he was whispering into the other end of my phone line.

"Did you like that, eh? Do you know why we took your shotgun? That's for you." The cops were urging me to egg the caller on, to keep him talking, but I lost my cool and exploded in rage.

"You bastards are working for a fucking crook! Do you understand? You tell that fucking Irving that he's nothing but a fucking crook."

The call ended at that point, as the party on the other end disconnected the line. The policeman on the other phone came back into the kitchen, while the cop listening in by my ear hung up the receiver for me.

As the police roamed about my house taking notes and conferring with Barbara and Brandi and myself, the reality of what had happened sunk in for me. As my emotions raged between anger and despair, I realized in those slowly settling after moments, that it was one thing for me to risk my own life playing cowboys and Indians with Irving. But if Barbara or my daughter were ever to fall victim to my indiscriminate lifestyle, my world would never be the same. This was not the way it was supposed to be. The war was supposed to be between me and Irving. If anything had happened to my wife or daughter, I would have gone to the ends of the earth for retribution, but where would that leave me if my family was harmed?

I realized then that as a man with a family that I cared about, I was at a serious disadvantage in a war with Irving. Irving had no such encumbrances because he cared about no one, including his girlfriend Jane. Irving was sitting in jail, safe and sound, while I was living at home like a ship at anchor. A sitting duck.

The police left a tape recorder hooked up to my phone and left behind their written report that was needed for my home insurance claim. I found some satisfaction that my blaming Irving in the police report would fuck up his day passes for a while, and at the same time, I was pissed that he was in jail where I could not reach him.

My sister-in-law and her husband became distant to Barbara and me after the home invasion incident. Brandi began to hang around with Chip "the Limey" Jenkins, whose humor and sarcasm she found enjoyable. Chip was an interesting character who, unlike many of his underworld friends, was intelligent as well as charming. While he was on bail and awaiting trial in Montreal on the Lebanon hash scam, he was unable to work legally without immigrant status. He began working under the table, for a local music promoter, to supply whatever drugs were needed by the performing groups that were booked into Montreal. Since Chip did not do drugs himself, he was the perfect candidate for the job. He was called upon to deliver an ounce of cocaine to the hotel room of the Rolling Stones when they were back in town to perform, and, as a fellow Englishman, he was invited into their suite for some conversation. I asked him about it the next day.

"So you were invited in by the Stones?" I said to him, trying not to sound like a middle-aged groupie.

"Yeah," he answered.

"Did you do a line with Mick Jagger?"

"No," he said, with that little schoolboy smile of his.

"Did you smoke a joint?"

"No."

"Well, what did you do with him?"

"We had a cup of tea."

I was hovering around Chip like a mother hen with chicks, in order to defend my stake in the bail money that had been put up for him. At the same time as the Limey was being shadowed by me, he was being threatened by Irving who was passing him messages from jail. Irving ordered Chip, by messenger, to collect the bail from the courts and give it up to Jane. I was telling Chip that it was my money and not to give it to anyone but me. The smartest thing the Limey could do, under the circumstances, was to leave town as quickly as possible, which he did after his trial ended. He chose to live in Vancouver, which is the furthest place from Montreal you can be and still remain in Canada.

He came up with an idea to stop me from pestering him. He suggested I get a seizure order on the bail money through the courts. That way, I would not have to worry about him absconding with the dough and turning it over to Irving. It was a fantastic idea, and I lost no time in contacting a civil lawyer who I had met when I was selling word processors. I gave the lawyer the bail ticket I had in my possession and had him put a seizure before judgment on the fifty thousand dollars bail money. That way, no matter what happened, the bail money was protected and no amount of threats or arm twisting by Irving was going to get it away from me. Check mate, I thought, as I completed the arrangements with the lawyer.

Barbara and I moved out of our house the day after the home invasion. We moved into a motel at first. Shortly after we moved, I phoned Fast Freddie who was out of prison on a weekend pass. Freddie was in contact with Irving whenever he went back into prison and I urged him to pass on a message. "Tell that fat prick Irving that his flunkies fucked up. Tell him he's never getting that bail money and I'll be waiting for him when he gets out!"

When Freddie started to warn me about the danger I was in and suggested I give up the bail ticket, it sounded to me like he was defending Irving's position. At that point, I told Freddie that I did not trust him anymore and hung up the phone.

I went to see my friend Hoss who was from a different milieu than either Freddie or Irving. Ron "Hoss" Kingsley was my age and came from a similar west end background as I did. Hoss ran his father's second Ford dealership and he had no other reason than enjoyment for hanging around with mobsters. Hoss and his wife both did the better part of two years in prison for importing dresses from Afghanistan, with buttons that were made of hash. Like a man born into a woman's body, Hoss did not fit properly into his station in life. Hoss was not just a fringer who hung on the sidelines with criminal friends. Hoss was a mobster in businessman's clothing. Hoss collected an arsenal of weapons that he was keeping to counter a possible Separatist revolution in Quebec. When I talked to him about my fight with Irving, Hoss advised me that the two men who were sent after me were there for a hit not a robbery. He would not tell me how he knew this, only that there was a contract out on me and that it was a fact, not a rumour.

Hoss was close friends with Allan "Hawkeye" Stone, whose partner was Big Solly Cohen. In the typical culture of the underworld, there were the usual ties between the players. Hawkeye had gone to school with Hoss. Hoss had had previous dealings with big Solly. Big Solly had once been a partner of Irving's. In fact, Irving used to proclaim his hatred of Solly so loudly and vehemently, whenever the other man's name was mentioned, that it was obvious there were bitter feelings between the two. Irving complained that Solly had ripped him off once, on a trailerload of hot televisions. Solly always denied the accusation, but I could not see Irving making something like that up and being so angry about it if it were not true. Irving's complaints about Solly also seemed credible because Solly never criticized Irving and the hate was all one-sided.

My friend Hoss confirmed to me again that the visit to my house was a hit and not a robbery and then offered to turn me on to his friends, Solly and Hawkeye. He said they could arrange a hit on Irving in jail, which Hoss said was the easiest place to get him. The offer came with only one condition. Fifty grand up front. I thought about the offer for several days before I passed on it. I was not too keen on paying Solly Cohen and Allan Stone fifty grand for a hit on Irving, when I had already heard that Solly was in the habit of pulling rip-offs. Not only that, but fifty grand represented the exact amount Irving and I were fighting over. I could not see the financial wisdom of giving away fifty grand to save fifty grand, especially when I knew that the offer from Hoss might be a con. Perhaps, more importantly, I was hesitant to enter into a murder conspiracy with two people I did not know, other than by reputation.

Instead of contracting out the job on Irving, I had my friend Little Joe buy me a rifle and scope through an ad in the papers. Then I bought a wig, a mask and an instrument to calculate the distance to a target and prepared to get Irving before he got me.

I made a special visit to prison to consult with my old pal, Big John Miller, who was not doing too well. John Miller had contracted cancer in jail and was being treated with radiation. He was furious with Irving for having encouraged him to go along on that fateful ride which led to prison and was even more bitter when he ended up with a colostomy bag on his hip. John Miller's advice on the subject of my war with Irving was apocalyptic. "What you have to do is cut his balls off," John Miller whispered across the metal table at the medium security visiting room. "Hit him where it hurts. Kill that bitch, Jane, who's running his errands and paying his goons."

I could understand that John Miller hated Irving, but I was surprised at how much he hated Jane. I could see no value in John Miller's advice to kill Jane, which would only stop Irving temporarily before opening up a war of retribution against people that I cared about. Besides it was not Jane that I wanted dead. It was Irv. Jane denied it, of course, when I confronted her about helping Irving prepare for my home invasion. But what better place was there for Irving's henchmen to hang out and watch me other than the house Jane was living in, which was right on my path home.

"Irving would never have arranged something like that," Jane replied to my accusation, and she seemed to believe what she was saying, even if I did not. Instead of killing her as John Miller suggested I wrote her off as Irving's flunky and never spoke to her again.

John Miller was unable to help me much with my war strategy, but he was kind enough to offer us shelter at his house. His wife Louise was a loyal friend and she opened her home to Barbara and me, knowing that there was a contract out on my head. In spite of her brave and kind offer of shelter, we did not stay for very long. I was a danger for Louise to have around, but I had other reasons for leaving. Between Louise's sorrowful face because John Miller had cancer and was in jail and Barbara who was shaking uncontrollably after the home invasion, I did not feel very comfortable there.

Within a couple of weeks of moving in with Louise Miller, Barbara and I were able to move into Barbara's mother's apartment after her mother left for Europe on a month-long vacation. Once we were settled into our own space, I took stock of my situation. I had lost my job when I reported the home invasion to my boss and he freaked out thinking I was back into crime. That did not really matter under the circumstances because I was not intending to return to work there anyway. I had no money to speak of, and I had no way of safely making money while this heated war with Irving was going on and any deal could turn out to be a set up. Irving still owed me over a hundred grand but I figured that was lost forever. I had no way to get to Irving in prison, unless I ponied up fifty grand, which was about all the cash I had left after selling off the Hawk T-1 aircraft. I had no desire to trust anyone else in a murder scheme but I could not continue to walk around town with a bull's eye on my back. Our house had been on the market for months but no reasonable offers had come in.

My friend Luc Lavoie said he had a friend who was interested in buying my house under the table. We came to a verbal agreement to transfer the house ownership, even though the amount was ten thousand less than I had paid for the property. Before I completed the transaction, I went to discuss the situation with my friend Jean Pierre Allard, the car dealer. Jean Pierre was a very nice fellow and he had come to several of my parties with his wife. His wife enjoyed herself thoroughly and got along well with Barbara, me and the others at the party. Jean Pierre, who loved his wife more than anything else on earth, told me one time that the toughest thing he ever had to do was to burn his own house down.

"You can't imagine the pain of losing all of your possessions," he told me, as he spoke of photographs and memories lost forever. He said that he had to burn his house down because he was deep in debt with no way out. His description of his financial situation at the time kind of reminded me of mine.

After discussing my situation with Jean Pierre I decided to book a three week vacation with my wife to Jamaica where we rented a villa in Ironshore. We shared the house with Barbara's friend, Heather Gilcrest, who was hoping her new boyfriend might stop by our villa to visit on his way back to Montreal from Colombia. Heather was a flight attendant with Air Canada and her free passes allowed her to meet and accompany Barbara and me in many parts of the world. Her boyfriend never did come by for a visit and his loss was my gain as I had two beautiful women to escort me all around the island.

But in spite of my two attractive female escorts, my world was truly a dark place with very little brightness shining in. When alone, I reflected upon my existence which revolved around guns and killers and thieves and lawbreakers of every type and I wondered what had happened to the hippie mentality that had come over me many years ago on my sabbatical to Mexico. I asked myself what had happened to my spiritual awakening that money was the root of all evil, and what had happened to those wonderful revelations of karma and peace and love that I once believed in. How, I asked myself, could I have strayed so far from the path of enlightenment and ended up on the one I was walking now?

One night, I was driving home alone from Montego Bay to Ironshore when I pulled to the side of the road. I got out of the car and stood in the pitch blackness at the side of the road looking upward. The stars were myriad in the heavens as I quietly called upon Him.

"Please, Lord. I don't know how this Irving business is all going to work out, but if you can somehow help me through this, I will end my gangster life."

I asked His forgiveness for the harm I might have caused others, especially Barbara and her sister and my mother who were all scared for their own lives and terrified for mine. I added that I was not yet a murderer and really did not want to become one, but what else could I do? My bed was made and I had no choice but to lie in it.

While I was still in Jamaica, I phoned Barbara's sister in Montreal to catch up on the news. Brandi told me that I had better come home right away. My house had burned to the ground and the fire inspectors were looking to question me about it. I told her the fire marshal would have to wait and that I would be home in a week when my vacation was finished. The world seemed a little brighter, as I broke the bad news to Barbara and Heather, who both looked at me with accusing glances.

When I returned to Montreal I cooperated fully with the police and the fire investigators as my insurance policy directed. The fire marshal told me my house fire was an arson and then quizzed me on why I had jammed an ax in the patio door frame. He suggested that perhaps it was done to stall the firefighters from entering during the fire.

"On the contrary," I said while pointing to the black-and-white photo he had taken of the ax. "I put the ax there to prevent another break-in or home invasion while I was away on vacation. If you want an arson suspect, go see Irving Goldberg in jail. He is on record for threatening my life and my home and for sending home invaders to take my possessions. There is already a police report on that."

I could sense that they did not believe me, but what could they do. I was in Jamaica at the time of the fire and as Irving himself used to say, I had an iron-clad alibi.

When the investigators questioned me about how I was going to deal with my situation with Irving, I told them not to worry about it. I was leaving Montreal and moving elsewhere.

"That won't work," the police investigator said, as he tried to bring me into the fold. "You should cooperate with us. No one escapes your kind of situation by moving. It always catches up to you."

"We'll see," I said, before leaving the investigators to their own agendas and opinions.

I returned to the rented home on the west end that the insurance plan was covering and started making plans for a trip out of town. I heard that Irving was not getting out on weekend passes anymore which was encouraging, but I also heard that he was the head of the Archambault prisoners' inmate committee which was a sign of his rising power in jail. I wondered for a time just what I had taken on. I had no idea who Irving might send after me next. It could be anyone. It might be someone fresh out of jail. It might be a contract killer already on the street. It might even be someone I trusted. One thing was certain. I would not know who was coming for me until the last second. The only smart thing to do was to find a safe haven until Irving himself came out of the slammer. Then, with a little luck, I would pick him off from a distance and be done with him. In my mind it was purely self-defence, although I knew if anything went wrong, the charge would be murder.

My insurance broker called me in for a conversation the next day. He befriended me like a brother and then suggested that the next time I had a financial problem I should call him for a loan rather than torch my house. I told him that I did not know what he was talking about and terminated the meeting. I liked the guy because we had spent quite a few hours talking business and getting close. He told me that my insurance claim had cost him his annual bonus and I felt sorry about that.

Next my lawyer called me in for a meeting. He had heard about my disagreement with Irving and he was concerned for his own well-being.

"I don't want any trouble from this guy Irving," he told me. "Who is he? I don't even know the guy!"

I calmed Sidney down and paid him his bonus for getting me off the importation charge. I told him Irving was in jail and not to worry. I was going to straighten things out with him when he came out.

After that, my mother called me. She was worried because her husband Jerry was out of town. She thought she saw three strange men driving slowly past her house and looking in. She thought they might be "bad men" looking for me. I didn't know if she had a jittery case of nerves with an overactive imagination or what. I told her to go into the bedroom safe and take out a gun I had left there for Jerry in case he needed it, in view of all that was going on around me.

"It's a revolver. Just point it and shoot," I told my mother who has always been a pacifist and hates violence, "There's no safety."

My mother had a very vicious German shepherd who was protective to a fault.

"Keep the dog close to you in the house," I told her. "If anyone tries to come in, set the dog on them. If that doesn't work, fire a warning shot into the ceiling and then call the police. Remember to stay low and use the gun only if you have to."

I called the local police detachment and explained the situation as best I could and asked them to look in on my mother. I described the station wagon with three men in it that my mother had seen cruising the neighbourhood, but I never heard anything more about the incident. I was surprised some time later to hear my mother confess that she was oddly comforted by having a gun by her side at that time and I found it ironic that even a pacifist can be comforted by the power of a gun.

My sister-in-law, Brandi, called. She was scared of what Irving might do to her and wanted to know what I was going to do about it. I was not unsympathetic but what was I supposed to do? He was in jail. "Give him the money," she said. I refused to do that. It was more than just the money at this point, I told her. It was about principal. But the truth was, I had painted myself into a corner with my stubborn refusal to submit to Irving's will and things had gone way too far to turn back the hands of time. I did not believe that Irving would trouble Brandi or anyone else in my family while his girlfriend Jane and his own family were still vulnerable.

At this point Irving was mad at me, not anyone else, and with his flunkies fucking up the first hit, he was bound to have less confidence in them than he used to. Throughout our years together, there had been many barbeques and family get-togethers involving Brandi and Irving. Brandi was so taken with Irv at one point that she was going to give him her fifty thousand dollar inheritance to invest for her. Even though Irving was my partner at the time and we were still close friends, I warned Brandi not to give him her money. To her credit she listened, which is why she did not end up standing in line with Irving's other creditors when the hammer came down on him. After the home invasion, Brandi gave in to her fear and accused me of "living my life like a movie" before dropping Barbara and me from her social calendar.

As if things couldn't get any worse, I drove into town one day and stopped into my old place of business to visit Luc Lavoie. The Modern Motors premises had been taken over by friends of Luc who, unbeknownst to me, were running a hot car ring out of the garage. I parked my car on the upper level to go to the washroom and stepped right into the middle of a police raid. I ducked into the bathroom when I saw the cops but there was no time to ditch my gun which was discovered in an instant when they pulled me out of the bathroom stall and searched me.

"Full bore," the detective who frisked me said, as he pulled my gun from my shoulder harness. "Do you have a permit for this?"

"No."

"Give him a break. He has a reason for carrying the gun," said Luc as the cops milled around me like salmon in a feeding frenzy. "Too bad you walked into this," Luc said to me. "I tried to warn you, but it was too late."

"Thanks anyways," I offered. "If you get out before me, call my wife and tell her I'm okay. When I don't come home tonight she's gonna think I'm dead."

The plain-clothes detectives sent me down to Station Number One for processing instead of taking me downtown for questioning with the other suspects in the hot car ring. I was disappointed to loose the .32 and shoulder rig but I was more disappointed to be in jail again.

"Back again," I scratched into the jail cell wall above my cot. Underneath I wrote my initials and the date. I had two joints in my shirt pocket that the cops missed in their excitement over the gun bust. I had no desire to add to my predicament and I flushed them down the toilet. The Montreal cops from Station Number One questioned me and seemed somewhat sympathetic to my plight with Irving and my need for a handgun to protect myself. They offered me a deal. If I would consent to a search of my house looking for more weapons, they would take me home. They said they would leave me there on my own recognizance if they found no other weapons. I agreed on the condition that I call my wife right away to spare her any more needless worry. "No deal," was their answer. The cops did not want any secret messages or warnings passed to Barbara that would interfere with their weapons search.

I had a pound of weed in the freezer that I knew the police would find, but I told them I would agree to their terms just to put Barbara's mind at ease. Even if they charged me for the weed, Barbara would know that I was in police hands and not someone else's. With all that was going on and my lack of regular phone calls, I knew she would be frantic with worry if I did not contact her soon. I didn't want to imagine how she would react if I didn't show up until the next day. Barbara was already down to ninety-five pounds and looked like she was disappearing with all of this Irving business. Her weight loss made me feel even guiltier than ever. When the police took me home, Barbara was so relived to see me that she started crying. The police searched our rented house and left after finding nothing unwarranted to charge me with. They did not even look in the freezer. I was home and safe. I put a fire on in the bedroom alcove and crawled into bed where I felt warm and protected under the covers. I talked to Barbara and I could see the strain in her face. This lifestyle was threatening to kill her before Irving killed me.

A few nights later, I spotted a white van in front of the house and I called the police to check it out. The van drove away and I never knew if it was innocently parked or if it was a police surveillance vehicle or another possible attempt by Irving's forces. The incident left me feeling insecure and I decided to find another house that was safer.

I found an ad in the paper that described a winterized cottage in Morin Heights, a few miles north of Montreal. I rented the place, and Barbara and I and our baby daughter stayed in the cottage for several months until my gun possession charge was dealt with. It was peaceful in the country and, for those several months, I slept without waking up five times a night to look around for intruders.

As my trial date moved closer, I had a few trusted friends come up for visits, people like Derrick the Doctor and Hoss the gun fanatic. Hoss and I had great fun shooting our guns off in the car graveyard, blowing out car windows and puncturing the car bodies with bullet holes. One time Hoss brought up his black powder rifles and I learned a valuable lesson. Never fire a black powder rifle from the hip. The powder discharges right under your chin and leaves it pockmarked with bits of burnt charcoal.

Luc Lavoie came up with my pal Bishop for a winter celebration at the cottage. Luc brought along two bottles of Remy Martin cognac that eventually saw Bishop puking on the lawn in a fetal position and me shivering on the bed with alcohol poisoning. Luc ended up sound asleep in an easy chair until morning. Only Derrick and his girlfriend survived the drinking binge to drive home unaided through the cold winter night.

I took long walks with Barbara around the small lake beside the cottage and because the TV reception was poor, I read many books that I had put aside years before. In time, I had my gun possession trial and paid my fine. Irving was still in jail with several years to go before release. There was no point in hanging around Montreal waiting for a bullet and with no other restrictions to hold me back after the gun charge was dealt with, I was free to leave the province.

I decided to visit my old friend Larry Williams in Vancouver. I purchased a camper and we went on a cross-Canada journey that brought back memories of our earlier days camping around Mexico. I liked the feeling of having all of my possessions with me everywhere I went, and with no fixed address, I felt as free as a gypsy.

When it was time for us to leave Montreal, my buddy Bishop was pragmatic.

"Don't tell me where you're going to be staying," he said. "If I don't know where you are, then I can't be forced to tell anyone."

I told him not to worry and that I was coming back to take care of Irving as soon as he was sprung from jail. Bishop once more offered to broker a peace between Irving and me, but I refused his offer, telling him that things between us had gone too far. I told him I had no choice but to take care of Irving. Everyone I knew lived in Montreal and there was no way I was giving them all up because of that fat prick bastard.

I know Bishop believed me, because for the first time in our relationship, I asked him to do me a favour and he refused. I stopped my car downtown and asked him to run into a wig store to buy me a wig. He adamantly refused. He was my best friend, he told me, but he drew the line at complicity in murder. I shrugged the incident off as one more reason to take care of business on my own.

I had no idea of the stress that I was under during this period, not until I jumped in my camper van with Barbara, our daughter and our dog and saw Montreal disappearing in my rear view mirror. When I hit the Ontario border, I removed the .45 from under my coat and put it away beneath the bench seat storage area, next to the unregistered rifle and scope that Joe Dudley had purchased for me. The next several weeks were a tonic for frazzled nerves, as my wife and I took our leave of Montreal and it felt just like a vacation.

We stopped in Toronto to see my old friend Manny, who had left Montreal after Jean Paul died to make a fresh start with his new wife. Manny had been in partnership with Jean Paul and it was his ex-girlfriend, Susan Braun, who had died with the loan shark in her Montreal apartment. Barbara and I stayed for several days with Manny and his new wife. We were able to relax in a way that we had almost forgotten was possible and I enjoyed the new experience of not being armed as we saw the sights and sounds of Toronto.

After a week of warm hospitality in Toronto, Barbara and I left to visit the northern forests of Ontario. We eventually reached Sault Ste. Marie and stayed with my cousin Bill who I had not seen for years. We had a great time catching up on gossip from our youth and he took me for a hike to a small stream where we caught hundreds of tiny smelt-like fish in nets.

When we moved on from the "Soo," Barbara and I stopped

at a government campground beside a frozen lake where we celebrated our journey with a bottle of wine. A magical moment is etched in our memories for all time: we sipped our wine on a deserted beach while the dog lay beside us and our daughter, Allison, played in the sand. As Barbara and I talked and laughed and smoked a fat joint of good weed, the lake crackled and snapped, sounding like champagne corks popping as the ice began its spring melt. That night, we slept in our camper beside the lake and it was the best sleep I had experienced in years.

We took the circular route around Winnipeg, because we had visited once before and found the best feature of the city to be the bypass. When we drove on towards Edmonton, we experienced the wide open spaces of the Canadian prairies which was immensely enjoyable. We kept looking for "Orbit," that was advertised as coming up on road signs, and were amused to find out that it was nothing more than a large orb-shaped garbage can alongside the highway.

When we arrived in Edmonton, we stayed with a friend that I used to work with in the printing and copier business, named Rolf Wolstrom. Rolf, as you might expect, was of German heritage. Rolf was taking care of a high-rise apartment in Edmonton and put us up for free in a fully furnished suite. He and his young girlfriend had left Montreal to have her baby, although they had not yet committed to marriage. They made us a dinner of potato pancakes and made us feel most welcome in a way that only ex-patriots can understand. We had a lovely time while we were there, but as nice as it was to have a free furnished apartment in Edmonton, warm weather beckoned us and we were anxious to move on to Vancouver.

The next highlight on our journey across Canada came as we stopped within view of the timeless Rocky Mountains. They were still as magnificent and spectacular as they had been the last time we saw them, ten years earlier. The granite peaks of the Rockies exceeded fourteen thousand feet in altitude and were so steep that even snow could not adhere until the lower reaches of the mountainsides. We stopped at the hot springs in Jasper, where we took a bath in the warm spring-fed sulphur streams that collected into a swimming pool. Barbara and I watched a vain, handsome man who looked like a movie star standing in the spring-fed pool, unaware that the sulphurous chemicals were making his hair dye drip in red trickles down his face. It sent us into giddy laughter that we had not experienced for quite some time.

On our way into Vancouver, we drove through Mission and I could smell the moisture from the mighty Fraser River before I even saw it. We drove on to Port Moody, where we inhaled the fragrances of apple blossoms and salt water as we rounded the head of Burrard Inlet. The weather was a balmy seventy five to eighty degrees and sunny. People in cars and on the street were tanned, even though it was barely the end of May. The streets were lined with flowers and fruit trees in bloom, as bird cries rang from eagles, gulls, crows and songbirds that were all competing for territory. The houses in Vancouver looked old but were well kept, and everywhere we looked around the city, the streets were pristine and without litter.

Spring in Vancouver was quite a contrast to spring in Montreal where melting snow reveals a winter's worth of dog crap in front yards all over the city. In Montreal, you might have found some warmth at this time of year by huddling in a sunbeam in some wind-protected alcove. A walk outdoors back there would have required fur coats and fleece-lined boots, in contrast to the pretty girls of Vancouver who were riding around in the back of pickup trucks wearing halter tops and shorts.

We arrived in British Columbia to experience the best summer that the province had seen in fifty years. Sunny days followed sunny days that followed more sunny days, stretching throughout the entire summer with nary a break. Barbara and I made jokes about Vancouver's reputation for rain and suggested that it was a ruse to keep the rest of Canada from migrating here. The two of us were having too much fun to miss our families or friends back in Montreal and every day was filled with new experiences. Barbara and I became closer as a couple than we had ever been before and I found myself forgetting that in a matter of months or years, I would have to travel back to

Montreal and take care of business with Irving.

We stayed with my friend, Larry Williams, who had honoured me as best man at my wedding several years before in Montreal. Larry and I had been workmates and friends at my old printing company job, before he grew his hair long and followed Timothy Leary's advice to turn on, tune in and drop out. When Larry visited me in Montreal, at the height of my flamboyance, he had been suitably impressed by the large home, the fancy cars and the lifestyle that I was leading at the time. But he showed no envy or jealousy and seemed quite happy in his own hippie sphere of the universe.

Larry was a car salesman on a new car lot in North Vancouver at the time we met him again in British Columbia. We stayed with him and his family for about three months, making certain to disappear in our camper every few weeks so as not to overstay our welcome. Barbara and I and the baby visited Long Beach on Vancouver Island and Brightside Resort on the Sunshine Coast and then went inland to the Okanogan Valley and the resort towns of Osoyoos and Kelowna. That summer, we saw all of the sights that British Columbia had to offer, including Victoria where we had "High Tea" at the Empress Hotel. With the approach of winter, we skied Whistler and Blackcomb Mountains which was nothing like the bunny hills in Montreal called Mount Tremblant and Saint Sauveur.

After nearly three months of living with my buddy Larry, it was time to move out on our own and we started to search for a place to stay in Vancouver. We tried looking for a place to rent, but we had two strikes against us as far as landlords were concerned. We had a young child and we owned a dog. I had never experienced anything like that in eastern Canada, where it was so easy to find rental accommodation. Vancouver, on the other hand, had a zero percent vacancy rate and the perspective landlords had you sign an application form before choosing who would get the honour of renting their dwelling.

For about three months we looked everywhere for rental accommodations, but in the end, we finally had no choice but to buy a house. We chose a small bungalow in scenic North

Vancouver, a stone's throw away from where my friend Larry and his wife Linda lived. The house was barely a thousand square feet in size and was a shadow of the house we had left behind in Quebec. I used to laugh that I could kick the house down with my feet and I was not joking. The tiny clapboard and shingle house featured two bedrooms and a huge, private fenced-in backyard. There were several Chinese maple trees there, as well as half a dozen fruiting plum trees. The house was apartment-sized but it was roomy enough for us all, once I converted one of our large shipping crates into a doghouse in the yard for Tania, our Doberman.

I had enough money for a year or two of living, with the insurance settlement from the fire, but a good chunk of that was already eaten up with the house purchase. We became less extravagant in Vancouver, but not enough to please one house-wife friend of Larry and Linda's. Bev found our spending habits outrageous. She took our free spending as a threat to her own frugal lifestyle and warned her car salesman husband, Carrie, about getting too close to us.

I began the interior painting and other house renovations myself, instead of wasting the money on a contractor and was surprised at my own abilities. I had never lifted a finger to do manual labor in the past, and this new experience of completing projects without spending a lot of money felt very rewarding.

I had been communicating with my lawyer in Montreal to make sure that Chip the Limey's bail money was secure and to have it paid out to me as quickly as possible. The money was being held in the Pronotary's Office of the Quebec Court and I was told that it was only a matter of weeks before I would be able to collect it. Shortly after telling me that all was going well, my lawyer called to inform me that there was a problem. The fifty thousand dollars in bail money had somehow been paid out to Andrea, Jane's sister.

"But we had a seizure order on the bail money. How can that be?" I asked my lawyer with amazement in my voice.

"We don't know how it happened," the lawyer told me. "Someone apparently removed the seizure notice on Chip

Jenkin's bail money from the Pronotary's file. There is an investigation underway, but it looks like it was an inside job. We have demanded payment and we expect to win, but you know how it is when you sue the government. It will take some time."

I was angry at first. Then I became livid with rage at the thought that I had been outfoxed again by Irving. I knew that my lawyer and I had taken all the proper procedures to seize the bail money, but how did Irving, who was in a maximum security jail, manage to get someone to infiltrate the Pronotary's office to pull the seizure order from the file?

Or had he? Could the Quebec Crown have ordered the Pronotary's office to release the money to Andrea to further spark up the confrontation between Irving and me? The authorities were not very happy about seeing me freed on the Lebanese hash importation charge, and now they were even less happy about my lawsuit against them for the bail money. It could have been a simple accident of some kind that saw the bail money doled out without the proper checks and balances. But in a conspiracy-driven mentality like mine, I found that to be the hardest of all theories to buy into. Whatever the reason, I had no choice but to instruct my lawyer to stay on the case, while I sorted out this latest twist in the never-ending saga of Irving versus me.

I marveled at what a mess it all was. I was lucky to have beaten the drug charges against me. But if I continued to make a nuisance of myself, the Quebec Crown could get angry enough to drag me back before the courts again. And if Irving or anyone else involved in my case were to rat and bring forward new evidence of my involvement, I would certainly be subject to a new trial.

Instead of being thankful for all of my blessings, I vented my anger over the lost bail money as I painted the interior of my new house in North Vancouver.

Checkmate for Irving, I thought to myself, as I slapped paint on the walls and stewed over his victory. I swore to myself that I was going to get him back for all that he had done to me. The invasion of my home, his goons terrorizing my family, double-crossing me for my money and leaving me to fend for myself on the streets.

But the truth was, it had been months since I had carried a gun in my pocket and I was beginning to like the feeling. I liked the slower pace of life in Vancouver. The weather on the west coast was beautiful and I wondered why anyone would want to endure the climate of Montreal when they could live in British Columbia. The people were polite, beyond anything I had experienced before. When merging in traffic in Vancouver, there was an orderly spacing of one car per lane whereas in Montreal, one line of traffic would dominate the single lane until some brave soul in the other lane jutted the nose of his car out.

The friendships that Barbara and I had developed in Vancouver became very close knit because of the absence of any relatives. We had holidays and dinners together with our new friends. We went to shows and parties together. The people we met were schoolteachers and lawyers and people from worthy trades.

When I called for news back east, I found that some of the friends I had left behind in Montreal had moved away themselves. Some had gone to Toronto to escape the volatile situation of the French Separatist movement in Quebec. There were some friends I stayed in contact with and others who I was able to leave permanently behind. Picking and choosing who I would remain in touch with became as easy as flicking a light switch.

A few well-chosen friends, like Derrick and Hoss and Bishop, ended up visiting me in Vancouver. It was a mixed blessing to see them because the talk always went back to the past, which I had left behind. I was less and less interested in retold war stories, and the more I thought about returning to my old life, the less appealing it was. Barbara's mother and both of my parents had come out to visit us on different occasions in Vancouver and we came to realize that our situation was no different than Barbara's two other siblings who lived in England and the United States.

Barbara's younger sister, Brandi, still lived in Montreal, and from what I was told, Irving had not approached her. He was not likely to cause trouble for her or any of my friends now that he had the bail money. I had a legal entitlement to the same amount of money from the Pronotary's office and that challenge was in the hands of the legal system. There was no need to pursue my vendetta with Irving if I did not want to.

I decided that if Irving contacted or bothered any of my friends or family, I would take that as a sign that I had to return and finish him off, and that would be that. But if Irving did not pursue our vendetta, I would let the matter drop and stay in Vancouver. The irony of it all came later, because it took twelve years to get the Quebec government to hand over the money they wrongly gave away. They tried every trick in the book to thwart me, including labeling the bail money the proceeds of crime. But that did not work because Barbara and I could show legal ties to the money, and in the end, the Quebec Pronotary's office paid me the fifty thousand dollars they owed, plus bank interest.

The big loser, in financial terms, was the Government of Quebec, but somehow I felt no satisfaction in winning my case. My lack of excitement over the payout of the bail money just showed me again that everything I had gone through was not worth fifty thousand dollars. If I had had it to do all over again, I would have conceded to Irving's demands right from the start.

I had a strange dream while sleeping in my new North Vancouver home. The stock market was going crazy at the time and I saw several news stories about a spectacular rise in gold and silver. That night, I dreamt I was talking to Barbara's father who had died some years before. In my dream he told me to buy gold, so, the next morning I went straight downtown and bought twenty thousand dollars worth of gold and silver. When the certificates were ready to be picked up some thirty days later, I had another premonition, this time to sell them, which I did. I cashed out with over twelve thousand dollars in profit in less than thirty days. The very next day, after I sold my shares, both gold and silver hit the skids. My luck was returning and I took the dream about Barbara's father as a sign that I was on the right path again.

I eventually heard from my friends back in Montreal that Irving was out of jail and on parole. He was selling cars in a small lot off Decarie Boulevard. It warmed my heart when I heard that two French speaking holdup artists came onto Irving's car lot and robbed him at gunpoint. They stole all of his gold jewelry, along with his Patek Philippe watch and took all of his cash. The two robbers also shot and killed Irving's dog, Nitro, as he bravely ran to his master's defence.

I couldn't help but wonder if perhaps it was because the boys on the docks were upset that Irving had spent all of their money on his hash scam and they had sent a crew over for a collection visit. Or perhaps Irving had had a falling-out with the same two gunmen that he had sent to my house. Whatever the case, it was all happening three thousand miles away and that was fine with me.

In leaving my past behind me, I felt at first that I had lost the battle, but I soon came to see that I had actually won the war.

Chapter Nine

Leaving Babylon

One of the first things I did upon arriving in Vancouver was to locate a reliable pot dealer. I had brought a pound of primo weed with me from Montreal when I moved, along with an ounce of good black hash. When that ran out, I had my wife's sister, Brandi, mail me another pound of Jamaican weed. It was seedy and mild, but at six hundred a pound it was reasonable. This routine continued for several months until I was introduced to Lou Berger, a North Vancouver pot dealer.

At first, I was blown away by the two hundred dollar price Lou was charging for an ounce of weed. But as soon as I lit up a joint, I was more blown away by the quality of the herb than the price. The weed that Lou sold me was grown locally but came with names like Thai and Hawaiian and Cambodian, with flavours that were sweet and spicy and highs that were spiritual and uplifting. I could buy weed back east for six hundred dollars a pound, but I preferred to spend two hundred an ounce for Lou's B.C. bud.

My friend Rolf Wolstrom moved from Edmonton to Vancouver and his pretty young girlfriend came with him. Rolf was promoting a 1950s designed sports aircraft on the Vancouver stock exchange. When he was not hanging paper at the stock exchange, he was flying German tourists on sightseeing trips around B.C. for a charter aircraft company. Rolf told me that the performance aircraft he was promoting had been designed as the way of the future after the Second World War. The aircraft never caught on in the fifties, but now that it was repowered and recertified with new turbocharged engines, the four-passenger plane was being hustled on the stock market once again.

The repowered aircraft was being promoted as a prototype for a new wave of pleasure aircraft and Rolf took me up for a test ride. It flew very well, particularly when landing against a crosswind. The aircraft handled like a sports car until take-off speed, when it would launch into the air like a fighter plane. It banked and turned in a very tight arc, almost as if turning in its own wingspan. It was a fun plane to fly, albeit so noisy that Rolf and I had to speak through radio headsets the entire time. Visibility was excellent with the entire front of the cockpit made from a bubble of unbreakable Plexiglas. I was impressed with Rolf's repowered flying machine, but not enough to invest any money with him.

By this time I had found a job in the newspaper business and become a salesman for the *Columbian* newspaper chain. The *Columbian* was Vancouver's oldest newspaper and had a paid circulation of twenty thousand, which was exaggerated to be over thirty thousand copies per day. Add to that another one hundred thousand *Columbian* weekly edition papers that were delivered door to door for free and you had a combined circulation of one hundred and thirty thousand papers. The job sounded better than it was, but there was really no other newspaper competition in its demographic.

The sales position was a slacker's dream. There were seven unions pulling the small paper towards bankruptcy, and as a *Columbian* employee, I was a member of one of them. My direct supervisor was the picture of a burnt-out newspaper man from Toronto, with baggy red eyes and a sagging smoker's face that matched his rumpled shirt and tie. He hired me and then quietly pulled me aside to give me some advice. He told me to just go through the motions and not to worry about achieving my sales quota.

"This is the *Columbian*," he told me. "It's not a real newspaper. Don't make waves and we'll all get along."

I had never heard anything like it before in all my years of selling and I quickly took full advantage of my sales manager's sage advice. I started driving my camper to work instead of my convertible Buick, so that I could drive down to numerous parks by the water to have a daily nap. I brought in enough advertising orders to satisfy my boss and I wondered where the other salesmen were napping because they were not doing any better than I was.

With all the free time I had on my hands and partially due to the literary environment I was working in, I began to write a novel. My wife had always thought that I had the talent to be an author, ever since I wrote an essay for her and got her an eighty percent mark in high school. Within six months of joining the *Columbian*, I told my wife that I could not stand my job anymore and suggested we take a sabbatical down to Jamaica. I was making decent money at the newspaper and the working conditions and benefits were excellent. However, I felt I was going nowhere in a job at a newspaper that was threatening to fall under the bailiff's lock and key every day especially with a boss telling me not to work so hard. None of the seven unions allowed for any of the concessions the newspaper publisher asked for and the province's oldest newspaper folded not long after I left it.

Barbara and I had been trying to conceive a second child since we came to Vancouver, and after almost three years, we were still unsuccessful. A relaxing trip to Jamaica might be just the tonic to produce our new baby, or at least that was my soothing sales pitch to Barbara. While I was down in Jamaica I would open a business renting motorcycles to tourists and at the same time, I would complete the work remaining on my book.

While working at the *Columbian* newspaper, I met a lawyer who had emigrated from Jamaica and he happened to be moving back down there now that the government had changed. His name was Vincent Chen and he was an ally of the new prime minister, Edward Seaga, a free enterprise capitalist who had defeated the socialist party of Norman Manley. Vincent offered to help me with my immigration papers and work permit, which he started working on even before I moved down to the island. I researched the type of motorcycles I would purchase and made a deal with a local supplier to ship them down from Vancouver. I sold my camper and my convertible to aid in financing the trip and I found a suitable tenant for a one-year lease on our North Vancouver home. To complete the preparations for our move, I bought a cheap Underwood manual typewriter, along with several reams of typing paper and plenty of correction ribbon. Barbara and I left our Doberman in the care of my friend, Tim, who was kind enough to take her into his house.

We flew to Toronto, which is a connection point for travel to Jamaica when flying from Vancouver. In Toronto we met with our old friends Manny and Bishop and their respective families. Manny had moved to Toronto shortly after he met his future wife in Montreal. He was part of our Montreal rat pack until he met his fiancé and disappeared with her like a thief in the night. It was a smart move on Manny's part, considering his wife's beauty and the nature of our mutual friends. The boys would have been after Wendy for sure had Manny stayed around in Montreal with her.

Manny no doubt had other reasons for leaving Montreal, since his ex-girlfriend Susan Braun had been murdered, gunned down along with his partner Jean Paul. My pal Bishop subsequently joined Manny in Toronto as part of the great exodus of Anglos who followed a well-publicized convoy of Brinks trucks that was filmed leaving Montreal for Toronto.

Barbara and I had a great time in Toronto reconnecting with our old friends and preparing for a year-long stay in Jamaica. The day before we were booked onto Air Canada's flight 992 to Jamaica, Barbara fell ill with stomach flu and went to see Wendy's doctor.

"Congratulations," Wendy said to me when they both returned from the doctor. "You're going to have a baby." After the shock wore off, Barbara and I came to accept the unexpected blessing and continued on our journey.

Upon arriving in Jamaica, we rented a car and I met up with

Duke, my Jamaican friend from my pot smuggling days. Duke came with us as a guide, while we scouted around Montego Bay for a nice place to stay. We found a villa eight miles from town in Great River Private, an almost exclusively white neighbourhood. The villa was situated on a hill, overlooking a plantation of fruit trees with the ocean about a half mile in the distance. The villa's main residence was a sprawling rancher with acres of space inside. There were four bedrooms, with two facing the front driveway and two that overlooked the ocean. The two ocean-facing rooms had louvred walls made with doors that folded open and closed. When the doors were pushed fully open, the entire west wall folded away so that the bedrooms were completely exposed to the sunny Jamaican sky. Each bedroom in the villa had its own ensuite bathroom and there was another bathroom in the main entrance next to the dining and living rooms.

The villa was owned by May, a lovely old Jamaican lady who lived in the maid's quarters at the far end of the house. I told her son "G," who was handling the transaction, that my Jamaican work permit would be ready soon and I rented the house at the local rate that was close to what a Jamaican would pay. The villa featured a spacious covered seating area under a peaked roof, next to a concrete pool that was fenced off for safety. I felt like Ernest Hemingway as I sat on that patio plodding away on my book, while overlooking a coral sea as tropical birds and insects filled the air with peaceful sounds.

I bought an old Fiat to drive to town and back, which worked out to be cheaper than taking a rental car over the long term. I would be able to sell the Fiat when I was done with it, thereby recouping most of the cost while still enjoying the privilege of having a car.

I ran into my old pal Brian Kholder from Montreal who was living with his wife in Montego Bay. Brian was drying out from his heroin habit, which he felt was a necessary intervention from time to time to keep him from becoming a full-fledged junkie. I caught up on the news from Montreal and he told me that the boys downtown on the docks were looking for me. It appeared that they wanted to continue the Jamaica scam, only this time without Irving. I thought about it some but I was in no rush to go back to Montreal and the games of cowboys and Indians. I liked my life in Vancouver and I liked my life in Jamaica and I had no interest in returning to my life in Montreal.

While I sat writing my novel on the shaded terrace by the pool, Barbara was writing letters to everyone she ever knew. She described our large villa and the view and then invited everyone she could think of to come down for a visit. I found it amusing that many of her invitees took her up on her offer and came to visit us in Jamaica, in comparison to how few came to visit us in Vancouver. There was no problem in terms of accommodation, with two unused guest rooms and plenty of empty space in the dining and living room areas of the house. The property we rented sat on five acres of cleared land, as did all of the villas in Great River Private. There was more than enough space for us and our visitors to enjoy quiet walks and conversations without anyone ever feeling crowded. Their visits were coordinated in such a way that every week or two, I was driving to the Montego Bay airport, either picking someone up or dropping someone off.

My father came down at Christmastime. He had recently split up with my mother and it was a good tonic for him to travel down to the island for a visit during the holidays. He enjoyed his two weeks of vacation and we enjoyed having him stay with us.

I met up with some friends of Brian Kholder's while I was in Jamaica. In particular, there was a husband-and-wife team from the West Island of Montreal who had started as low-level helpers for Brian before they moved off to their own scams and into the big time. The husband and wife team were manufacturing honey oil in Jamaica and they were transporting it in huge amounts to the U.S. and Canada. The couple lived in Hopewell, not far from us. Their villa was situated high on a mountain overlooking the entire west coast of Jamaica. It had the most awesome view I have ever seen on the island. You practically needed a mountain goat to get up to there, and I felt afraid for my little Fiat, as it climbed up potholed streets that would be next to impassable in the rainy season.

When I finally made it to the top of the mountain, I was struck by how cool it was compared to the heat down below. The West Island couple needed their lofty location on the mountaintop in order to communicate with the regular flights of small aircraft that their buddies were flying into Jamaica, to pick up oil.

The smugglers in their planes were forewarned by the West Island couple about the schedule of the American AWACs that were patrolling the Caribbean. Their information came from an associate who lived in Miami near the airport. The associate was able to see when the AWACs were in for servicing and when they were assigned to fly. When the AWACs were down for servicing, the drug runners would fly over to Jamaica, pick up their oil or weed and fly back to the States to a drop zone. The West Island couple charged fifteen thousand dollars per flight and their fee covered the AWACs schedules, access to a remote landing strip in the jungle, aircraft refueling and as much oil or ganja as required at a decent price.

The couple offered me honey oil at eighteen hundred a pound, but I passed on the deal. I told them I was not in Jamaica on business. I was there for pleasure. Although their oil was exceptionally good, the price I could get for it in Canada was not worth the premium to be paid in Jamaica.

Like the West Island couple, my buddy Brian Kholder was also in Jamaica to set up a scam. It was like old home week as Brian and I and Barbara and Karen rekindled a friendship that had not wavered in spite of time or distance or a heroin habit. When I met Brian and his wife on the beach in Montego Bay, they were low on cash. We invited them to stay with us in our villa. Brian made more money than anyone I ever knew in the drug business, most of it smuggling weed from Jamaica. But Brian was a junkie, and one hundred thousand dollars is just a drop in the bucket to a man with a high-grade heroin habit.

Brian was a walking oxymoron. He was a gentle man with hippie tastes and values but he also had a multimillion dollar heroin habit. Brian and Karen were trying to get it together again after several separations that began after Brian was sentenced to three years in Edmonton. Brian and Karen's daughter, Brooke, was almost the same age as our daughter. They used to call her their little angel and Brooke often slept in their bed until she was about eight. It was a pleasure to have the Kholder family stay with us as our young daughter Allison enjoyed Brooke's company. I, for one, enjoyed Brian's intellect and my wife enjoyed Karen's earthy reality and lack of pretension. Karen was jogging to lose weight and she would laugh out loud about the Jamaicans who drove past her and yelled "Run Fatty!" Jamaican nicknames reflect the people who carry them, unlike North American nicknames. In Canada a fat man is called "Slim" while in Jamaica he is called "Bigga". There was plenty of room at our villa and for a while we projected a family image that looked quite normal. Brooke was in school in Jamaica during the day while Allison, who was not yet school-age, was with her mother and Karen. Some nights Brian would wander into town alone. With no car of his own, he took the local minibus that was crowded with Jamaicans. Brian would come home stoned in the wee hours of the morning. On some nights there would be no moon and zero visibility. One time he was accosted by an armed police patrol as he staggered up the Great River Private service road that led to our villa. The Jamaican police officers turned their flashlight on Brian as he approached their parked car.

"What are you doing wandering around in the dark?" one of the cops asked him.

"I'm going home," answered Brian pointing in the direction of our villa.

"But it's so dark. How can you see where you are going?" the cop asked him.

"I can feel where the pavement ends with my feet," Brian answered.

"Aren't you afraid of duppies?" the cop asked, meaning ghosts, which most Jamaicans believe in.

"Nah," answered Brian before tip-tapping his feet along the pavement towards home.

Pinot Mufasantii was both our neighbour and the developer of the Great River Private Estates. He lived a few villas above ours and he occasionally came down to visit us. On one occasion, he had a conversation with Brian and posed a question.

"What are you going to do in Jamaica?" the millionaire developer asked.

"I'm going to make some money," Brian answered.

Without demanding the specifics of how Brian was going to make his money, Pinot asked him again. "But what are you going to do when you make your money, Brian?"

"I don't know."

"Don't you think you should have a plan?"

"Yeah, I guess so."

"So what are you going to do when you make all your money down here in Jamaica?"

"Open a nightclub maybe."

I could see where Pinot was leading with his questions, even if Brian could not. Pinot was trying to say that it was not enough to make money dealing ganga, unless you have a plan to do something with it.

In the evenings Brian would sometimes confide in me and he told me that he had fifteen hundred pounds of sensi that he was going to air freight into Montreal in two shipments. The scam was a mind-blower, with almost a half a dozen customs officers at Mirabel Airport in on the deal. Brian told me he had to wait until all six Canadian Customs officers were on the same shift in order to get the load through. Customs in Jamaica were already paid off and they took good care of Brian's weed for him while he waited several months before the time was right. He finally got the green light from Canada to send his cargo off and ended up getting one seven hundred pound shipment through while the other one was lost. Brian's end was about two hundred thousand dollars, which in his world was barely enough to last a year.

Brian told me a story about his partner Hank who was a heroin dealer in Montreal. Hank had a pretty young girlfriend, half his age, who was going out with Hank and fucking Brian on the side. Brian told me a story about how another friend of his named Moe tried to move in on Hank's girl and how he would not be warned away. One night Brian and Hank were watching a movie about a man cutting another man's throat over a fight for a woman. The next night Hank went to Moe's apartment with a delivery of heroin and a loaded .45. He had a friend with him as backup, which was a good thing because, just like in the movies, the gun jammed at exactly the wrong time. Hank and his accomplice had to finish Moe off with a knife and according to Hank, he and his accomplice barely got out of the apartment in one piece. Brian figures Hank was watching the movie and came away with the idea. After hearing this, I asked Brian how he could be crazy enough to fool around with Hank's girlfriend after telling me that story.

"Hank wouldn't do that to me," Brian explained, with a curious logic that only a junkie would understand. "It wasn't that she was fucking the guy. It was a matter of respect. The guy wouldn't take a warning. It's too bad too cause I liked him. He reminded me of you."

A few weeks later, Hank came down to Jamaica for a visit, and after asking if it was okay, Brian brought him over to my house to meet me. I was surprised to see that Hank was an elderly man with receding hair and an ample girth. I felt sorry for any young chick who had to fuck this old guy for her fixes, but he was very polite and I really had no reason to feel as uncomfortable around him as I did. Hank was another leg shaker who nervously bounced his legs whenever he sat down. My old partner Irving was a leg shaker, too, and I wondered if all these leg shakers had the same troubled consciences.

Brian and Karen left shortly after his load of sensi was sent off to Montreal, to join in the feast of the kill. I did not mind. More guests were coming and we needed his room. Barbara's mother and sister, Margaret, from England came for a visit after Brian and Karen left. I was getting smirking looks as I walked the two blond sisters down the beach, both women being several months pregnant.

Then Rolf Wolstrom and his new girlfriend, Sierra, came for a three-week visit after Barbara's mother and sister left. The two spent much of their time exploring the island by motorcycle. It was nice to have their company, although I thought it somewhat cheap of Rolf to throw us a ten dollar bill for the maid before leaving for the airport. A bottle of good wine for his hosts might have been more appropriate or at least he might have treated us to dinner out somewhere.

Derrick the Doctor and his wife came for a two week visit from Montreal after Rolf and Sierra left and we had an exceptionally good time with him and his wife Marion. Marion and I were approached on a beach in Negril by the cast of a Jamaica Tourist Board film crew. They wanted us to do a commercial, along with my blond-haired daughter who was the focus of the shoot. Marion and I were supposed to walk along the beach as backdrop to the scene, while a colorfully dressed Jamaican woman sat under a Mango tree with my four-year-old daughter, Allison, on her lap. As Marion and I walked the beach, the director had to coach me several times to look more amorously at Marion, which was somewhat difficult to do with her husband Derrick looking on. The filming experience would have been tedious had we not partaken in some of Ma Brown's magic mushroom tea before the shoot. The tea had us laughing out loud on the set and made the seventy-six takes that followed somewhat bearable. Marion and I were paid seventy-five dollars each in U.S. funds and I received an additional seventy-five dollars for our daughter's participation. In addition to the union scale payments, we were all put up that night in a posh hotel on the beach and were invited to eat dinner with the film crew.

After Derrick and Marion left us to fly home to Montreal, Manny and his family flew down from Toronto. It was great to have Manny visit and his young son had a ball diving for coins that I threw into the deep end of the pool.

I thought of our own baby who was coming due and I tried to convince Barbara to have the birth in Jamaica. I was hoping to gain dual citizenship for our child, thinking that it might help us if we ever immigrated to Jamaica permanently, but she would not hear of it. My lawyer friend Vincent squelched that idea completely, informing me that there would be no benefits to our child being born in Jamaica. He advised Barbara to have the baby in Canada where universal health care covers everything and where the best nurses and doctors and facilities are available.

At that point, Vincent was still waiting for my work permit to be processed and I was glad I had not yet ordered the motorcycles from Vancouver. Barbara wanted to go back home to have our baby. And besides, if the truth be told, I was getting bored with Jamaica. I knew every bump in the roads, and I was tired of going to three different food stores in order to complete one grocery order. After a while even the beaches and water were uninviting and I began to understand why everyone living in Jamaica said they wanted to "get off the rock." There was nothing to do besides watch videos and smoke ganja and I was getting tired of living in paradise. The things I missed most were small things, like a real McDonald's hamburger or a glass of milk that did not taste like goat's milk. I longed for a breath of cool fresh Canadian air that had been flavoured by the Pacific Ocean and washed clean by the Rocky Mountains. I missed the efficiency of Canada, with customs officers who don't take bribes and service industry employees who don't move so slowly as to look like they're working underwater. I missed telephones that worked. I missed conversations with my Canadian friends whose views were cosmopolitan, compared to those in Jamaica.

I had a surprise visit from Rolf, who flew back down to Jamaica in a twin engine plane that he had been hired to fly from Vancouver to Miami. He was alone on this trip and in spite of his chintzy cheapness on his last visit we welcomed him to stay with us again. Even though he was tight with money, Rolf was free with his opinions and I must confess that I enjoyed his company as I was brought up to date on world events.

While we shared some wine and pot on my pool deck, lying on chaises lounges, Rolf informed me that he was here in Jamaica to meet with a man named Errol. Errol was supposed to front Rolf some weed, which he was supposedly going to fly back to the States. I say supposedly because I never believed Rolf's story for a minute. As far as I knew, Rolf had no contacts in Jamaica and he was always very straight and exceedingly cautious. Rolf was having money problems, he told me, while we both lounged, taking in the ocean view. His aircraft stock was in the toilet. No one was buying his shares, which had fallen from a high of several dollars to barely a few cents in value. When his supposed contact Errol did not show up with the weed and Rolf was forced to depart with his luggage holds empty, I suspected his trip to Jamaica was a dry run. Before he left, I pulled Rolf aside and made him a proposition. Come back down with a bigger plane, I told him, and I would fill it with weed. I would arrange to procure the weed in Jamaica and I would arrange to sell it in Canada. His hands would remain clean. All he had to do was fly. The payout would be in the hundreds of thousands, I promised him, all of it tax free. He agreed to give the idea some thought. After a fun sightseeing flight around the island in his plane, Rolf dropped me off at the Montego Bay airport and headed back to Miami.

After his departure, it was almost time for Barbara and me to leave Jamaica as well. She was in her ninth month when we arranged our bookings to Vancouver and time was running out. In the final two months before we returned to Canada, neither Barbara nor I set foot in the pool or the ocean, as our daily routine was established to the point of boredom.

Breakfast was a highlight. After a sumptuous feast of bacon and eggs and fresh fruit on the patio, I would log several hours of typing while Barbara would read or contemplate life by the pool. Our daughter would occupy herself with the simple daily activities at the far end of the house, often playing with a new brood of puppies or chasing the free range chickens that May allowed to run loose in the yard. After lunch, the three of us would drive into Montego Bay to pick up provisions and newspapers and magazines. I would buy rolling papers and wine while Barbara would shop the fashion shops and duty free stores. We would pacify our daughter Allison with an ice cream or a Cisco, which is a Jamaican frozen fruit popsicle. Sometimes we would drive to the larger hotels like Seawinds or the Holiday Inn and watch the crab races or the limbo dancers. Or we would just people watch as the tourists played volleyball in the hotel pool.

We were home by four most afternoons for the second highlight of the day which was supper. Barbara, being pregnant, neither drank nor smoked but I tried different imported wines with our dinner almost every other night. I never found any that were exceptional. I suspect that sitting in a container for weeks at a time in ninety-six degree heat might have had something to do with that. Dinner was usually bought fresh at the market with fish being a favourite or freshly killed chicken. Red meat was an occasional staple, but Jamaican beef was usually as tough as old leather due to the herds of cattle grazing on the mountainsides instead of on flat ground. Lobster was a treat that we bought on occasion from industrious young Jamaicans who stood at the side of the road, with diving masks and spears in one hand and a brace of fresh lobsters in the other. My dinner was always finished off with a marijuana spiff and a generous round of discussion. With no TV to watch, the stars and the jungle entertained us at night with a chorus of chirps and whistles and hisses and screeches as the forest came alive after dark. When the local DJs down the road added their boom box music to the chorus of insects, Saturday nights became as noisy as a New York restaurant at lunch hour.

Towards the end of our stay, it seemed that our intended departure was not getting any closer as the Jamaican days crawled by. We called our tenants in Vancouver and asked them if they would like to end their lease early and we were ecstatic when they agreed. Barbara and I immediately made arrangements to return home. We went to the beach one last time on the day before our departure. Barbara came grudgingly with Allison and me, as she was into her ninth month of pregnancy and not really in a swimming mood. Barbara was so anxious to return home that we did not even bother to stop in Toronto on our return flight and passed straight through to Vancouver without even seeing our friends.

When we arrived home in Vancouver, our house was exactly as we had left it with not a pin out of place. Our tenants had found their own place and they were considerate enough to have left our house in perfect condition for our return. When our son was born a few weeks later at Lions Gate Hospital, I was the happiest man alive, even if he did look just like my father without his false teeth. Our baby had pudgy red cheeks and sparkling mischievous blue eyes that gave only a hint of what was to come. He was blue when he first came out of the womb, and while I was fascinated to have witnessed the miracle of birth again, I could have lived quite happily without that experience.

After our son was born, I quickly found a job selling printing machines, a job I was referred to by a pot smoking buddy of mine. I worked at the job diligently, but between high-speed Xerox copiers that were fast replacing dedicated printing presses and a new breed of high volume computer reproduction equipment, it was like swimming upstream to make any money at the trade. It often took months to get paid for a sale and if anything went wrong in the chain of credit and financing approval requirements, the deal would fold up like a cheap lawn chair. I liked the work in spite of its drawbacks, but I was paid on a straight commission basis and my pay was completely unreliable. However, apart from money issues, I was reasonably happy with my job.

One night, while sipping a Grand Marnier with Rolf back in Vancouver, the subject of a weed run to Jamaica came up again. We discussed the idea in detail and we decided that the first step would be to take care of the financing. I said I could take care of the weed and the Jamaican expenses if Rolf would take care of the plane and the fuel. Rolf lined up a chartered twin engine King Air for the run, and he had a friend who had committed to financing a part of our deal. Between them, they came up with about half of the money required to finance a seven hundred pound load of weed.

I started polling my friends for investments and several came on board with five thousand dollar increments. Heather, our stewardess friend, was in for five. Bishop came in for five. Derrick put up five and so did I. The other five thousand of the twenty-five thousand cost of the weed would be covered by my Jamaican friend Bossa, on a front. All of my investors stood to make three times their money, with a payout that would come within a few months or less.

I contacted my old friend, Lou Berger, to see if he wanted to drive a camper down to Florida to meet Rolf and drive the weed from there up to Seattle. Lou was eager to join the crew, at a promise of fifty thousand dollars for his end, and he had a trustworthy buddy to go along with him as a helper. Since Lou still had his credit card maxed out, I cleared it up for him with a two thousand dollar payment. Then I had him rent a camper in his own name. I explained to Lou that my name was too hot in the United States to rent the camper for this mission and I promised to cover the actual expenses when they came in. What I told Lou was the truth, but I also wanted no connection to Lou and the camper if he got busted. There were no borders for Lou to cross, so apart from the pickup at a remote airstrip, transporting the weed to Seattle should be a snap.

To complete the Seattle to Vancouver leg, Rolf was going to fly the weed into Canada with a smaller plane. He said he was going to take a flight path that would be only a few feet above the water. That way, he would be well below the radar and could then fly the weed into British Columbia using the San Juan and Gulf islands as cover. Rolf told me he had used the same route to smuggle liquor into Canada. He planned to pick the weed up from Lou at a private airstrip in Seattle and then fly it to a small runway near Squamish, B.C. My crew would be waiting there to drive the weed to a stash house in Vancouver.

When our financing was finally in place, Rolf chartered the twin engine King Air for a month and took it down to Seattle to have long-range fuel tanks installed. This was totally against FAA rules, but any fine he received would be more than covered by profits from the weed.

I flew down to Jamaica and went to see my old friend Bossa in the parish of Saint Ann's. I had first met Bossa through Brian Kholder during the old days of our Montreal weed scams. Bossa was an old hand at large weed shipments, and the soft-spoken Jamaican agreed to supply six hundred pounds of Saint Ann's weed for twenty-five thousand dollars Canadian up front, with the balance to be paid on the cuff. The weed was not sensi quality, but with only a few seeds per bud, it was better than the usual Saint Ann's coli. Bossa was proud of his new high grade sensimilla, having pulled out all of the male plants he could find in his crop. He would have had pure sensi but, unfortunately, the rest of his neighbours in the surrounding hills of Brownstown were not as enlightened as he was and some of their male plants fertilized some of Bossa's female plants.

Bossa not only supplied my weed, but he also helped me scout out a perfectly paved runway for the weed transfer. He took me to the Ican plant in Boscobel which is halfway between Ocho Rios and Montego Bay. Ican's private runway was chained off to prevent smugglers from using it, but Bossa had chain cutters and he also knew the local cops. I could see that Bossa wanted this scam to turn out well for me. He said he would personally load the weed on the plane and see that it got off safely.

When I came back to see Rolf in Vancouver and told him we were prepared to go, I could see that he was nervous. I tried to assuage his fears, but I figured I would have felt the same way if I were in his place. After a couple of delays and false starts relating to the preparedness of the aircraft, I committed everyone to the plan one last time. Rolf would fly down to a small town in Georgia, a few hundred miles north of Miami. From there he would make contact with Lou in the motor home.

"Don't stay in the same hotel together," I cautioned Rolf and Lou. "With your Canadian licence plates and accents, you guys will stand out like sore thumbs. And don't spend all of your time in the hotel bars. Keep to yourselves until the work is done."

I explained that planes like Rolf's were known to ferry loads from the Caribbean into Florida and Georgia all the time and that the best thing Rolf had going for him was the element of surprise. He had to fly that plane into North Carolina on one day and head to Jamaica the very next. On arrival in Jamaica, he had to load up, fuel up and turn around and fly right back to the drop zone in the U.S. The plan was for Rolf to fly back into the States on regular air traffic lanes and, upon reaching U.S. territory, he would make contact with the tower. They would direct him to the designated international airport and when they had done so, Rolf was going to radio in mechanical problems. Then he would duck below radar and fly to the alternate landing strip. On the ground he would have only minutes to unload, sweep the plane and then take off again into radar coverage. He knew he would catch hell from the tower for pulling a stunt like that and he might even be fined by the FAA and have his licence suspended. But by that time, the weed would be rolling towards Seattle in Lou's camper and at that point, Rolf would be able to afford the fine, since his end would be over three hundred thousand dollars.

After one last meeting in Vancouver, Lou, Rolf and I set our watches, arranged our phone codes and then set off on our adventure. Lou was driving a new twenty-eight-foot camper with plenty of room under the bunks for storing the weed. Rolf flew down to Seattle and removed the seats from the aircraft to make room for the weed and then filled the plane with fuel. From there he planned to fly non-stop from Seattle to North Carolina.

I booked my Air Canada commercial flight to Jamaica and arrived in time to make the last-minute preparations for Rolf's arrival. When the weed was pressed and packaged and ready for transport to the Boscobel runway, Bossa had his transport crew on standby. I had ten thousand dollars cash in my pocket to pay off any police, in case they came to the runway before Rolf was loaded and ready for takeoff. I was excited to be pulling off my own weed scam, and for once, I was in full control. But along with the control came a tremendous responsibility to see the plan through to fruition. The weight of success or failure rested on my shoulders alone and no matter what happened, I was determined to see our plan through.

Chapter Ten

Striking Oil

It was a typical day in paradise with the temperature hovering around ninety degrees and not a cloud in the sky. I had flown down to Montego Bay a few days earlier to prepare for Rolf's arrival and I was staying at the Holiday Inn, where there was a bank of telephones in the lobby as well as one in every room. I left my name with the front desk of the hotel to be paged when my telephone call came in from Rolf. I needed to hear from him that everything was ready to go and to make any final adjustments to our timing. When Rolf's call was two days overdue, I started to get concerned. I was expecting him to call with some kind of problem or other because everything to Rolf was problematic. I was beginning to think that his complaints were a stalling tactic but I was not ready for what I heard on the day before he was to fly in and pick up the weed. The front desk paged me at the pool bar and I hurried to pick up the courtesy phone in the lobby. It was Rolf.

"How's it going, Rolf?"

"Not very well."

"Are you ready to fly over here?

"Yes, but I don't like it," he said.

"What do you mean you don't like it?"

"I have been talking to some of the pilots in the hotel bar and they tell me it's not a good idea."

"What do you mean you've been talking to the pilots in the bar?"

"There's a bar at the hotel next to the air strip where all of the local pilots hang out."

"You are not supposed to discuss what you're doing with anyone."

"I didn't tell them anything. I just listened in to their conversations. What you are asking me to do is dangerous. The authorities are on the lookout for that kind of thing."

"Of course it's dangerous. That's why you're being paid so well."

"Money is no good to me if I'm in jail."

"It's a little late for this, Rolf."

"I don't care if it's late. It's my neck on the line."

"That's why you were supposed to get over here quick. Get in and out fast. Not sit around drinking with a bunch of red-necked crackers who happen to be pilots. Is Lou there yet?"

"Yes. He's staying at the hotel."

"Which hotel?"

"The same one as me."

"Jesus Christ! I told him to stay at a campground!"

"I don't think it matters anymore."

"Why not?"

"Because the mission is too dangerous."

"You had plenty of time to decide that it was too dangerous before we invested all of our money in this deal. I have six hundred pounds here waiting for you."

"I can't carry that much. I can take five hundred at the most."

"You said you could carry a thousand."

"That was before I calculated the weight of the extra fuel in the long-range tanks."

"Fine, then come over and get the five hundred."

"I don't know."

"Look, Rolf. I have all my money and all of my friend's money tied up in this deal. I'm not going back to Canada empty-handed."

"I have my money invested, too, but there's no point in continuing just to get caught."

"If you move right now you won't get caught."

"I don't know."

"Look, I have to go up to Saint Ann's and tell Bossa you're not coming today. He's waiting up there with everything ready. The landing strip is reserved and it's the nicest one on the island. It's even paved, for fuck's sake. All we're waiting for is for you to fly your ass over here like we planned."

"I'm not sure."

"Call me back tomorrow and tell me when you're coming. I don't want to hear anything else except that you're ready to fly."

I hung up the phone with a loud slam of the receiver and it took a few moments for the conversation with Rolf to settle in. It was obvious what had happened. Rolf had developed cold feet and he no longer wanted to do what he said he would do. I was beginning to think that his participation in our mission had been nothing more than a scam from the very beginning. The smooth-talking prick had been sucking money out of our venture from the get-go and he never had any intention of flying a load of weed up from Jamaica. His bullshit lies were just another way to keep his head above water, by using our expense money to cover his day-to-day needs.

I thought about his initial flight down to Jamaica to meet Errol, who supposedly had some weed for him. There was no Errol. Rolf's flight down to Jamaica had been nothing more than a worm on a hook and I was the guppy he went fishing for. I still had hope that he would fly over to Jamaica as expected, but in truth, I was not even expecting him to phone back again. I was quite surprised when his call came through the next day. I was hoping that Rolf had regained his nerve, but his first sentence squelched that idea.

"It's over," he said.

"What do you mean it's over?"

"I'll tell you when I get back home."

"Fuck you! Tell me now."

"They know all about me. They know what I'm doing."

"Who knows all about you?"

"The FAA. The police. They are probably listening in to our phone call right now."

"Listening in to what? You haven't done anything yet."

"They know what we are planning."

"How the fuck would they know that?"

"They looked in the plane and saw the long-range tanks I had installed. They saw that the seats had been removed."

"Who let them into your plane?"

"They don't need anyone to let them in. They have this mirror thing on a long pole that lets them see into the windows of aircraft that are parked on the tarmac."

"How do you know they looked in the plane?"

"They told me."

"Who told you?"

"An FAA guy and the police who work at the airport. They pulled me aside and told me that they looked inside my plane and saw the missing seats and the long-range fuel tanks. They told me they know what I'm up to and they warned me not to try it."

"Take off from that airport right now and go park the plane somewhere else. You and Lou scout out a better site and I'll wait over here until you're ready."

"It's too late."

"What do you mean it's too late?"

"They chained my props."

"Wait a minute. The authorities think you might be doing a dope run so they chained your fucking props? Get Lou to buy some bolt cutters and just cut the chains off."

"You don't understand. They seized the plane."

"Why the fuck would they do that when you haven't done anything wrong yet?"

"The FAA called the owner of the plane in Alberta and asked him about the long-range tanks. The owner said the tanks were not authorized and told the FAA to seize the plane. I am probably going to be in big trouble with the CAA when I get back to Canada. They might even seize my pilot's licence."

So there we were. That was it. There was nothing more to say except goodbye. Checkmate Rolf. You got me good. If you had not been hanging around the airport bar drinking your fat ass off but instead had flown over to Jamaica like we had planned, the mission would have been completed by now. I cursed Rolf every which way from Sunday as I drove back up to Saint Ann's to see Bossa and tell him the bad news. When I told him our plane had been seized in Georgia, Bossa took the news without any visible concern. He offered to keep my weed safe until I could arrange to get another aircraft to come over. But the plane was not the problem. The pilot was.

I discussed the situation with my Jamaican sidekicks, Duke and Righteous, on the way back to Montego Bay. When we stopped to burn some weed with Sunny in Hopewell, Duke offered me a solution to my problem.

"Have Bossa make the weed into oil," he suggested. "I will carry it up to Canada for you."

"What do you mean?"

"I can carry it on my body."

"You would do that?"

"Yes, mon, no problem. I already carried some oil to New York."

"Six hundred pounds of weed will make more oil than you can carry up to Canada by yourself, Duke."

"I can carry some oil too," said Righteous.

"And me as well," said Sunny.

"It's not a bad idea," I answered. "No one will expect someone from Jamaica to body pack drugs all the way to Vancouver. Usually the oil runners get off in Toronto or Montreal."

"Yah, mon," said Duke. "All I need is a return air ticket and a letter from you inviting me to visit you in Vancouver."

"You know, I think it might work."

"It have to work, mon."

The plan made sense. And the alternative was to leave six hundred pounds of weed behind in Jamaica while I scurried back to Canada with my tail between my legs. I drove back the next day to Saint Ann's and spoke to Bossa about the idea. To my surprise, he agreed to convert the weed into oil for me and before I left for Vancouver, I put him in touch with Duke. There was no need for me to stay around Jamaica until the oil was ready. Duke was capable of picking up the oil from Bossa himself and wrapping it onto his body. Unlike Duke, I had no experience in body packing and I would never have considered such a bush-league scam unless I was in a jam. With little other choice, I flew home to Vancouver to wait for Duke to arrive.

Rolf was back in Vancouver when I arrived but I was in no hurry to see him. He had let me down and I could not get over the feeling that he had been scamming me all along. Lou called from somewhere in the States. He was driving the camper home to Vancouver and was out of money and out of fuel. At first, I told him to buy a hose and siphon his way home because he went against my orders and stayed in the same hotel as Rolf, but in the end, I Fed Ex'd him some money.

When Lou arrived home in Vancouver he asked me about paying the mileage charges for the camper. I was glad I had not rented the camper in my name and I let him squirm for a while. I told Lou I would pay him for the mileage charges when the bill came in later. There was no rush because I knew Lou never paid his credit card debt anyways.

When Rolf called me up and asked me to meet a friend of his who had invested money in the scam and to explain what happened, I was only too happy to oblige. I met Rolf's investor at his father's office in a high-rise tower downtown that featured a view of the ocean. I was surprised to see that the friend's father was also in on the scam. He asked me what went wrong.

"I'll tell you what went wrong," I told the father. "Rolf here chickened out. He fucked around in Georgia, drinking with the FAA, instead of flying over to Jamaica to get the load of weed and then he went and got his plane seized."

"Can we get our money back for the weed?"

"No. The money is all gone."

"What about the weed?"

"It's sitting in Jamaica if you want to go and get it."

"Then what can we do?"

"Ask Rolf that question. He took your money, not me."

"Can't you help us out in some way?"

"I have my own investors to deal with."

"I guess that's the way it is, then."

"Yes, that's the way it goes sometimes."

I did not cut off communication with Rolf completely after the failed scam but I did not see him for a long time afterwards. I could not be totally certain that he had scammed me all along, but my gut instinct told me that he had. I still had my job selling printing equipment on straight commission to go back to, so things were not too bad financially.

I called all of my friends who had trusted me enough to invest in my scam and told them the sorry news. Without going into detail, I told them that I might have a way of recouping their investment but they would have to wait a while.

It was almost a month before I heard from Duke and I was beginning to think that my Jamaican friends were as untrustworthy as my Canadian pilot. Then I got the call.

"Hello."

"Yah, mon."

"Hey, Duke. Where are you?"

"I'm in Toronto."

"Is everything alright?"

"Everyting cool, mon."

"When are you coming to Vancouver?"

"Tomorrow."

"I'll meet you at the airport."

"Yah, mon."

Beautiful! Duke had already cleared Canadian customs in Toronto.

When Duke arrived in Vancouver, I met him at the airport and drove him straight to our home in North Vancouver. There I helped him to unwrap the layers of tape that were holding almost twenty pounds of oil around his midriff. The next day was spent packaging the oil in one-ounce brown bottles. It was a messy business but well worth the effort. I paid Duke five thousand dollars up front and promised him another five when the oil was sold.

After a few weeks visiting with me in Vancouver, Duke went back to Jamaica to wait for his second payment while I called upon my pot smoking friends in Vancouver to help me sell the oil. At two hundred dollars an ounce wholesale, when the oil cost twenty dollars a gram retail, my friends were all making money. The spread allowed my dealers to double up on their investments. I could have charged them more for the oil, but I learned a long time ago to set up my dealers to be dependent on me, by giving them good profit margins. By giving better margins, I had my street dealers protecting me as the source of their livelihood rather than flipping me to the cops for a quick buck.

I fronted the oil first to Lou so that he could make some money to compensate for wasting his time driving the camper to Georgia and back. My electrician friend, Ben Jessup, also moved some product for me, as did another friend named Brandon Penfold.

Brandon was a big oil mover and a lot of fun to be around. He was a rounder who liked to hang out in the seedier places of Vancouver. He was the person who introduced me to my commission-based job and he had become a close friend and confidant. He was a little jealous of the action I was into, but became much happier when he was given the bulk of my oil to sell.

My Vancouver friends and dealers were happy. My Jamaican friends were happy. I was happy. My investors were especially happy when I paid them all back. I paid everyone back in full except Bishop, who received a thousand dollars less than he invested. I could have covered Bishop's investment in total, like my other investors, but I held back the thousand to cover the rotten stock he sold me in his now-defunct company called Montreal Toner and Supply. It took a few months before everyone was reimbursed, but eventually they were all paid back. It wasn't as good as getting a three-fold return on their money, but it was much better than they might have expected, considering the nature of the business they had invested in. I could easily have told everyone that their money was forfeited, just as I had told Rolf's investors, and they would have had to accept that.

After Duke returned to Montego Bay, my Jamaican pal

Sunny came up with some oil strapped to him. Then came Righteous. Then Duke came back again. It was great for me. I sat at home doing nothing until a phone call came. Then I would go to pick up another visitor from Jamaica.

The money was flowing in pretty nicely and there was plenty of jingle in my jeans to cover both my needs and wants. The sales job Brandon had turned me onto was perfect for my lifestyle. I could work when I wanted, leave when I wanted, stay away for weeks or months or years and then return to selling printing equipment. It is not in my nature to sit around and do nothing for very long, and even though my oil business was prospering, selling printing machines allowed me to fill in some of those daytime gaps.

The time came when Bossa's oil from the six hundred pounds of weed ran out. Then I had to start paying for the oil in Jamaica before it could be body packed up to Canada. At first, Duke was able to supply me with oil, but his price was too high. So I started flying down to Jamaica myself to purchase and prepare the oil to be body packed to Vancouver. My old friends from Montreal, who were still dealing in ton loads of weed and oil, would have probably laughed at my little scam. But I had no interest in getting any bigger and any more exposed than I already was. I felt comfortable dealing in Jamaica, where the customs agents were corrupt and most of the cops could be paid off. I also felt comfortable in Vancouver where I was relatively unknown to the police. As long as more Jamaicans could be found to come to Canada body packing oil, my business would continue to bring in several thousand dollars per week for as long as I ran it. Next, Duke sent his girlfriend up with a dozen pounds of oil. I had her take a taxi from the Vancouver Airport to my house and paid her immediately for the oil.

Eventually Barbara and I had to look for a larger house after our son was born. We could not afford to upgrade in the North Vancouver area because house prices had doubled in the few short years that we lived there. I was looking for a place large enough to house our family of four and I also needed space for one more item. I wanted a grow room. The grow room would supply my weed requirements, with a little left over to supplement my inconsistent commissions. The house I eventually chose was next door to my pot smoking buddy Brandon in the Maple Ridge area. Ben, the electrician, wired my new basement with four one thousand watt metal halide lights. The conversion worked out beautifully and while I sacrificed some storage room in the basement, I always had a larder full of weed and a pocket full of cash. Not too many people were growing pot indoors at that time and the authorities weren't really checking for it the way they are today.

I read up on the subject of cannabis cultivation until I became a veritable expert. I loved the hobby aspect of growing pot and the bonus of having valuable buds at the end of the process just made it all the more worthwhile. My friends were growing pot and I was growing pot. We all used our legitimate incomes to pay our household bills and used our illicit income for luxuries.

My oil business must have looked like I had a licence to print money to my ex-partner Lou because he started to pester me for the chance to be an oil runner. I had no wish to use Lou as a runner since I had more than enough Jamaican volunteers. As well, my friend Brandon warned me not to do so.

But I felt sorry for Lou, who had never made a real score in his life, and after much consideration, I finally agreed to take him down to Jamaica and pack him up with oil. I rented May's house in Great River Private on this occasion because it was remote and secluded, in a high-end area that had its own private security. Lou loved the exotic Jamaican experience, with the ocean view and the spicy food and the warm summer nights full of jungle sounds.

Duke, who had been supplying some of my oil, was having trouble securing enough, so I went with him hunting for oil suppliers in Montego Bay. I was pulled aside by a young man who I was told later belonged to the Chicken Gang. The young Jamaican man offered to sell me some oil. I told him I was interested but his price was too high. I told him I might see him again next trip down to Montego Bay because I already had enough oil for now on this trip. He asked me where I was staying in case he came up with a better deal and I told him to come and see me at May's. Duke said that was a mistake as soon as we drove off.

"What do you mean?"

"Those guys work with the cops."

"So what," I told him. "We're staying at May's and the oil is all stored at Righteous' house."

"I'm just telling you, mon. You can't just talk to people on the street. You have to be careful."

"You're just being paranoid."

A few days later, on the very day we were to leave for the airport to body pack a dozen pounds of oil to Vancouver, I was driving back to May's house with Duke. It was time to pack Lou up for the trip home and we were heading back to May's to get our suitcases. It was Righteous' idea to pack Lou at his house in Hopewell instead of Great River Private. He felt safer working in his own kitchen rather than wrapping up Lou in May's house. As I pulled off the main road into the private road to the Great River Private estates, I noticed a Jamaican work crew standing around a water main with a green Land Rover parked nearby. I sped past them and drove a half mile further to pull into the driveway of our villa. As I stopped at my front door, May's niece, Mercy, came running out to greet me.

"The police were just here."

"The police? When?"

"They just now left."

"What did they want?"

"They wanted us to let them into your room, but I did tell them I did not have a key."

I thanked Mercy for the warning and I quickly unlocked the grillwork that protected the bedroom quarters and ran into my bedroom. I rummaged through my drawers in search of my weed and rolling papers and handed the works to Mercy, who ran off to hide it all somewhere outside.

As she left my room, an unmarked Jamaican police vehicle pulled up the long winding driveway and stopped in the yard outside of our villa. It was the Land Rover that I had passed on my way in. I went outside to greet the visitors and met three plain-clothes Jamaican police officers who were standing by my front door. One of them asked if I was the renter of the house, before showing me a hand-written search warrant. After they asked me my full name, they added it to a line at the top of the search warrant and then asked me to escort them inside the house. The three policemen nodded at Duke, who was well known to them in the same way that everyone knows everyone on the small island of Jamaica. The cops took down Lou's name as well as mine and then they went straight into my bedroom. Without much difficulty, they found about half an ounce of weed I had missed in my haste to clean house, but they did not find the oil that they were looking for. They kept looking around the bedroom quarters until they satisfied themselves that there was nothing else in the house and then one of them held out the brown paper bag with the weed they had found in my room.

"This is illegal in Jamaica."

I resisted the impulse to remind him that the Jamaican economy was dependent on the marijuana trade, which brought in money equal or greater to the tourist industry and bauxite production together.

"It's not mine."

"It was in your drawer."

"That's not my drawer. I only rent the place."

"You have the only key to the room."

"That weed was left here by the last guest. Not me."

"You are responsible."

I knew where this was leading and I looked over at my friend Duke who was standing by with Lou, neither of them saying anything.

"Let me speak to my friend for a minute," I told the cops

The cops nodded and then stood aside while I spoke to Duke in a whisper, "Fix it up man."

Duke screwed his face into the proper expression of concern mixed with exasperation and walked over to talk to the three policemen. Duke huddled with them muttering in a conspiratorial silence and then walked back to me a minute later.

"Do you have a thousand dollars?"

"Jamaican or U.S.?"

"U.S."

"All I have in cash is five hundred."

"Give it to me."

I did so and Duke walked back to huddle with the three policemen. There was a rustle of bills changing hands and ten seconds later the three cops were gone.

"That was close."

"Yah, mon."

"They were here for the oil."

"Yah, mon. Sent by the Chicken Gang. When you don't buy their oil, they turn you in to their friends in the police.

"Did you see their warrant? The cops down here just carry them around blank and fill them out whenever they need them."

"Yah, mon. Jamaican style."

"I'm glad you were here, Duke."

"Yah, mon."

"Those pricks would have taken me to jail for half an ounce of weed."

"No, mon. They wanted money."

"Five hundred U.S. wouldn't have done shit if they had found our twenty pounds of oil."

"Yah, mon. Them would want a whole heap more money dan five hundred."

"I don't have any more money. I would have been fucked."

"Yah, mon."

"I guess it's over for this run."

"What do you mean?" said Lou, having finally found his voice.

"We've been spotted, Lou," I answered. "They could be on the lookout for us at the airport."

"They never even looked at our air tickets."

"Are you telling me you still want to go through with the run after all this?"

"Yes."

"Aren't you afraid you'll get busted?"

"No."

"I wouldn't do it."

"I want to."

"What do you think, Duke?"

"Them cops working wid de Chicken Gang. Them not work for no CIA."

"You think we can still pull it off?"

"Yes, mon."

"Okay, we go."

I made Lou a promise as I drove out of the Great River Private estates. If anything went wrong, I told him, I would pay him five thousand dollars and take care of his lawyer as long as he didn't rat me out. I told him I would pay him out of my own money, even if we lost the load of oil.

When it became apparent that the three policemen had left for good, Lou and I drove straight to Hopewell where my friend Righteous was waiting for us with twenty pounds of oil. There was barely an hour to spare before our flight departure, when we finished wrapping Lou. I was surprised at both Lou's greed and his lack of fear as we placed bag after vacuum-sealed plastic bag of oil around his midriff. I was suggesting that he stop at around fourteen pounds but Lou, who was being paid by volume, kept saying, "More, give me more." We packed him up until he had the entire twenty pounds of oil on his person and when Lou put on his suit jacket, there wasn't even a trace of a bulge.

We drove to the Montego Bay Airport with Lou in Righteous' car and Duke in mine. I was concerned, in case the cops recognized my rental car and stopped me again on the way to the airport, but that did not happen. At the airport check-in, Lou passed through the first hurdle and was whisked ahead of me into the in-transit lounge without being frisked. With that major obstacle overcome, we had a four-hour flight to Toronto to face. The flight went by very quickly, with an unexpected tail-wind pushing us into Toronto a half hour early.

I let Lou deplane ahead of me, so I could keep an eye on him as he went through Canadian customs. I saw him again waiting in the immigration line and I noticed that he wore an impatient, grumpy look on his face. It contrasted with the tired but smiling faces of the other returning air passengers around him. I lost sight of Lou at the baggage conveyor, when his suitcase came down the baggage ramp ahead of mine. I was tagged by immigration for a baggage check, so I picked the shortest line I could find. I waited my turn in line, still looking for Lou, until I reached the customs counter. There was much movement and talking in the half dozen or so customs lines, as several hundred passengers waited impatiently to get through to the outer terminal. It was difficult to see what was going on with Lou until finally it was my turn to have my luggage searched. I lifted my bag on to the customs counter, along with my briefcase, and my attention was caught by a minor commotion in the customs line two counters over. I thought it might be a scuffle between two passengers but I was unable to discern what was causing the commotion. I was still unable to locate Lou, who I hoped had been waved through without a baggage check. The female customs agent who was working my counter looked through my bags and my briefcase.

"What's this for?" the female customs inspector asked.

As she asked the question, my eyes focused on a briefcase sitting open on the customs counter two lines over where the commotion had occurred. I could not tell for certain, but it looked like Lou's briefcase sitting open over there. The passengers in that line were being shuttled to a new line as that customs counter was suddenly closed. I had a sinking feeling as I looked back at my own customs agent who was asking me questions. She was pointing to a roll of expansion bandages that I had in my briefcase.

"What's this for?" The female customs agent repeated her question, as she pointed to the roll of bandage tape that was to be used to rewrap Lou's oil in his Toronto hotel room for the second leg of his flight to Vancouver. It was the same bandage tape that Canada customs agents were probably peeling off Lou right now.

"I have a bum knee," I said, surprising myself at the efficiency of my unrehearsed answer. I thought I detected a flash of suspicion in her eyes, but the agent found nothing further to ask me about in my luggage and she waved me through to the outer terminal.

I was relieved to get through the customs screening, as I walked through the frosted doors to the outer area of the terminal. I waited several minutes in the outer terminal for Lou but he didn't appear. As the seriousness of the situation set in, I went into survival mode. The last thing I wanted was to be arrested in Toronto and be charged there on a conspiracy beef. I had no idea how strong Lou was going to be in the face of a possible seven-year sentence for importing drugs. He could be inside spilling his guts to customs and the RCMP right now, I thought, as I started walking away from the terminal.

I took a cab to the Airport Hilton where Lou and I were booked into separate rooms. I took a seat in the bar and had a drink before I made some phone calls. First, I telephoned the front desk to see if Lou had checked in or left a message for me.

No, he had not.

I called home and spoke to my wife, asking her if she had heard from Lou or his wife Lucy.

No, she had not.

I told Barbara to call Lucy and check on whether Lou had called her. Then I left the bar and checked into another hotel under my first and middle name. I paid cash for my accommodation, and then went up to my room and threw my suitcase on the bed without unpacking it.

If Lou had been busted at the airport and gave me up to the RCMP, they might be waiting for me tomorrow at the Air Canada flight I had pre-booked to Vancouver. I called Canadian Airlines and booked myself on an earlier flight, using my second and last name. It was not a great change of name but it was enough of a difference to foil a hasty name search if anyone was looking for me via computer. I called my wife again in Vancouver but she had been unable to reach Lou's wife Lucy. I called the Hilton Hotel one last time and found out that Lou had never checked into his room. I was on pins and needles until my plane took off from Toronto the next day and then I had six hours to sit and reflect on what had gone wrong.

Had the Jamaican cops passed on the intelligence to Canadian Customs about Lou and me being investigated for drugs? If that were so, why had I not been pulled out of line for interrogation and a body search like Lou had been? I remembered the last time I had seen Lou, when he was standing in the immigration line with that impatient scowl, as though he were a businessman upset with the delay. His attitude was different from all of the other tired travelers who had just returned from holiday and I wondered if that had twigged Canada Customs on to him. The second-guessing was making me sick to my stomach and my friend Brandon's words began ringing in my ears.

"Don't use Lou as a runner. You know he'll fuck everything up."

Hindsight is perfect vision, I told myself, as I made up excuses, but there was no doubt I felt guilty. I should have scrubbed the deal after the cops raided us in Jamaica. Forgetting the jail and the money aspect of Lou getting busted, my scam was now blown since the element of surprise was gone. I had let my own greed coax me into agreeing with Lou when he insisted on continuing with the run, even after we were investigated and questioned in Jamaica.

When I got home to Vancouver, I hugged my wife and children and decided that I had had enough of Jamaica and smuggling. What did I need Jamaica for? My grow op in the basement covered my weed needs and provided me with extra money. My job selling reprographic equipment was beginning to show dividends after years of sporadic returns for my efforts. And I felt a deepening responsibility to stay out of trouble with two children and a wife to take care of.

I eventually heard from Lucy Berger, who informed me that Lou was in jail in Toronto and she had moved to Vancouver Island to live with her mother. She told me about Lou getting pulled from line and being busted at Pearson Airport in Toronto. She told me that Lou had not given me up to the RCMP and I subsequently gave her the five grand I had promised Lou. It took a few weeks to pay her off, using the proceeds of my grow room and some oil that I had left. I even threw in an extra three thousand because Lou copped a plea to three years and it cost me hardly anything for his lawyer.

When the dust settled, I felt I got off easy and I had to give grudging credit to Lou for keeping his cool when many men wouldn't have. Lou served a little over one year before he was paroled. I saw him again in Vancouver and we ended up still being on good terms after he got out of the slammer, which is unusual in these types of situations.

I lost some of my enthusiasm for smuggling dope from Jamaica after Lou's bust, but I did not lose my ambition for making money. With my sales job as a cover, I continued to grow weed in my basement and discussed the merits of expanding my operation with some of my other grow op buddies.

But before that could happen, I received a phone call from my good friend Derrick the Doctor in Montreal. Derrick said he had some friends who wanted to offer me a business proposition. I knew the two friends he was referring to, one by reputation and one through a meeting in Jamaica.

Allan "Hawkeye" Stone had been a friend and partner of my old buddy Brad the "Wild Man" Wilder. I first met Allan Stone when I was down in Kingston with Big John Miller working on our scam. Hawkeye was there with the "Wild Man" working on their own scam. Hawkeye had a partner named Solly Cohen who was a well-known figure in the Montreal underworld and who was once a partner of Irving's. Irving always hated Solly, and as the Arabs say, any man who is an enemy of my enemy is my friend. Therefore, I had no hesitation in meeting Solly and Hawkeye to discuss some business. From what I could gather from the brief telephone conversation with Derrick, Solly and Hawkeye had a door into Canada and they needed someone with good connections in Jamaica.

I agreed to fly down to Montreal to discuss the business proposition on three conditions: One, I was not obligated to take the deal. Two, they were to cover my expenses to Montreal and elsewhere. And three, I was not going to touch anything with my own hands. When I received these assurances, I flew to Montreal to begin the tightest damn smuggling scam I had ever seen.

Chapter Eleven

Make Money, Not War

I met with Allan Stone and Solly Cohen at Derrick the Doctor's house in the West End of Montreal. Derrick's house was a beautiful New England–style cottage that looked like it was furnished out of a magazine, with all of the finest appliances, cabinets and hardware. Derrick now had a very successful medical practice, established many years before, and his wife had a long-standing job as an executive for Mary Kay Cosmetics. Between them, the two professionals were pulling in enough income to impress even their mobster friends.

Derrick was a fringer. A fringer in the underworld is someone straight who likes to hang around with criminals. Derrick grew up with one of the two men he was introducing me to on this day, having gone to school many years ago with Allan Stone. Derrick knew Allan's partner Solly from his reputation around Montreal and by smoking hash and doing lines with him when he came around on visits with Allan.

"Hawkeye" Stone had made his bones as a teenager when he was unfairly targeted for a beating by the local bar bully. Hawkeye went home after the beating and got a .32 pistol and waited for the older bully in the parking lot of the Holiday Inn. It was winter and Hawkeye wore a hooded jacket that concealed his face from fresh falling snow and from passersby. After a couple of hours of waiting, the bully finally presented himself in the parking lot and Allan capped him one in the thigh. The bully fell down screaming in pain and Hawkeye made like a bunny and fled the scene. Everyone knew that Allan had done the deed, even though the cops could not prove it, and Hawkeye gained the reputation as someone not to fuck with. He told me later that he went to make peace with the bully in the hospital but when the bully saw Hawkeye come into his room, he was so scared he almost passed a kidney stone.

Hawkeye had also been the object of much awe and respect for his friend Ron "Hoss" Kingsley, who use to talk about Allan and Solly like they were part of Al Capone's mob.

"Those two can get someone killed quicker than anyone I know," Hoss used to say, and I almost believed him.

In fact, I always wondered about Hoss himself doing clip work on the side. He was a fanatical gun nut, with a collection of unregistered guns from flintlocks to Uzis. I went to visit him one time and he took me into his basement to show off a new gun. To my surprise, he loosed off a round in the basement that ricocheted around the ceiling and ended up bouncing off a wall before hitting me in the leg. There was no injury because the little .32 caliber bullet was spent of energy by the time it hit me, but I told Hoss that I didn't appreciate getting shot.

Hoss had faced the wrong end of a gun himself one time, when he ripped off Solly and Allan on a hash deal. It was their money that financed Hoss and his wife Janice's scam to ship home a load of dresses and skirts with buttons made of hash from Afghanistan. The first load came through fine, and instead of sharing the loot with their partners, Hoss and Janice told Hawkeye that the shipment got lost and tried to sell the hash on the side. They got caught red-handed. The two were lucky to talk themselves into a settlement, with Solly holding a machine gun on them while the husband-and-wife team shamelessly pointed the finger at each other. Hoss and his wife made arrangements to pay back the ends they had ripped off from Solly and Hawkeye, and in the typical fashion of the underworld, they were forgiven and reinstated as friends again.

In the early days of their relationship, Hoss used to pull rip-offs with Hawkeye. The two men would catch up to a dope dealer and rob him at gunpoint. Hoss lost his taste for that action when he stitched the wall with machine-gun fire around one dealer from the States and the guy didn't even flinch. They got the money they were after and then got out of there, but Hoss figured they were starting to push the envelope. After that, he moved onto smuggling, which in his mind was a much less dangerous occupation.

No one felt sorry when Hoss and Janice got busted and went to jail for three years for their Afghanistan button scam. Hoss's father owned two very large and successful car dealerships, and it was a common sentiment in the underworld that rich people shouldn't be involved in crime. Of course, anyone who really knew Hoss knew that he was into the gangster life for the action not the coin. The same was true, to a much lesser degree, for his buddy Hawkeye and Hawkeye's partner Solly. They too, were into the lifestyle for the action, but the money was far more important to them than it was for Hoss.

One time, Solly and Hoss had an athletic challenge match to prove who was in the best physical condition. You would have thought that the outcome would be easy to predict, when you compared fat Solly to Hoss. Hoss was at least ten years younger than Solly and about a hundred pounds lighter, even if he was somewhat fat himself. A bet was made for a thousand dollars cash and Allan Stone was the officiator. Since it was winter and about thirty below outside, Hoss and Solly measured off a five mile distance inside of a high school gym. It came to about a hundred laps. The footrace started off well, with Hoss in the lead, but halfway through the race, Hoss's dope smoking habit began to catch up with him. Before the race was over, Hoss was gasping for breath while fat Solly sailed by him, laughing all the way to the bank. To add insult to injury, Solly did the last lap running backwards while Hoss dragged his tired ass off the gym floor to go get his wallet.

Solly and Hawkeye were multitaskers, never satisfied with dealing in one scam at a time. They would be manufacturing and distributing Quaaludes at the same time as they were running hash from Afghanistan and shipping weed up from Jamaica. Solly and Hawkeye did not have wide doors that would allow them to bring in large loads of contraband into Canada, but they had enough small doors to make quite a good living. They also dealt in guns, stolen merchandise, booze, hard drugs, pharmaceuticals — you name it. My private name for them that I shared only with Barbara was Heckle and Jeckle, after the two conspiratorial crows of cartoon fame. I picked that name because like the two crows, there was nothing that these two guys wouldn't do or get involved in.

Hawkeye, Solly and I sat down for our first meeting at Derrick's house and the appropriate greetings were exchanged. Everyone knew my history with Irving, so I started out by stating that I wasn't into the gangster life anymore. I said I was prepared to discuss a business venture, but if it was going to end up with everyone shooting everyone else, I was going to walk. Period.

At this point, Solly enlightened me with some recent history about my old partner, Irving. Apparently, after Irving came out of jail, the crazy Jew decided he was going to kidnap and ransom a well-known coke importer named Ryan "Tooney" O'Toole. Tooney was supplying the Hells Angels with tons of coke and he had a reputation as the only smuggler in Montreal who could raise a million dollars with one phone call. Irving and Roger Ouimet, the thug he had sent to my house to kill me, conned Tooney into meeting them at a motel in the west end of Montreal. They used Freddie Peters to lure Tooney to the motel with a fabricated story about having located some guns that had been stolen from Tooney's house earlier that year. However, there were no guns waiting for Tooney in the motel, except for the shotgun in Irving's hands and the .45 automatic in Roger Ouimet's hand. Irving was hiding in the bathroom when Toonie came into the motel room, expecting to get his guns back. When the door closed behind him and Roger Ouimet pointed a gun at him, Toonie saw that it was a trap and smashed a chair through the motel window as he attempted to flee. There was a struggle between Toonie, Freddie Peters and Roger Ouimet but the cocky little Irishman was winning the battle. Roger Ouimet fired one shot, hitting Toonie in the chest, but when he tried to shoot him again, his gun jammed. There was a further struggle between the three men and Toonie was still full of fight, when Irving ran out of the bathroom where he had been hiding. Irving blasted Toonie in the neck with his shotgun, as he ran over the prostrate Irishman, then continued straight out the motel door and fled the scene. Irving was followed by his cohorts who made good their escape, leaving Toonie dead on the floor. After killing Toonie, Roger Ouimet went downtown and bragged to the world. "I killed the king. Now I'm king."

But Roger Ouimet was not king for long because Toonie had a partner named Ron "Smitty" Smith. Smitty told members of the Hells Angels that he would settle a five hundred thousand dollar coke debt and give them another two hundred pounds of blow for free, if they took out his partner's killers. Somewhere along the line, the Angels caught up with my old pal Freddie Peters who traded a confession for his life and named names.

Within a month of Smitty's contract being given to the Angels, Roger Ouimet was blown out of his toupée while watching television in his high-rise apartment downtown. Roger died along with four of his cronies, including Ronnie McGuire, by a bomb planted in a VCR. In typical fashion of the underworld, one of Roger Ouimet's friends, Jacques "Apache" Francois who had done contract hits with him, brought Roger the VCR to watch the Grey Cup football game and a video about the Hells Angels. After the blast, which blew out walls and sent two of the apartment's elevators crashing to the ground, the only thing left to identify Roger Ouimet was his hair piece.

The Angels had their first installment on the deal with Smitty and the hunt for Irving was next. A few months later, two hit men were almost successful when they located Irving at his house and walked up his driveway with guns drawn. Like a cat with nine lives, Irving spotted them first and hopped a backyard fence to escape. The hit men found Irving's gun where it had fallen out of his pocket on the other side of the fence, but there was no sign of their target.

The Angels were still looking for Irving when Solly brought me up to date on his recent activities. Solly told me that he, too, was part of the search party looking for Irving and that he was hoping to pick up a cool chunk of change if he could find him. The Angels held the contract from Smitty, but they would eagerly share it with someone if they could find the last of Toonie's killers. Solly told me he was even going to come out to Vancouver to strong-arm me for Irving's whereabouts, until he found out that Irving and I were on the splits. I wondered how Solly could have known so many of the details of what had happened to Toonie when he wasn't even there. But I had seen his kind of insight before and like I have said before, there are surprisingly few secrets in the underworld.

As you might imagine, I ate up the news about Irving's misfortune like a shop vac sucking on a mohair rug, and I sat on the edge of my seat to hear more. The coke and the weed that Solly and Hawkeye were providing for our meeting fueled the fire in me and I found my blood starting to pump as the story unfolded.

Solly asked me if I still wanted to kill Irving and I told him no. Solly was surprised at my reluctance. He told me that he would not have allowed anyone to get away with handcuffing his wife and coming into his home with guns drawn.

I told Solly that I felt that way for a long time, while Irving was still in jail. But then, I added that so much time had passed since it all went down, I no longer had any interest in pursuing it. I told Solly I was back in Montreal to make money, not war.

"Besides," I told him, "look at all the trouble Irving is in, without any help from me."

The Angels were after him. The cops were watching him. Most of his friends were dead and any left had deserted him. He was on parole. He was out of money. Why did I have to do anything more to Irving than what was already happening to him?

Solly and Hawkeye nodded their acceptance of my logic and then moved on to an explanation of their scam and what they needed me for. A friend that Hawkeye used to go to school with was the head of a cleaning crew at the Montreal airport. The cleaner told Hawkeye that he was willing to pull small loads of hash off the planes, if someone could get the hash safely on board. Since one of the routes that he serviced was a direct flight to Jamaica, the aircraft cleaner needed someone in Montego Bay who would be able to get the hash into a special cavity on the plane.

That's where I would come in. Hawkeye and Solly knew from Derrick that I had lived in Jamaica and they knew of my past involvement with smuggling weed to the boys on the Montreal waterfront. My experience in smuggling gave me the credibility they were looking for and my relationship with the boys on the docks gave me the references they wanted. Plus, I was a trusted friend of Derrick's. I made my terms and conditions clear and agreed that if their plan worked, I would share my end with Derrick for turning me on to the score. It would be a four-way split, with half of my end going to Derrick. Solly, Hawkeye and the aircraft cleaner would get a full end each. The plan seemed good to me and I was not greedy enough to want more than I was offered. I would be handling nothing in Canada. My hands would be clean. If anything went wrong, it was worth half of my end to have Derrick as insulation between me and his two criminal friends.

I flew down to Jamaica immediately after our meeting to see if I could find the connections I needed and I lucked out right away. I found Righteous in Hopewell and Duke in Montego Bay and we started our inquiries. Righteous asked around the island and located a Jamaican named Topsy who could help us. Topsy was a member of an airport cleaning crew in Montego Bay and he was known to have placed weed on planes before. I met with Topsy to discuss our plan and had Righteous come along as intermediary. I described the hiding place on the aircraft to Topsy and he said he could do what I needed. I offered Topsy one full end of the profits and we quickly came to terms. Then I went back to Montreal and told the boys we were good to go.

Solly and Hawkeye gave me the cash to buy twenty pounds of hash in Jamaica for a test run, as well as the expense money to pay off Topsy and the others in my Jamaican crew. Righteous,

Duke and Sunny became my executive assistants and were immediately put on my payroll. They found me the hash I needed in Jamaica and pressed it into slabs that were handed off to Topsy. I went near nothing and I touched nothing as I oversaw the operation from a distance and put the scam together. At first, Topsy was unable to locate the secret hiding place in the plane, even with the detailed instructions I gave him. He put it elsewhere and within a few days of my arrival in Jamaica, a plane was winging its way to Montreal with twenty pounds of hash concealed on board. We almost lost the first load but Hawkeye's aircraft cleaner in Montreal was able to get to the hash before it was discovered and before the scam was blown.

The next time Topsy shipped the hash up to Canada, he found the right stash spot and the amusement park ride began. Week after week, I shipped hash to Montreal, with loads that escalated from twenty pounds to seventy pounds. It was not long before we were all rolling in dough and feeling like we had a licence to do what we were doing.

My routine was as follows. I would come to Montreal from Vancouver and I would meet with Solly and Allan to pick up the investment money. Then I would head for Jamaica to buy more finger hash. When the load was shipped off, I came back to Montreal from Jamaica to pick up my end in cash, along with some personal hash. Then I would fly back to Vancouver. A week or two later, I would repeat the whole itinerary. It was clean. It was neat. And as far as I was concerned, I was in complete control because, without me, Solly and Hawkeye had no way to get their hash on board the aircraft.

I was determined not to relinquish that control for as long as possible. Eventually, Solly and Hawkeye started coming down to Jamaica for visits. At first, I maintained a distance between us, even though they were fun to hang around with. Solly was a party animal. The fat man was able to pick up a phone and order women and cocaine like the rest of us order pizza. At first, I thought he was paying for the girls that he brought down to Jamaica for entertainment, because at three hundred plus pounds, Solly was not exactly a ladies man. But the guy had character and a never-ending supply of money, coke and Quaaludes, and there were plenty of women who wanted to come to Jamaica with him. I couldn't help but like Solly, with his easy laughter and constant joking, and it was hard for me to reconcile that he was also a professional killer who tracked down fugitives for the mob.

"I can always tell when someone is being hunted," he told me one time, when I pointed out someone I knew on the beach. "That guy," he said," is being hunted. See how he checks out everyone who comes onto the beach."

"That's because he's an undercover cop," I argued good-naturedly, but Solly was adamant.

"No," he said, "I know that look. He's on the run."

I met another part of the "Solly and Hawkeye Gang" when I returned to Montreal after several successful shipments of hash. Sandy "The mule" Mullins was an interesting character that I had seen here and there in my travels around Montreal. I had always wondered about the guy with the gray hair in a biker ponytail and what he did for a living. It turns out he did the same thing I did. Sandy came across as rough and tough, with a raspy, deep voice and a dry, sarcastic wit. Sandy was the kind of guy you could show two bodies to in your trunk and without blinking an eye, he would pick up a shovel to help bury them. Sandy was a serious old school gangster and I was careful to keep on his best side. In the beginning, he was very helpful when he defended my spending habits with my guys in Jamaica.

"That's how Toonie treats his guys overseas," said Sandy, when Heckle and Jeckle began haranguing me about the expenses. "Leave him alone."

And for a while they did. Sandy also supported me regarding the security concerns I had about Solly and Hawkeye coming down to Jamaica.

"Don't get involved in their parties," he warned me. "Just stay focused on business."

I was glad Sandy agreed with me about certain things, but as time went on, he dug deeper and deeper into his bag of coke until no one was listening to his mad ramblings anymore.

Following Sandy's earlier advice, I was pretty loose with the purse strings in Jamaica and I made sure my boys down there were well paid. It was easy for Solly and Hawkeye to gripe about expenses, but it wasn't their asses on the line in Jamaica. I bought Sunny a motorcycle with a 125 cc engine. It was plenty peppy on the road but easy on the gas. I also paid enough for Righteous to buy his first car, a Lancer that came with air conditioning. I set Duke up in a small convenience store and bar at the decrepit hotel where he lived with about twenty other Jamaican families.

I honestly can't say how much cash we were making on each run. The flights were flying weekly, and usually we shipped between seventy and one hundred and fifty pounds of hash, worth about five thousand dollars a pound wholesale. Even if you split that between six people and deduct expenses, it still left a tidy profit for everyone. When I look at the numbers, I am amazed that my money could ever run out, but the gangster lifestyle, which might leave a person dead or in jail at any moment, encourages spending. It's like being told you have six months to live and then being given a million dollars to spend. You just don't think about investing in the future.

I stayed at Derrick the Doctor's when I was in Montreal, and for about a year we continued on with our fifty-fifty split. But after a year of doing all the work and taking all the risks, I felt it was unfair that Derrick continued to get such a large cut of my end. It took Solly and Hawkeye to push me into discussing the issue with Derrick. They heckled me for being a chump and effectively talked me out of continuing to piece the Doctor off. I came up with a proposition. If Derrick would become more involved and carry the money to Jamaica for me, I would continue to split my take with him. If he refused to help me, then our deal was over. After all, Derrick was a doctor and didn't need the money like the rest of us who had no other income. To his credit, Derrick was charming about his decision not to become involved any deeper in our scam. He agreed to stop taking a cut, and for a while, I continued to stay with him when I went to Montreal.

As time went on, Hawkeye and Solly began to come down to Jamaica more frequently to party. It is hard to blame anyone for wanting to enjoy the exotic splendor of the island, but with a thousand other areas in the world to choose from, why pick the one place where our business was being conducted? Why not just wave a red flag at Canada Customs and advise them that three well-known smugglers were hanging around together in Jamaica?

I thought the problem had solved itself when Hawkeye got himself arrested in Montego Bay with a bag of weed in his hotel room. He spent several weeks in jail, until he was finally judged and released with a fine. I was secretly glad about Hawkeye getting busted, figuring that he would never come back to Jamaica again after that. But Allan Stone loved that island so much he could not stay away.

Don't get me wrong, I really enjoyed the good times when Solly and Hawkeye came down. They were so much fun that I could hardly keep away from them. Solly and Hawkeye loved fine dining and high rolling and the party was non-stop whenever they showed up in Montego Bay. They supplied the beautiful girls and the Quaaludes while Jamaica supplied the coke and the weed.

The parties were fun, but I soon began to miss my wife and children and I knew that my constant traveling back and forth between Vancouver, Montreal and Jamaica was bound to be drawing some heat. So I found a lovely villa in Ironshore, Jamaica, and flew my wife and children down to live with me. We enrolled our two children in school. My work permit, which I had applied for years ago, finally paid me back some dividends by giving me resident status. The work permit also legitimized my stay on the island, and when I took my overflow cash to the Cayman Islands for deposit, the Jamaican work permit removed any possible drug stigma from my money. After all, who could blame anyone for wanting their money in a safer place, when the politics in Jamaica were so volatile?

When I informed my two partners that I had a bank account in the Caymans, they immediately became concerned that I was siphoning off the expense money. They began to hover around me, trying to get closer to my contacts. I also had some concerns about them holding back on the amount of hash money they were really receiving in Montreal. Even if they were holding back fifty cents per gram, it would have far exceeded anything that I could ever skim. The mistrust was to be expected in our line of work and I am sure that there was a little skimming on both ends of the scam. But there was so much money coming in, there was no need for concern over small potatoes.

During this period, I received some more news on the whereabouts of Irving. It seems that crazy Irving had tired of being pursued by the Angels and had sought the protection of the police. Irving, who always professed undying hatred for rats, became one himself in exchange for a new identity and an escape from his past. He was being housed in Parthenais Detention Centre and he was now suing the RCMP for not following through on their promise of a new life and a hundred grand in cash. Irving was held incommunicado in Parthenais for months, as the cops and Irving reached a stumbling block. The cops wanted Irving to confess to pulling the trigger on Toonie, which was a condition Irving would not agree to. The RCMP then cut off his visits from his girlfriend, Jane, until she eventually left him. The story ended with Irving being released from jail. He was thrown back on the street, without his new identity or money, after he had spilled his guts on everyone he knew. I can not say I was unhappy to hear of my old partner's misfortune and I felt that he deserved everything that came to him. One thing was certain. The RCMP were fully aware of my role in Irving's past and I expected some kind of retribution if they ever twigged on to my visits to Montreal and Jamaica.

At this very time, a war was brewing between the Hells Angels and the Rock Machine motorcycle clubs in Montreal. Because Solly and Hawkeye were selling the bulk of our smuggled hash through members of the Angels, I was careful to keep my distance from the two men when I was in Montreal. One time, when I came to town on my way through to Jamaica, I checked into in a cheap little motel near the airport that

Hawkeye had recommended to me. I had been visiting Derrick's house, snorting lines of coke, when I returned to my motel around midnight. The previous week I had flown from Jamaica to Montreal to complain to Hawkeye's partner Solly after Hawkeye had shown up in Montego Bay with the Cowboy. The Cowboy was a well-known drug dealer from Ottawa who was famous in drug dealing lore for being one of the pioneers in the industry. I, myself, had used him on occasion to sell some of my Mexican weed that I brought in from Arizona. Bringing the Cowboy down to tour our operation in Jamaica was as stupid a move as I had seen yet from Hawkeye, and I was seriously thinking that he was trying to scare me out of my own scam with his infantile behaviour. I left Hawkeye in Jamaica to return to Canada to complain about it to Solly.

Hawkeye returned to Montreal behind me and was furious that I had spoken to Solly. He proposed that I should quit the scam and give my end over to Righteous. He suggested that I was trying to split him up from his partner, Solly. Even Sandy "the Mule" was of no help to me on this occasion, and I felt a bad vibe of things to come. I wondered, at one point, if I was going to be removed from the scam by force. But Hawkeye and I settled our differences grudgingly, with Solly as mediator.

So, on my next visit to Montreal, when I rented that cheap motel room in Dorval, at Hawkeye's suggestion, I was on my guard. When I returned to the motel from Derrick's that night, there were several Harley Davidson motorcycles parked on either side of my motel unit that were obviously part of a biker gang. I saw that I would have to pass through the bikers to get into my room and I made a U-turn as soon as I saw them. I went straight to the nearby Holiday Inn where I booked another room. Then I called the front desk at my original choice of motel. I told them to go to my room and pack my bags and send them by cab to my new address.

This was happening at a time when the body count was beginning to rise in the Montreal biker war and I am unhappy to report that my old friend Hoss was killed in that war. Hoss, who consoled me during my war with Irving and warned me that no one was going to say "draw," when I showed him my gun, never had a chance to pull his own gun, either. Someone used a remote controlled bomb to blow up his car in his driveway as he was leaving home to begin his daily routine. There was a time when gangsters would refuse to hit a man in front of his family, but those days were long gone by the time Hoss met his fate.

My friend little Ziggy Epstein got caught up in the biker war as well and had to flee to Florida to save his life. Ziggy was riding with the Angels in Montreal and he helped set up Freddie Peters for a hit outside of a bar near Decarie Boulevard. After the Angels had pumped enough information from Freddie, he was of no further use to them. The Angels would have let Freddie live, if Allan "Smitty" Smith had not demanded further retribution for Toonie's killing. Ziggy knew he was in trouble when Irving started calling him with death threats from Parthenais, after Irving heard about Freddie being gunned down. While Ziggy was hiding out in Florida, his lawyer, Sidney Goldman, began spreading it around town that Ziggy was going to rat about Freddie's murder. I do not know why Sidney would have said that if it were not true, but after the rumours started flying, Ziggy's coconspirators in Freddie's murder ordered two hit men from Quebec to kill Ziggy. According to court transcripts, the two hit men were known to Ziggy and he had no idea what was coming when they took him out for a one-way ride in their car. I was sorry to hear about his fate, although little Ziggy had quite grown up into a strong, strapping young man when I saw him last at Derrick's house in Montreal. Ziggy was a friend and a reliable accomplice when I left him behind to make my life in Vancouver. I would have liked to have remained in touch with Ziggy, but I suspect I would have been dragged into a similar fate had I stayed in Montreal.

I was glad to be living outside the Montreal war zone by residing in Jamaica and in Vancouver. While bodies were piling up in Montreal, Barbara and I lived a life in Jamaica that was one of quiet luxury, with an up-scale villa that came with maids and gardeners. I was finally able to convince Barbara to drive our car, even though it was a stick shift, and she chose to volunteer to help at the school where our children were enrolled. I gave generous donations to local charities through well-known local personalities such as Doris Hugh, the realtor, and every Wednesday I allowed the school to hold swimming classes in the pool at our villa. I spread my wealth around in other ways, as well. I was generous to a fault with the average Jamaican and overpaid for everything, as far as they were concerned.

I was content to live in Jamaica for a time, but after almost a year of it, I became bored silly. The same boredom was evident in the face of a stranger who sat next to me at the counter of the Pelican Grill in Montego Bay. The man started up a casual conversation with me and I soon found out he was working at the American Embassy. When the conversation turned to marijuana, the man began to tell me how the weed in Jamaica was grown with rat bat shit and I knew then that he was not working in the embassy typing pool. I figured him for a narc, and I wondered if he knew who he was talking to.

Barbara was forced to return home to Canada because of a bad case of pneumonia, so I began commuting again. Leaving Jamaica spelled the beginning of the end of my participation in the hash scam, although I spun another year out of it before it died on me. It ended soon after Allan and Solly began spreading their wings and started to look for their own contacts in Jamaica. They discovered a Jamaican named Lenny, who lived in Saint Ann's and who offered good deals on finger hash. Up to this point, the hash had always been procured by my team of friends. Sunny, Righteous and Duke traveled the length and breadth of the island to gather up the hash we needed.

Solly and Hawkeye now started to buy our hash from Lenny in bulk, and then used my Jamaican friends to move the hash around. As well, Hawkeye began showing up unannounced to stay in the same Ironshore villas that I rented. I found him partying with girlfriends, which was no problem, but I was totally pissed off when he started bringing down his drug dealing friends from Montreal to show off his Jamaican connections. Both Solly and Hawkeye were bringing heat to our scam and, to quote a phrase from my old partner Irving, "they seemed to think they had a fucking licence."

Allan started doing freebase cocaine, and for a few times, I did it with him. I enjoyed the initial rush of smoking cocaine but I was never able to repeat the effects of the first high. Subsequent visits to the crack shack produced less and less enjoyment and I ended up returning to my first love, weed.

Solly came on to me in Jamaica with another proposition. He said that he was in touch with my old crew who controlled the Montreal waterfront. When he told them he was working with me, the boys downtown offered him the same deal they offered Irving and me. If we would ship up a thousand pounds of sensi the boys would grab it off the Montreal waterfront for us.

I was thrilled to be back in the big leagues, but there had been some changes since I was last involved in multi-ton load shipments. You could no longer ship out a container full of weed without paying someone off in Jamaica. The dockworkers were wise to container scams, and the crane operators could feel by the strain on the cables if the container weighed more than the amount reading on the manifest. If they were not in on the scam, the dockworkers would rat out the container of weed for a finder's fee from the police. Righteous came through for us on that issue by locating a Jamaican customs broker who could guarantee that the container of weed would be placed on board a ship without drawing any heat.

Putting together a half ton of sensi was a lot of work, but I had many willing hands to help me as my sphere of connections in Jamaica grew broader. Sensi came from the west end of Jamaica where my black friends lived, not from the Saint Ann's side of the island where Solly's contact, Lenny, came from. After Righteous supervised the gathering of a thousand pounds of sensi, I accompanied him to Kingston to discuss payoff terms with the customs broker. The cost of the weed was outrageous, compared to the Coli weed I had purchased in bulk years before. With inflation factored in, the Sensi weed cost one hundred to two hundred dollars per pound, depending on the farmer who sold it. We cleaned out the year's supply of several villages to put together our load. The weed promised a return of a million dollars or more when it sold in Canada for a thousand dollars a pound. That would work out to roughly five to seven times our investment, which is a normal standard for smuggling profits that has held true for my entire smuggling career.

We had an investment of several hundred thousand dollars in the scam. At every phase in my dealings, I emphasized the seriousness of the people behind our scam to the Jamaicans involved, so that everyone knew not to pull any ripoffs. Hawkeye had made the acquaintance of a crooked cop named Franklin on one of his trips down to Jamaica. When a Jamaican helper named Moe got caught with his hands in the till, so to speak, Hawkeye offered his new found friend Franklin a contract to kill Moe. I could not believe my ears when he told me what he had done, and I told Hawkeye he was crazy to start that kind of shit in Jamaica where everyone knows what's going on. I was mad at Moe for being such a rotten prick as to rip us off for two kilos of hash after all we had done for him, but it was not enough to kill him over. I told Righteous to go and find Moe and warn him, which he did, but I never saw Moe again. Someone told me that Moe went off to America and someone else told me he went back into the countryside around Mandeville where he had been born. I never knew for sure what happened to him, but like I said, I never saw Moe again.

It was probably Hawkeye's karma backfiring on us when the first shipment of weed that we sent to Montreal disappeared without a trace. Solly said the boys on the Montreal docks couldn't get to it safely, but the customs broker in Jamaica said he had heard nothing about a container bust in Montreal. The broker felt that the drugs had gotten through and that we had been ripped off. I must confess that I had the same concerns when I remembered back to how the boys had never missed a container for Irving and me. It was inconceivable that Canada Customs or the RCMP would bust a thousand pounds of pure sensimilla without generating a few headlines and photo ops for themselves.

It took the better part of a year to recoup the losses involved in that one container shipment and I was hard pressed to invest that kind of money a second time. It wasn't only money that was lost. It takes a lot of time and energy to compile a ton of sensi. Several months at least. Then, there is the risk of moving the weed from Negril to Kingston. After that comes the risk of getting it shipped to the docks and clearing export customs. And last but not least is the effort involved in getting a full container of weed onto a commercial vessel without the authorities twigging onto the contraband.

But after a few more hash loads came in by air, and after assurances from Solly that the scam would work this time, I did get talked into another try at smuggling up a container shipment of sensi. This time, we used Solly's connection, Lenny, in Saint Ann's instead of our last customs broker who no longer trusted us after the container disappeared and we did not pay him the bonus that he was promised. Lenny claimed to have an inside man on the Kingston waterfront to place our weed on the ship.

This time, we decided to send two thousand pounds of sensi, to make up for the first container that was lost. We are talking about a major investment of over three hundred and fifty thousand dollars for the weed, the expenses and the payoffs. It was an endeavor that was complicated by the fact that we were still running the charter flight hash scam twice a week. Our Jamaican connections were successful in buying the weed, driving it to Kingston, and having it placed on a container ship to Montreal. Once again, the container was busted, only this time I actually located a news story about it in a Montreal paper.

After that, I told Solly and Hawkeye that I was no longer interested in putting my money into a container scam. I could see the writing on the wall, as Solly and particularly Hawkeye began to ignore more and more of my advice. One time when I was in Montreal, Hawkeye showed me half a million dollars in cash in a shopping bag. Then he hid it under his bed while we went out for a coffee. Talk about loose. On that same visit, Hawkeye drove me in his Mercedes to visit the aircraft cleaner who was pulling off our loads and Allan invited me into his house to meet him.

"No fucking way!" I told him. I slunk down low in the passenger seat, while Hawkeye ignored my concerns and went inside without me. I waited about fifteen minutes for him to come back out, all the while wondering what he was trying to pull by bringing me there. A raid by the cops would have pulled the three of us in the smuggling scam together and would have completed a connection that could have sent us all to jail. Hawkeye snapped at me when he came back to the car, as though I was a coward for not going inside to meet the cleaner. I reminded him that I was not in town to make new friends. From the very beginning, I had told him that I never wanted to meet his contact and I felt it was a serious breech of security to bring me there. I don't know what he had in mind, but it seemed to me that Hawkeye had some kind of death wish hoping to get himself caught, or more importantly, to get me caught.

I was starting to look at my new partners with increasing suspicion and when Solly insisted that I bring the number of the shipping container to Montreal myself, so that he could pass it on to our waterfront contacts, I felt a warning flag being raised. We had a dozen people that could run that number up from Jamaica to Montreal for us, but he wanted me to bring it up personally.

Part of the reason for my mistrust was due to several intimate conversations between Solly, Hawkeye and me while we were together in both Montreal and in Jamaica. Jamaica was where the parties rolled the longest and the drug use was the highest, as a vacation mentality would merge with Solly's festive spirit. I have a pretty high tolerance for drugs and when most people are toppling over, I am still firmly in command of all my faculties. Some of the questions that came from Solly on those late night stoned-out chats came with a sharing of information that was somewhat one-sided. He told me all about his past and the various hits he was involved in. Solly was another leg shaker who exhibited nervous tendencies unconsciously. In addition to leg shaking, Solly had itchy palms that he was always scratching. His troubled conscience notwithstanding, Solly was a true soldier in the sense that he was always ready and willing to drop anything to help his buddies.

One time, he told me that he was called out of bed to run downtown and help a friend named Riley Robertson who was being beaten up by a black American football player at a downtown speakeasy. When Solly arrived at the sixth-floor apartment where the speakeasy was located, he covered the room and handed his buddy a gun. When Riley was ready to shoot the football player on the spot, Solly cautioned him.

"Not here in front of everyone. Take him out on the fire escape, at least."

When I asked what happened next, Solly told me the black visitor to Canada ended up falling to his death from the sixth floor fire-escape.

"What happened?" I asked again and Solly made a pushing motion to indicate that the black man had been pushed over the fire-escape. I knew he was telling the truth because I remembered the headline about an American visitor falling to his death at a speakeasy and how all of the witnesses had mysteriously vanished from the scene.

Another time Solly was called out of bed by one of his buddies in the middle of the night. Fearing there was a serious problem, Solly strapped on his guns and ran downtown to a hotel to find his partner at the time, Robert Lavigne. He found him alright. In bed with a three hundred pound woman.

"Look, Solly," Robert said as he lifted one of her fat legs. "She's got rolls of fat everywhere. You can fuck her anywhere. In the arm. In the leg. Anywhere."

Solly told me he did not appreciate the humor at three in the morning and told me it was a good thing in a way that Robert was gone. Robert was the guy who died with Charlie Wilson in a hail of bullets in a club north of Montreal.

"I liked him, but the guy was crazy," Solly told me. "He was going to get us all killed."

In amongst all of his stories, Solly asked me pointedly if I had ever killed anyone. Warning buzzers went off in my brain, cutting through the layers of cocaine, marijuana and alcohol that dulled my senses.

"No," I told Solly. "But I would never tell anyone if I did."

SMUGGLER'S BLUES

"Why not?"

"Because there's no statute of limitations for murder."

"But I told you about mine."

"I never asked you to."

Solly was miffed at my lack of forthrightness, as though I had failed to reciprocate his honesty. I was not sure if he was trying to bond with me or searching out fodder for future use. I even wondered if he and Hawkeye were confidential informers, although the idea almost defied belief. How could you rob and kill people and still work with the police? But how else could Solly know so much information about Irving and others that could only have come from the source or from the police? He told me that Irving was thrown out of the witness protection program because he would not own up to killing Toonie. How would he know that? He told me that Irving killed a man, a nice young Jewish fellow who was a fringer, who had invested money with Irving. I remember the man from his frequent visits to our car lot to buy and trade in vehicles. He had apparently continued his relationship with Irving after I left town. When the Jewish man threatened to go to the cops after a bad deal, Irving killed him. But how could Solly know this? Was he just passing on rumours?

Hawkeye told me stories about his past that had me wondering about him, too. He told me about being apprehended for an offense that put his partner Solly in the can for three years. It was a gold bullion robbery at Toronto's Pearson International Airport. Solly was doing time for the score and Hawkeye was on bail, headed for the same fall. He told me that he tried everything to avoid it. He told me he cooked up a scheme which he first ran by Solly in jail for approval. After getting the green light from Solly, Hawkeye made a deal with the Crown to provide undercover information. The first thing he did was arrange to have a hundred pounds of weed left in a motel room for the cops to find. The cops and the Solicitor General were happy with the publicity from the find, but soon pressed Allan for more information if he wanted to keep himself out of jail. Allan told me about arranging for a pound of diluted heroin to be placed in a locker downtown for the police to find. He did not sound at all concerned that someone delivering the heroin to the locker went down with the smack.

"Fuck him, he's a heroin dealer," Hawkeye replied to my query.

I don't know if he realized it or not, but no matter how cool he thought he was being with the cops, I knew he was traveling down a slippery slope when he started playing ball with them. In the end, Hawkeye was not able to avoid his sentence, because in spite of his help to the cops, the Solicitor General himself called to put a stop to the deal that was brokered.

Hawkeye and Solly both went into prison with an OC stamp on their files. OC stands for organized crime. When Hawkeye finally exhausted all avenues and he finally had to face the music, Solly was already in line for a parole. But they got out at almost the same time because Solly served three years of a seven-year sentence and Hawkeye ended up serving less than two.

To get out early, Hawkeye told me he had made a deal with a guard at the prison he was in. Hawkeye was on a work detail, cleaning brush in the forest with an axe, when he had a run-in with another inmate. The other inmate had been mercilessly picking on a young lad who was new to the work team and Hawkeye took offense to it. He warned the guy off and when the other inmate would not listen, Allan swung his axe near his foot and told him to leave the kid alone. His axe would have cut the inmate's foot off, if he hadn't moved his leg out of the way, and he screamed like he was being murdered when the axe cut into his boot. The head guard saw the whole thing and pulled Hawkeye out of line.

"You don't like it here, do you?"

"Not much."

"How would you like an early release?"

"How can that be?"

"Anything can happen once you're in the system."

"How do I make it happen?"

"My truck is getting old. I need a new one."

"I'll have a new one in your driveway Monday."

SMUGGLER'S BLUES

And that's how Hawkeye won an early parole after serving barely a year of a seven-year sentence. At least that's how he told me it had happened. It crossed my mind that he might be stroking me, but I saw the same thing happen with Simon Steinberg, who was out on parole in two years, after receiving a twenty-year sentence. His family must have contributed to some fund or political party, but whatever they did, it worked.

The more I thought about it, the more I began to have serious concerns about the integrity of my Montreal partners. With all the trouble brewing in Montreal at that time between the Hells Angels and the Rock Machine, I wondered if the police might be investigating me as well. In all 150 people died in that biker war before it was ended in a truce. When an innocent seven-year-old boy was killed in a car bombing of a biker, the police became proactive about shutting down the bikers. On paper, I looked bad enough to be a possible player in the biker war and my mysterious travels between Montreal and Vancouver could certainly be considered suspicious.

Add to this the fact that my ex-partner in crime, Irving, was known to have been involved with killing Toonie, why wouldn't I be a suspect? When the fire marshall investigated my house burning down, I blamed it on Irving. What if Irving had blamed me for killing Toonie when he was in witness protection?

The proof of my hypothesis followed shortly thereafter, when I was waiting in the Dorval Airport terminal for my plane to Toronto. The plane was connecting to flight 992 to Jamaica, where I was meeting Solly and Hawkeye who were already down there. As I waited alone by the coffee bar for my flight to depart, a lone individual came rushing into the lounge as if late for his plane. He carried no hand luggage and I saw no ticket. He sat himself beside me at a small table beside the food counter. The stranger was short and unshaven and he wore jeans, sneakers and a T-shirt. His casual dress looked somewhat out of place amongst the other business passengers sitting around the coffee bar. Cops do not realize it, but they present an image that looks as much like a criminal as the criminals do. Same leather jackets. Same three-day growth of beard. Same swagger and demeanor. I spotted him in a second, as he began a casual conversation that I was unable to avoid. You know the routine. Nice day, eh? Should be a good flight. Where are you headed? That kind of shit. I did my best to ignore him and I was pleased when he finally excused himself and left with the statement that he had to collect his hand luggage from a locker before the flight. I knew he was full of shit because there were no lockers in the in transit lounge where boarders had been pre-cleared for their flights. The friendly stranger still had no hand luggage when he returned and sat down beside me again to continue his deception. I did my best to avoid further conversation with him and was relieved when I was finally called to board the aircraft. I was especially glad to see that his seat was not the vacant one next to mine. However, as soon as we were in the air, he appeared beside me again to carry on with his force-fed chat.

"I am going to Mexico to be a guard at a gold mine," he said after some mindless conversation about nothing. "It pays good money. Do you want a job? They need more people."

"No, thanks."

"Do you know how to use a gun?"

"No," I answered. "I am into the peace scene."

"Really, you never owned a gun?"

"Years ago, for hunting maybe. Not anymore."

"Where are you heading from here? he asked.

"Vancouver," I lied.

"What flight are you taking to Mexico?" I countered.

"Flight 463 out of Toronto at noon."

He pressed me with more questions relating to guns and violence, until I left my seat and went to the bathroom. I figured for sure he was a cop and I wondered if his barely concealed interrogation was a prelude to my arrest in Toronto. While I was in the bathroom I popped a Quaalude to take the edge off, before returning to my seat.

Damn! He was still there.

There was no getting away from him, I thought, as I sat down and feigned sleep. After several minutes with my eyes closed, I couldn't believe it when I felt him elbow me in the ribs. I

SMUGGLER'S BLUES

opened my eyes and he looked into them. He said nothing for the longest interval, as we held a staring contest at thirty thousand feet above sea level.

"You seem very calm" he said after the pause. "But is your heart racing inside?"

"Huh?"

"Are you scared inside?"

"Scared of what?"

"You know."

I knew alright, but I wasn't letting on to this guy.

"No, I don't know," I persisted in a louder voice. "Now leave me alone. I want to have a nap."

He left me alone from that point on and the stranger was nowhere to be seen when I awoke and deplaned in Toronto. The first thing I did when I got off the plane was to check the video monitor for the time and flight number he had given me. There was no flight of any kind to Mexico within hours of noon, and his flight number was a phony.

I continued on my way to Jamaica and was relieved that the pest was nowhere to be seen on the next leg of my voyage. When I arrived in Montego Bay, I saw Solly and Hawkeye in the waving gallery.

"I told you never to meet me here at the airport," I growled, as they both meandered over towards me outside of the inbound terminal. I gave them the story about the cop on the plane and I was miffed at their lack of concern. Hawkeye acted like it was an everyday occurrence. Solly just laughed and had me repeat the part about the cop elbowing me in the ribs and then laughed harder.

When Barbara and I left Montego Bay on the return leg of a later flight, I saw a man in a suit in the waving gallery. He was taking a picture of Barbara and me as we walked across the tarmac to the plane. He was either taking a picture of us or he was taking a picture of the bare tarmac and we just happened to be in the way.

I knew the heat was on and my fears were reconfirmed when I was returning with Barbara from another trip to Jamaica that was purely a pleasure trip around Christmas. For some reason, Barbara and I were having an argument on the plane ride home via Toronto. We had both been drinking and the booze was starting to speak, as my wife and I exchanged insults. By the time we reached Customs and Immigration, we were so angry with each other that we retrieved our bags separately and went through different customs lines. Canada Customs must have seen this as unusual behaviour and no doubt already had me on a watch list. I saw Barbara clear customs in the next line over and scowled at her, as a female customs officer searched my bag and found nothing. I was expecting to be sent on my way, when a male customs officer of a more senior rank came behind the counter and told the girl to step aside. He said he was taking over the search.

"Hand me your jacket," the male customs officer said to me.

He was referring to the jacket I always wore on plane rides or carried through customs. The suede jacket gave me an air of legitimacy and offered a number of extra pockets to pack money and other trifles into. The jacket was clean on this occasion, or so I thought. The senior customs officer took the apparel from my arm and started carefully removing the lint from every pocket in my jacket. As he placed the bits of lint on the counter, I quickly saw that it wasn't just lint. It was bits and crumbs of marijuana that had fallen out of joints that had been in my pockets over the course of many years. The weed bits came from joints in Canada and in Jamaica. In fact, I could tell by the bright shade of green that most of the marijuana crumbs were from Canada, having been transported to Jamaica and back again. When he had finished picking through my pockets, the customs officer arranged the lint in a little pile on the counter and I was surprised to see that there was enough weed in that pile to roll a huge fatty. I wasn't really worried if the case went to court, because it was no big deal. But at the same time, I remembered how Phil Robson had been stopped in Toronto by Canada Customs with half a joint that his girlfriend had accidentally packed into his suitcase. Canada Customs made him go to court on that little beef and he had to hire a lawyer. Then he had to travel back and forth between Montreal and Toronto for months while the case meandered through the Canadian justice system. Montreal was only three hundred and sixty miles from Toronto and it was a major hassle for Robby. I was living in Vancouver, which was three thousand miles away from Toronto, so I was none too pleased when the senior customs officer looked at me with a satisfied grin and turned to his female associate.

"Bring me an evidence envelope, would you?"

The prick. He was going to bust me for that little pile of lint. That was all the incentive I needed. As he turned his back to take the envelope from his junior officer, I gathered up a lungful of wind and let go a blast that scattered that pile of lint to the four corners of the universe. There was nothing left. Not a sprig. I knew that with all the dirt and dust on the floor, this guy would never be able to retrieve the evidence. He was not aware of what I had done until his female associate called him by name.

"Sandy."

"What?' His tone was impatient.

"Sandy, he blew it away."

"What?"

The senior customs officer turned back to look at me and then searched for the pile of lint and weed on the counter, which was gone. It took a moment to register what had happened and he looked at me with fury in his eyes.

"I found drugs on you," he said. "That gives me the right to strip search you."

So into the little room we went, which was a first time experience for me. I was confident that I had nothing to fear. I stripped to my underwear and stood waiting while he checked my clothes.

"Take off your shirt."

I did as ordered.

"Take off your pants."

I complied again.

"Hand me your socks."

I watched as he went through them.

"Pull down your shorts."

I did as told.

"See any drugs?" I asked in a wry tone, as I stood nude before him. I was glad that I was still drunk enough not to feel any embarrassment standing there naked. The customs agent had no choice but to let me go, and I groused about the inconvenience when I joined my wife later. She had a good laugh at my expense and our argument ended on that note.

The highlight of my final days in Jamaica, before making the decision to return home to Canada to live, was Righteous' wedding to his girlfriend Donna. I was the best man. In the end it was an honour that I regretted, as I stood melting in the one hundred degree heat. I was wearing a suit, and I wished that I had not done such a large hit of coke before the ceremony.

Some weeks after the honeymoon, I was driving with Righteous to conduct some business in Kingston. I was feeling him out to see if Hawkeye or Solly were trying to put a wedge between us, which was something I could feel happening from day one. The answer to my question came in a roundabout way, when out of the blue, Righteous slammed me with a put-down. I was talking about how coke makes me talkative and Righteous said, "Yah, mon. On coke you got a whole heap of mouth."

It was the first time Righteous had ever shown me any disrespect and I knew then that my suspicions were on the right track. I made the case to Righteous that without me, the boys in Montreal would treat him like shit. They would bump him from his position as soon as it suited them to do so. I gave him the "we are like brothers" routine and reminded him of our long friendship. Then I promised him that when the hash scam ended, I would bring him to Canada and show him how to make money growing weed indoors in Vancouver. I even offered to set him up in an operation. In spite of my sales pitch, I knew by the end of that ride that the end was in sight for my relationship with Righteous as well as with Solly and Hawkeye.

The day finally came when the scam died a natural death, with a phone call to me in Vancouver that came from Allan "Hawkeye" Stone.

"Don't bother coming back to Montreal," he said. "It's over."

Hawkeye went on to tell me that his aircraft cleaner was finished pulling bags from the plane. The cleaner had accepted a transfer to Toronto, and he was close to retirement. Since I had never met the cleaner, I could only accept what Hawkeye was telling me as truth and I remained in Vancouver to tend to my grow op and contemplate my own retirement. I stayed in touch with Righteous and Hawkeye for the next short while, to make certain I was not being scammed out of my scam. But I had to admit that the scam had grown tiresome in spite of the money. I felt that my partners in Montreal were acting like children, which was easier to see now that I had kids of my own. It had been a good, long run and no one was in jail. A perfect ending to a perfect crime. I saw no problem in remaining in Vancouver with the mother of my children to begin repairing the fabric of a relationship that had suffered from years of stress and extended absences.

Chapter Twelve

Growing Up and Growing Op

The grow op scene has changed the smuggling scene forever. Who needs to run the risk of importing marijuana thousands of miles across fortified borders when you can simply grow the stuff underground with halide lighting? House basements are ideal for growing pot indoors because they provide a measure of protection from busts thanks to Canada's privacy laws. Indoor grow ops started as ma-and-pa operations with everyday people growing pot in their homes to supplement their incomes. It has since grown to an organized business worth millions of dollars and is often run by members of the Vietnamese communities or by members of the Hells Angels.

When I returned to Vancouver I attended to my grow op and I expanded the operation. I had eighty grand left in my attic from the hash scam with Solly and Hawkeye and enough money secreted away in the Caymans to pay off my house mortgage. The bank draft from the Caymans Bank legitimized the money I had earned in the drug trade and I sank it into equity in my home in Vancouver. I used that equity to buy a second house for growing marijuana and I set up a third operation in the house of a friend. The cash in the attic paid for our unexpected expenses and some of our luxuries, while the grow ops covered my day-to-day needs like food, gas and entertainment. If you think eighty grand cash is a lot of money, try living on it for a couple of years. Everyday living can suck up a chunk of money in a flash the way an alcoholic sucks up booze on a bender. My savings were lasting longer than usual because of my grow op income. But while my grow ops were keeping pace with my financial requirements, I was irritated to be dealing at street level again. I had people knocking on my door all the time and no one buys pot without staying for at least an hour to shoot the breeze.

I started back at my old job selling printing machines to add to my income and to give me something that was lacking in the grow business: intelligent conversation.

I called Hawkeye in Montreal from time to time. He continually assured me that the Jamaica scam had ended, which I did not believe. I called Righteous several times but I could feel that he was avoiding me. I made a phone call to Jamaica and checked around with some people I knew in real estate and working at certain hotels. I discovered that Hawkeye and Solly were still making regular trips to Jamaica. I was also hearing stories about Righteous visiting Derrick the Doctor and Hoss in Montreal, and I knew then that I had been bumped out of the scam.

I could have blown the whistle on the double-crossing pricks, but I did not have it in me to be a rat. In truth, I didn't really give a damn about working with them anymore because in my mind, they were all idiots with more balls than brains. More importantly, I was about to launch into a major expansion of my grow op business and I figured that I could pull in a couple of hundred thousand dollars per year tax free, without any dependence on anyone but myself. The cops were putting values of a thousand dollars per plant on weed seizures, which was way in excess of reality. Each plant might fetch between two hundred and four hundred dollars, which is not bad when you multiply it by one hundred to two hundred plants, harvested every two or three months. I was pulling in about a hundred thousand or so a year tax free at the time, and I figured that would double when my three grow ops got rolling. Barbara had started working full-time as a nurse, which was her profession, and between her income nursing, my income selling printing machines and the grow op income, I was looking forward to a comfortable retirement.

As I look back now, I can see that I was way too loose with my grow operation. I had been growing pot for several years and I was starting to act like I had a licence. Between the guided tours for my friends and my carelessness in purchasing large amounts of hydroponic equipment and supplies, I was calling attention to myself. I made a call to Righteous to see if he wanted to come up and start working with me in the indoor cultivation business. I was surprised when he answered no. If that didn't tell me a story about what he, Hawkeye and Solly were doing in Jamaica, nothing would.

About six months into the expansion program of my three grow ops, I was beginning to see some decent profits when the worst possible thing that could have happened did. I had been away with Barbara and a girlfriend partying it up in Whistler. After two days of wining and dining and fireside après ski, I came home to thank my father, who had been watching my house and children. Black Monday began as I approached my house, around the time my two children would be home from school. As I pulled up to my house, I saw what appeared to be a police van in my driveway. I continued on past my house, without stopping, and I saw that my grow equipment was in the yard and that the police van was full of healthy mature marijuana plants. I drove away to make arrangements with my dad to come over and wait for the kids and then I returned home to face the music.

The cops were as nice as one could expect them to be about a drug bust, even to the extent of making jokes about my green thumb. The cop who interviewed me at my kitchen table was an older man with thinning hair, who complained about his summer cold as he kept sniffling throughout my interview. He kept leaving the kitchen table to run upstairs to the bathroom, which is next to my bedroom. After I had been taken away, my wife arrived home. The police were still there taking reports and photos. They were occupied in the basement and did not see Barbara walk into the house and go straight upstairs to our bedroom. Barbara saw a small flap of cocaine that the police had found, sitting open on our night table and she immediately took the flap of coke and flushed it down the toilet. As soon as she did, the cop who had been interviewing me came running upstairs to confront her.

"Where's the coke?" he asked.

"What coke?" she answered.

The cop was choked, but what could he do? I'm pretty sure he was snorting the coke during my interview, but I will never know for certain. I just know that he went up to the bathroom several times during my questioning, yet I never heard the toilet flush.

The policeman who took me into the station let me cover the handcuffs I was wearing with my jacket when he took me to his squad car, so that the neighbours would not see them. I was booked and released on my own recognizance and I was back in my bed that same evening.

For some reason, my little pot bust for fewer than sixty plants was placed in the cross-Canada byline so that it hit every newspaper in the country. Miraculously, the only person who read about the bust at my work was my friend Mike Morrison, who was the credit manager at the company. There was no problem with that because it just so happened that Mike himself had a grow op in his basement, as did most of his friends. It was Mike who gave me my starter plant called Mavis, which was one of the best production strains of marijuana I ever saw. I immediately closed down my two other satellite operations the day after my bust and I kept them closed until my trial and sentencing were over.

Through good fortune or divine intervention, one of our old neighbours and friends in the North Vancouver area was a partner in a law firm of great renown. Our neighbour set me up with his senior partner in the firm named David Gibbons, who was so well respected that the judge in my case gave recognition to him from the bench. The judge actually stood up and welcomed my lawyer into his courtroom, which I felt was an exceptionally good start to the proceedings. David Gibbons was overkill for the small charge of cultivation, and I was let off with a three thousand dollar fine and no probation. I was worried that my previous criminal record would make things worse for me, but the proof of my lawyer's competence became evident in his handling of the old gun charge. My lawyer told the judge that the charge was many years old and besides, it could not have been a very serious offense, as evidenced by the fine and suspended sentence I was given. The judge, in turn, remarked that my charges seemed to fall exactly ten years apart.

"Let's hope I don't see you here in another ten years," the judge said, as he banged his gavel and fined me three thousand dollars. The judge thanked my lawyer for gracing his court with a personal appearance, as opposed to sending some junior flunky, and then closed my file.

It was practically an invitation to start up my grow ops again. I still had my job and Barbara still had hers, so our income kept at pace with our needs, in spite of the bust. But there was nothing extra for high-flying vacations or new cars and I was back to buying my personal weed on the street at thirty-two hundred a pound. When my weed bill started to annoy me, I was forced to start up one of my satellite grow ops again. It seemed ridiculous to spend my hard-earned money for shit weed that I could grow better myself.

I waited until my senses told me that I was no longer a heat score, and then I restarted my grow op. After first transferring the house I had purchased into my father's name, I found a third party to sit on the bomb. I had learned during the course of my trial that in order to convict someone for operating a grow op, the Crown had to prove access and control. That meant that in order to convict a person for growing marijuana, the authorities had to find that person in possession of a key to the grow premises, as well as prove that they worked there on the cultivation of the marijuana. My third-party friend took care of all those risks in exchange for free rent, free food, expenses and one third of the profits after I sold the weed. After I took my personal weed out of the crop and after I deducted the expenses, I split the remaining profits with the house sitter. I ended up with very little money from the operation, but it was enough to satisfy my weed requirements and it was also enough to add a little comfort cushion to my income. My job selling printing machines was becoming more reliable after so many years of being in the business and I was actually developing a decent client base. I enjoyed the work and I developed several close friends at the company.

Shortly after my pot bust, I received a call from my old Jamaican pal, Righteous. Righteous had immigrated to Florida, where he was working with his wife at a Hertz Rent a Car dealership. He said that he was ready to come up and start growing pot with me in Vancouver. I told him of my recent bust and I told him that I was no longer interested in dealing drugs. Righteous began to complain about how hard it was living in the States, with his and his wife's salary barely keeping up with their needs. He asked me what he could do to get ahead. I told him to keep working hard at his job if he wanted to get ahead. After that, I never heard from Righteous again. I figured the hash scam he had going with Solly and Hawkeye was finally over and Righteous had been flushed down the toilet by the Montreal crew.

After the call from Righteous, I heard from Hawkeye Stone one last time. He called me out of the blue in Vancouver to tell me that he had access to several thousand pounds of Columbian weed in Montreal. He said that he would front me a couple of hundred pounds to sell in Vancouver, if I wanted to come to Montreal and get it. He went on to tell me that his aircraft cleaner from our hash scam had moved off to Toronto to retire and because I had heard the same thing from Righteous, I finally believed him. Even though I told Righteous that I was through dealing drugs, I decided I would check out Hawkeye's weed in Montreal and see if there was any benefit in selling it in Vancouver, where the prices were astonishingly high. A price of a thousand dollars a pound was established on the phone, which left room to double up on my investment. That meant a potential two hundred thousand dollars in profit, with no cash outlay.

I spoke to my electrician pal, Ben Jessup, and he agreed to go partners with me on the deal. Ben had wired up my first grow op for me and I trusted him as well as you can trust anyone in this business. Ben had been busted at his own home grow op, just like I had, and he was pretty cool about it. When the cops came to the house to bust him, he just smiled and said, "Oh well. I guess you got me."

Ben's pal, Jim, was the pot dealer who sold Ben's weed in Vancouver and Jim had never been arrested. Jim was a smart cookie. He moved every six months to a different location and changed his cell phone at the same time. If he didn't think you were worth knowing, he wouldn't give you his new number and that would be the last you would ever see of him.

So the plan was for the three of us to fly from Vancouver to Montreal to pick up the load of weed from Hawkeye. Ben was going to kill two birds with one stone and buy a couple of cars in Montreal at the same time as he picked up the weed. Two hundred pounds of pressed weed could easily fit in the trunk of an American car. He and Jim would ferry the cars and the weed back to B.C., with Ben in the chase vehicle and Jim driving the bomb. Ben, being the consummate businessman, figured to make money on the weed and the cars, both of which were cheaper on the east coast. The only reason I was to be in Montreal was to act as the intermediary between the two sets of people who did not know each other.

When Hawkeye first called me in Vancouver, we had chatted about our plans in roundabout terms on my cell phone. When I called him back to confirm that I was indeed coming to see him, he warned me about the danger of talking business on a cell phone.

"You're probably right," I answered into my cell phone, "But I'm not discussing details."

"Just remember, I warned you."

I knew he was right, but I had no reason to think that I was being watched when I was up to so very little at the time.

I arrived in Montreal on a separate flight from the one Ben and Jim were on, and then checked into the Holiday Inn in Dorval. It was the same hotel that Ziggy Epstein and the crew had started out from to meet the plane from the ill-fated Bahamas scam. I couldn't help but think back to those wild and crazy days, as Jim and Ben went off to purchase the two cars they wanted. Ben bought two bread-and-butter models, as they say in the car trade. One was an Oldsmobile Cutlass and the other was a Pontiac Grand Prix.

When I informed him we were ready with the cars, Hawkeye was slow in producing the weed, for some unknown reason.

Sometimes, the only thing that stands between a criminal and his being caught is his own unreliability. He says six but arrives at eight. He says he'll have the stuff with him, but he shows up without it.

Well, it turned out that our asses were saved because Hawkeye couldn't get his shit together to complete the deal on time. Just before Hawkeye was finally ready to deliver the weed to my runners, two things happened which set me on edge. First Hawkeye had instructed me to have the transport vehicle parked in the parking lot of a local truck stop and restaurant near our hotel. The truck stop backed onto a large parking lot and I instructed Ben to park the Cutlass at the very back of the lot. If all went as I expected, the transport car would be driven off by one of Hawkeye's runners and returned with the weed in the trunk that same afternoon. I drove past the truck stop on several occasions and was dismayed to see the Pontiac still sitting in the parking lot alone and untouched all day. On one of my drive pasts, I noticed a four-wheel-drive Jimmy parked near the Pontiac with its engine idling. The Jimmy had a large CB antenna on its roof and an older, gray-haired man was sitting in the car drinking coffee. A few hours later, when I passed by again, he was still there. Then as I returned to my hotel and drove into the parking lot, an unmarked cop car peeled away just as I arrived, and I got a funny vibe from the scene.

I went upstairs to my room and met with Ben and his runner and we did a line or two of coke. I told Ben and Jim of my suspicions about the Jimmy in the parking lot and told Jim to go and see if it was still there. When he came back with the news that the Jimmy was still in the parking lot of the truck stop, I left the hotel and drove straight to my friend Derrick the Doctor's house. I had not seen or spoken to Derrick for a couple of years,

SMUGGLER'S BLUES

when I pulled into his driveway and asked him if I could use his phone. I called Hawkeye from Derrick's phone and told him to stop the deal immediately and to come right over to Derrick's house to meet me. Then I made small talk with Derrick who must have thought that this was my rudest behaviour yet.

Hawkeye finally arrived in his Mercedes. It was the same Mercedes that he had driven for years, although it had had a top-to-bottom restoration done on it. Hawkeye was skeptical when I told him about the man in the Jimmy, as Derrick stood listening to our conversation. Hawkeye told me to hop in his car and we'd go back and check my story out. With the weather clear and the sun shining brightly off the glistening snow at the side of the road, we drove slowly along the service road that led to the truck stop. As we pulled up to the truck stop, we saw that the Jimmy was still parked at the drop. But as soon as he spied Hawkeye's Mercedes, the driver of the Jimmy pulled out and left.

"Look, there he goes," I said with excitement in my voice.

"We'll follow him," said Hawkeye.

We followed the Jimmy in Hawkeye's car for about a city block until he turned down a side street.

"If he's a cop, he's blown it now," said Hawkeye as he followed the Jimmy. "This is a dead-end street. We'll stop here at this end of the street and wait. If he's what you say he is, he'll have to come back past us."

It took only a minute before the Jimmy came back up the dead end street, with the driver sheepishly avoiding our stares as he drove past us.

"I guess he's a cop," said Hawkeye.

"The deal is off," I said to Hawkeye. "Forget it."

I drove back to my hotel where I put two and two together. We were all hot. Hot like firecrackers. There must have been an undercover team on Ben, Jim and me at the Holiday Inn and they were probably listening to our every word from the hotel suite next door. I thought again about that ghost car that I had seen speeding away from the hotel and figured that it was probably part of the same surveillance operation. I told Ben and his runner the facts of life. Although we all felt disappointed, we aborted the mission and headed back to Vancouver. Ben consoled himself with the fact that he had purchased two cars that he would make a profit on in B.C.

The second near miss came right after that. Since I was flying back to Vancouver empty handed, I decided to bring the better part of a pound of Colombian weed that Hawkeye had supplied me with as a sample when I arrived in Montreal. I broke the weed into several small packets. I wrapped them up with masking tape and I addressed them to a person from the phone book. Then I put a stamp on each parcel. I did this hoping to use the postal privacy laws to my best advantage, if the weed were ever discovered on me. I put a package in each pocket of my jacket and slacks, making certain that there was nothing metal on my person to trigger the airport security alarms. I had done this a dozen times at least in the past and I had never had a problem on domestic flights. But this time I was departing from Mirabel Airport rather than Dorval.

"Mirabel is an international airport," warned Hawkeye, when he saw what I was planning.

"Yes, but it's a domestic flight," I replied ignoring his warning. "I've done this a million times."

"Suit yourself," Hawkeye sighed with a shake of his head.

His warning came back to haunt me as I stood in the screening line at Mirabel Airport, waiting my turn to pass through the metal detectors. Something was unusual, I noticed, with a small lump forming in my throat. The screeners were pulling people out of line and body searching them, as well as using the electronic wand. They were taking things out of people's pockets and checking through their items and articles. If they started pulling things out of my pockets, I would be screwed. I was perhaps six passengers away from being checked through the gate, when I stepped out of line and went back to the main terminal washroom.

What a nice tip for the washroom attendant, I thought, as I began tossing packages of weed into the garbage can. Even though I knew the danger of carrying weed through the screening line, I could not bring myself to throw away all of the packages of weed, thereby making the trip a total loss. I kept two of the eight weed packs in my inside jacket pockets, as I returned to the screening line and prepared to board my flight home. I have to ask myself now why I would take a chance like that, in the face of all the near misses on that trip. Had I been caught with those two packs of weed, I would have spent months, and maybe years, commuting back and forth to Montreal from Vancouver to deal with the bust. Fortunately, I passed through the screening line without any problems and without a body search, and as soon as I did, I regretted the fact that I had thrown the rest of the weed in the garbage.

The flight back to Vancouver was uneventful and I returned home with a new attitude. I was tired of taking risks. I was tired of leaving home all the time to pull scams. I was tired of playing cat and mouse with the authorities. I was tired of the double-crosses. Tired of the danger. Tired of risking jail. I finally saw my life for exactly what it was. Blessed. It has always been blessed. I had a nice home. A nice family. Good friends. Barbara and I both had good jobs. I no longer felt alienated from society. If anything, I felt alienated from Hawkeye and Solly and just about everyone else I knew from my past.

I closed up my satellite grow house shortly after arriving back in Vancouver. I was no longer interested in dealing, even in petty amounts of weed. I didn't care that my dealer of many years pulled a final rip on me for the outstanding money he owed. I made a hundred grand in profit, just from selling the satellite house, and instead of using the money to finance another scam, I sunk it into the house of our dreams. Our home has a view of the ocean and we put in a pool not long ago, using our legitimate, hard-earned money from our jobs. Even though our income dropped dramatically after I stopped scamming, it was not so bad. I did a calculation and was surprised to realize that even though I had earned hundreds of thousands of dollars in my illegitimate movements, I would have been better off had I stayed at my legitimate sales career right from the beginning. The money I earned illicitly disappeared like water down the drain, in a drug-and-alcohol fueled orgy of unnecessary excesses and indulgences. Once I was back living like the rest of the world, I no longer felt the need for vast sums of money.

Today Barbara and I are living quite well, without me resorting to crime. Our savings reside in a bank, like everyone else's money, and I can enjoy my successes without hiding my assets.

I find myself echoing the law and order proponents in our society, and I have no shame at my hypocrisy because my thinking has changed about a lot of things. I no longer believe that manners are an unnecessary encumbrance on society. I no longer believe that religion is for cowards and fools. I no longer believe that a stolen apple tastes better than a purchased one.

In hindsight, I see that the money I earned was secondary to the main reason for my criminal behaviour. I wanted to be a cop before I started into my life of crime. I wanted adventure. When I was rejected from one side of the law, I developed an affinity for the other side. Had I been accepted into the Montreal Police Force or the RCMP, I would probably never have started smoking pot, which has helped to shape my life into what it is today. Because I survived the dangers of my life in the underworld, I can truthfully say that I am glad to have experienced life to the degree that I did. Not that I enjoyed the shitty parts. I did not. But so many folks reach their retirement years, after a lifetime of scrimping and saving, and never really get to enjoy the fruits of their labor, whereas I feel that I have already had my rewards. There were no wars for my generation to exploit in easing our youthful angst, and I always said that if I was going to have to fight in a war, I may as well pick one that pays well. While I am not particularly proud of my past, I can honestly say that I stayed true to my principles. I did not deal in powders. I did not rip anyone off. I did not kill anyone, thanks to the grace of God.

I was going to call my book "Last Man Standing," but that title should really go to two people I know who last I heard were still in the smuggling game. One is Allan Hawkeye Stone and the other is Buddy Kholder, Brian's brother. I don't know for certain what Hawkeye has been up to for these past years. His partner Solly Cohen is dead, and no one knows who did it. My old pal Big John Miller is dead, after gaining compassionate release from prison and surviving less than a few years with a colostomy bag on his hip. Ron "Hoss" Kingsley is dead, blown up by a bomb during the Quebec biker war. Ziggy Epstein was gunned down in Florida after the hit on Freddie Peters. Freddie Peters is dead, killed by Ziggy and an accomplice. Charlie

Wilson is dead, killed by Jean Paul LaPierre and his partner. Jean Paul LaPierre and Susan Braun are dead from gunshots delivered at least in part by Jean Paul's partner. Jean Paul's partner, Joseph Lemieux, is dead, killed in a jailbreak after he killed a guard. Joseph's younger brother, Rene, was also a victim of gunplay, having been killed in a bank robbery shootout. Irving is either dead or in jail or back on the streets and running from the Angels or who knows who else. I don't know and I don't care. Shaun Palmer went to jail. Myron Wiseman has disappeared after he took on a new identity to avoid a jail sentence for the Lebanese hash scam. Simon Steinberg went to jail after getting caught on our Lebanese hash scam. He came out on an early parole, only to fly a plane full of coke from Colombia to Canada. Simon was caught again and I heard that he ratted on the Colombian cartel in his plea bargain. The last I heard about Simon, he had overdosed on heroin in jail, but was still alive. Brian Kholder is dead at forty-five years of age, from natural causes brought on by the ravages of heroin. His wife Karen is dead of leukemia, perhaps also aggravated by years of heroin use. Dave "Kaka" Klein died at thirty-eight years of age from a heart attack caused by a combination of too many drugs and high living. The boys on the docks retired, but not before one of them was taken for a ride by Mickey McDonald and shot four times in the back as he made good his escape at a stoplight. The couple from the West Island that were friends of Brian Kholder's and who were running aircraft filled with pot and oil from Jamaica to the States split up after they were busted. The wife and the husband and all of their high-flying buddies were caught and got long prison sentences in an American prison. Brad "the Wild Man" Wilder died of a brain aneurysm, several months after he turned himself in and completed a seven-year jail term for smuggling bags of weed on his father's airline. Irving's hit man, Roger Ouimet, was blown up along with four of his buddies by members of the Hells Angels.

My lawyer Sidney Goldman was murdered during the war between the Hells Angels and the Rock Machine. It might have been a biker gang hit or perhaps Sid was punished for losing a drug case involving a high-ranking female member of the Colombian drug cartel. The Montreal chapter of the Hells Angels killed the entire chapter of the Laval Hells Angels and sunk all five of their bodies, wrapped in sleeping bags, in the back river of Montreal. The Laval Hells Angels were murdered in part because they were too deep into the coke bag, but mainly because they owed Tooney half a million dollars and would not pay. Ryan "Tooney" O'Toole is dead, murdered by Irving and Roger Ouimet in a motel room. Tooney's partner, Ron "Smitty" Smith, is serving a life term in an American prison.

In large part, the ones who escaped the carnage in Montreal were the ones who moved away. Me. Bishop. Manny. Ryan McCaan. Robby Robson.

Derrick the Doctor is still in Montreal, although he is not hanging with a criminal element anymore since most of his gangster friends are dead or in jail. Shaun Palmer moved to Ottawa after he finished his jail term. Chip "the Limey" Jenkins moved to Vancouver and escaped Montreal justice but unfortunately, his wife died shortly after he won freedom from his importing case. My Jamaican partner Righteous moved to Miami with his family and is chasing the American dream. My Jamaican friend Sunny married a black woman and moved to the States ending up in Texas. I wonder how Sunny finds the ganga down there?

The second guy who was still "standing" in the smuggling game when last I heard, is Brian Kholder's younger brother, Buddy. Buddy built a hotel in Jamaica with the proceeds of his smuggling activities and appears to be doing well. I went back to Jamaica several times after quitting the smuggling game, and on one occasion, I brought two of my work friends down from Vancouver with me. We surprised Buddy, as he sat with his sister Bonnie by his hotel pool. Buddy's face turned white when he saw me and I realized later that it was my two friends, who looked like mafia enforcers on either side of me, that were bothering him. When he realized that I was just paying him a social visit, Buddy relaxed a little, but not enough to stop his habit of bouncing his leg up and down.

Buddy told me that just that same week he had witnessed his best friend Hans being killed in front of him and Hans' daughter. It happened at a seaside bar that Hans owned down the street from Buddy's hotel. Three Jamaican hit men had come into the bar, with guns drawn, and warned Buddy and the daughter to step aside, before they gunned the German down and left. That might have been part of the reason why Buddy was still a leg shaker. I had a great time with my two Vancouver buddies on that trip and I finally came home without the nagging feeling that something bad might come out of my visit to Jamaica.

There will always be a connection between me and that island, even if most of my old friends have left. The last time I returned to Jamaica, Barbara and I went, as we always do, to visit the house on the hill in Great River Private to pay our respects to the owners. May is no longer living there, since she came down with Alzheimer's and had to be moved to a home in the countryside near Mandeville. Her son G, who is now retired from the police force and who has known us for decades, offered us the use of May's house for free anytime we wanted it.

"May is gone and the house is empty," he told us. "This is your house now. You should be living here."

We thanked G for his offer, but I doubt that we will choose to live in Jamaica anymore.

Like everywhere else in the world, crime has gotten worse and even I am careful to stay only in the safe areas of Jamaica these days. I used to carry a pneumatic spear gun for protection in my smuggling days, but a spear gun is no match for the AK-47s carried by Jamaican thieves today. I have decided that the key to happiness in this life is to stay low profile. I no longer wear my gold bracelets and chains and gold watches, which sit unostentatiously out of sight in my safety deposit box. Instead of a Mercedes, I drive a newer domestic model of convertible, and my wife has a similar but older model. I am still working at my same old sales job and although I am not rich, I am finally living the Great Canadian dream that I have always wished for, but never realized I had.

If there is any advice that I can give, it is contained in these poetic words from Jamaican musician Peter Tosh: "Live clean and let your works be seen."

But who listens to advice these days? I have seen people lose their very lives because they refused to take advice or refused to do what they did not want to do. You would have to be blind not to see that my story is one of danger and excitement mixed with despair. It is a story of high highs interspersed with low lows that exceed anything you might expect in the normal world. The danger kept on coming and the rewards never lasted. If I had it to do all over again, I would have gone to university and toughed it out to earn a degree. I would have left my gangster friends to their own lives and started saving towards retirement and a pension, like most people do. I doubt that I will ever really retire, although my friends might argue that I retired years ago. My life is comfortable in its present form, as I watch my children grow and move along with their own lives. I get up in the morning and have my coffee and read the daily papers as I always have. I take note from the news stories that the next generation following behind me is making the same mistakes I did. Every day there is another headline about a vengeance killing or a rip off killing connected to drugs. It seems to me that the world is getting crazier than ever. There is so much for young people to learn, I think to myself, as I read about their misguided exploits.

But I have learned my lesson.

"Live clean and let your works be seen."

Yah, mon!